"Funny, engaging, courageous, *No Map to This Country* is a roadmap for anyone embarking on the journey to understanding what helps kids with autism."
—**Patricia Stacey,** author of *The Boy Who Loved Windows*

"Our society is riddled with vexing problems; bullying, drugs, and Internet safety are just a few of them. How do we cope with these problems? In a corporate environment solving problems would require an organizational leadership that would set rules and steer the company in an appropriate direction. At home, these same problems demand, more than anything, caring parents and community support.

Data from longitudinal studies on autistic patients who have improved enough so as to lose their original diagnosis show the importance of aggressive and tenacious parenting. These are parents who initiated interventions long before a diagnosis was obtained. Furthermore, the number of therapeutic interventions for recovered patients was large and intensive, requiring many hours of parental involvement each week. Parents soon find that there are, and will be, many competing demands for their time; too many to be handled by any single individual.

Jennifer Noonan's book, *No Map to This Country*, could be the story of a race, in this case a marathon rather than a sprint. Preparing for a marathon is not something to be taken lightly. You need to break down different aspects of the race in order to achieve your goal. You also need information on your state of health (physical check-up), what shoes to wear, hydration, weather conditions, diet, and a rigorous training schedule.

Jennifer Noonan picks up the gauntlet of Clara Claiborne Park and Bernard Rimland as devoted parents preparing for a marathon and finishing it. In *No Map to This Country* Jennifer talks about her lifetime goals, the hopes she has for her children, her struggles with coping, and freely admits to her own personal shortcomings. It is also an educational book where Jennifer identifies autism related problems before they snowball uncontrollably. The book provides a guide path to those new to the world of autism, pioneers in their own right, as to what to expect and how best to proceed.

Maybe writing this book for Jennifer has been an exercise in grief shared is grief diminished; one where she narrates a journey of healing and redemption. Truthfully I had a feeling of despair in reading the first few chapters because I could readily identify with Jennifer's plight and the problems she encountered. This feeling has been superseded by hope and confidence in knowing that the Noonan family is in good hands. I am looking forward to the postscript several years from now."
—**Manuel F. Casanova, MD,** SmartState Endowed Chair in Childhood Neurotherapeutics, University of South Carolina, Greenville Health System

no map
to this
country

no map
to this
country

One Family's Journey
Through Autism

Jennifer Noonan

Da Capo
∞
LIFE
LONG

Da Capo Lifelong Books
A Member of the Perseus Books Group

Set in 12 point Granjon LT Standard by the Perseus Books Group

Cataloging-in-Publication data for this book is available from the Library of Congress.

First Da Capo Press edition 2016

ISBN: 978-0-7382-1904-2 (paperback original)

ISBN: 978-0-7382-1905-9 (ebook)

Published by Da Capo Press

A Member of the Perseus Books Group

www.dacapopress.com

Note: The information in this book is true and complete to the best of our knowledge. This book is intended only as an informative guide for those wishing to know more about health issues. In no way is this book intended to replace, countermand, or conflict with the advice given to you by your own physician. The ultimate decision concerning care should be made between you and your doctor. We strongly recommend you follow his or her advice. Information in this book is general and is offered with no guarantees on the part of the authors or Da Capo Press. The authors and publisher disclaim all liability in connection with the use of this book.

Da Capo Press books are available at special discounts for bulk purchases in the U.S. by corporations, institutions, and other organizations. For more information, please contact the Special Markets Department at the Perseus Books Group, 2300 Chestnut Street, Suite 200, Philadelphia, PA 19103, or call (800) 810–4145, ext. 5000, or e-mail special.markets@perseusbooks.com.

10 9 8 7 6 5 4 3 2 1

To the scar on Andrew's leg

Contents

CONTENTS

Author's Note

Some of the names and identifying details have been changed to protect the privacy of individuals, but the events and conversations in this book have been recorded as I remember them. This is, however, only one story of one specific family, and nothing contained within is intended to be taken as medical advice. Readers should consult with the appropriate physicians regarding any symptoms or conditions that may require diagnosis or medical attention.

Foreword

AUTISM SPECTRUM DISORDER (ASD) is now estimated to affect one in sixty-eight children, and surveillance of its prevalence only demonstrates that it continues to increase. It may be one of the most profound medical disorders affecting us in our lifetime. In this book, Jennifer Noonan takes us with her through her journey of trying to find answers and effective treatments for her son with ASD. Like many parents, Jennifer forged a unique journey using incomplete information and sometimes misinformation as a guide towards an unknown destination. The book provides some insights into the tireless, sometimes unforgiving road that only some parents and families have the wherewithal to travel. The fact is that many of the people and professionals whom she meets along the way have little appreciation for what she has gone through and what remains on her path.

The essay by Emily Kingsley is very pertinent to the story but incomplete, as the book later points out. For some families, the journey is like arriving in Holland when you are planning to spend your vacation in Italy, but for others, it is like landing in Beirut, not Holland. The trip is very different for each family, and it is hard to predict at the onset. Many times the symptoms of autism do not appear until the second year of life, and they often get much worse before they get better, so for many, it is like starting a vacation in Italy and then one morning coming out of your hotel room and finding yourself in Holland. Then, after you get used to Holland, the next morning you find yourself in Beirut.

At this time behavior therapy is commonly believed by most professionals to be the primary mainstay treatment for children with ASD. Experts believe that full-time (forty hours per week) applied behavioral analysis (ABA) or an equivalent behavior therapy should be provided to children with ASD, and studies have indicated that this type of therapy can have amazing positive effects for children, especially if started very early in life. Despite the significant impacts of behavioral therapy, its benefits are limited in many children and may provide suboptimal recovery. Of greater concern are the practical limitations that prevent this therapy from being delivered to the children who need it. For example, an ABA therapist typically is paid between $50 and $100 per hour. Thus, a full-time program would cost from $100,000 to $200,000 per year. It is not surprising that it is often very difficult to get insurance to pay for this therapy. Schools often have few or no behavioral therapists, and when they do, the therapists are in such high demand that they can provide only a few hours of therapy to each child. Many families that have the means pay out of pocket, and those that do not have the means cannot get the needed behavioral therapy for their children. This highlights the impact of ASD on the medical and educational system and demonstrates the urgent need for medical therapies that can accelerate and optimize the effects of behavioral therapy in order to ensure complete and lasting recovery.

The fact that a full-time therapist is needed for each child with ASD is a testament to the widespread effect ASD has on the community at large. If one therapist is needed for each child, the number of individuals affected by ASD is no longer one in sixty-eight but one in thirty-four. If you add the need for a parent to be a full-time care coordinator, the number of people now affected is one in twenty-three. Add siblings and the rest of the family, other teachers, and medical professionals, and it is easy to understand why ASD touches all of our lives. The emotional, financial, and societal costs of ASD are great.

This highlights the urgent need for good answers regarding the causes and effective treatment.

More and more medical studies are discovering the biological basis of ASD and investigating new treatments. Symptoms that were previously dismissed are starting to be recognized by some. The involvement of the gastrointestinal system was dismissed for many decades, despite symptoms almost always being noted in children with ASD. In fact, some of the first case reports published over half a century ago noted prominent gastrointestinal systems in children with ASD. We have come a long way—about five years ago, several autism societies supported a multidisciplinary panel of nationally respected physicians and scientists to carefully consider the evidence of gastrointestinal disorders. They concluded that these gastrointestinal disorders are real in children with ASD and that the symptoms are sometimes unusual and include ASD-type behaviors. Thus, it can be very difficult to diagnose gastrointestinal disorders in children with ASD if the physician is not well aware of the different ways in which children with ASD can manifest gastrointestinal disorders.

Recently, research studies have started to clarify the biological basis of gastrointestinal disorders. Studies from respected universities have demonstrated the deficiencies in the machinery in the gut that breaks down certain components of food, such as carbohydrates and protein, and have linked imbalances in the microbiome (the trillions of organisms that live in the gut) to ASD. In fact, one study in mice suggests that altering the bacteria in the gut can substantially improve ASD-like symptoms—at least in mice. Could this be the basis of many of the observed positive effects of specific diets, probiotics, and other treatments that are not uncommonly used to treat children with ASD? Perhaps. However, the clinical trials to answer these questions are sorely lacking, leaving physicians and parents with little good-quality information by which to guide treatment for children with ASD.

This lack of evidence is sometimes interpreted as meaning that many treatments such as changes in diet are not effective and shouldn't be applied. However, nothing could be further from the case. Many of these treatments may be effective, possibly in a subset of children with ASD, and warrant a trial on an individual basis—especially since many of these treatments are very safe. The truth is that most medical treatments—even common treatments like those for hypertension—don't work for everyone, so they are applied on a trial basis to see if they are effective for that particular person. The key is to know which treatments are most likely to be effective, and that is the piece we are missing for children with ASD. Until we have more knowledge and better treatments, parents will continue desperately to try treatments that have little or no scientific basis. There are few physicians with the knowledge to help guide parents to the more useful and safe treatments and away from treatments that are unlikely to be helpful and may even be dangerous. However, without good scientific studies, it is difficult for even knowledgeable practitioners to be confident in their recommendations. The lack of knowledge has essentially created a vacuum that is filled with both potentially helpful treatments and those that are the latest fad. We urgently need to fill this void.

Jennifer Noonan provides insight through her realization of her son's diagnosis of ASD. The atypical pattern of development she describes is rather unusual for children with ASD, making the diagnosis difficult, or at least not obvious. The fact is that many children diagnosed with ASD have their own unique developmental path, and the exact path or paths that lead to the development of ASD are still not known. In fact, the recent criteria for diagnosing ASD underwent a major revision. This is a testament to how much we still need to learn. Given the preliminary understanding of this disorder, it is clear that we all need to have an open mind. Indeed, autism may have its greatest effect in challenging our preconceptions and prejudices.

RICHARD E. FRYE, M.D., PH.D.
Director of Autism Research,
Arkansas Children's Hospital Research Institute

Welcome to Holland

by Emily Perl Kingsley

I AM OFTEN asked to describe the experience of raising a child with a disability—to try to help people who have not shared that unique experience to understand it, to imagine how it would feel. It's like this . . .

When you're going to have a baby, it's like planning a fabulous vacation trip—to Italy. You buy a bunch of guide books and make your wonderful plans. The Coliseum. The Michelangelo David. The gondolas in Venice. You may learn some handy phrases in Italian. It's all very exciting.

After months of eager anticipation, the day finally arrives. You pack your bags and off you go. Several hours later, the plane lands. The flight attendant comes in and says, "Welcome to Holland."

"*Holland*?!" you say. "What do you mean Holland?? I signed up for Italy! I'm supposed to be in Italy. All my life I've dreamed of going to Italy."

But there's been a change in the flight plan. They've landed in Holland and there you must stay.

The important thing is that they haven't taken you to a horrible, disgusting, filthy place, full of pestilence, famine and disease. It's just a different place.

So you must go out and buy new guide books. And you must learn a whole new language. And you will meet a whole new group of people you would never have met.

It's just a *different* place. It's slower-paced than Italy, less flashy than Italy. But after you've been there for a while and you catch your breath, you look around . . . and you begin to notice that Holland has windmills . . . and Holland has tulips. Holland even has Rembrandts.

But everyone you know is busy coming and going from Italy . . . and they're all bragging about what a wonderful time they had there. And for the rest of your life, you will say, "Yes, that's where I was supposed to go. That's what I had planned."

And the pain of that will never, ever, ever, ever go away . . . because the loss of that dream is a very, very significant loss.

But . . . if you spend your life mourning the fact that you didn't get to Italy, you may never be free to enjoy the very special, the very lovely things . . . about Holland.

Chapter 1

An Odd Sense

ONE OF THE unwritten rules of any autism story is that it must begin with a perfect birth, to serve in dramatic contrast to the downfall that is coming. The baby is beautiful, the parents are full of joy and hope, and the nurses sprout wings and halos as the idyllic music swells over the hospital intercom.

That is not our story.

The truth is, we had to fight with fertility treatments for a year and a half just to get to the moment of conception. I would later learn that women who undergo fertility treatments are more likely to have an autistic child, though no one can say whether that is due to some effect of the medications or simply because women predisposed to having autistic children are also more likely to have trouble conceiving in the first place. But after a slew of invasive testing; varying doses of drugs that made me a hormonal nightmare to be around; and over $1,000 in labs, office visits, and prescription co-pays, I was finally rewarded with that positive pregnancy test I had so desired.

I would also later learn that $1,000 was petty cash when it came to medical bills.

My delivery was likewise more difficult than average. After twenty hours of labor with minimal progression, I was wheeled away for a C-section, which was a pretty big disappointment for someone who had intended to deliver naturally. Again, I would later learn that C-sections are correlated with a higher incidence of autism, but still no word on which direction a causative relationship, if any, might be going there.

But as in the proverbial scenario this story is supposed to be starting with, once they handed Paul to me, none of the hardship mattered anymore. I was in love.

That evening he cried, and continued all night long. He was eating well, he wasn't gassy, he was swaddled in a dozen different ways, but still he cried on and on. We had to reluctantly send him out to the nurses' station for a few hours to be comforted by someone else, because after two days with no sleep, there was a genuine danger that either of us might pass out with him in our arms and drop him. I will never know for sure what was going on inside his little body, but all my experiences with newborns both before and since tell me it was not normal; there was something wrong. By the next morning he was doing better, though, and soon we were home and happily living our lives with our perfect new son.

Perfect, but weird. As any new mother would be, I was secretly proud of all the small things that made my child noticeably unique, even to strangers. Everyone who touched his little hands commented on how surprisingly strong he was. At six weeks old he could grip your finger hard enough to hurt. As he got older I became scared to let others hold him, because they were never prepared for how fast and hard he would suddenly arch his body out into the air for no apparent reason. Even once they got used to the tumultuous physics of my son, it was impossible to actually leave him with anyone unless they were willing to endure hours of wailing until I returned. This included my husband and other close family members, much to everyone's dismay. Yet despite such severe separation anxiety, he wasn't clingy, as one might expect. In fact, he almost never wanted to be held, and certainly never cuddled. My arms were meant only for lifting him higher to reach some object or moving him to a more exciting place. He was hyperaware of everything around him and desperately wanted to be free to grab a piece of it all, as long as I remained reassuringly nearby.

At three months old Paul began the screaming game. He would let out an ear-piercing shriek, short and deliberate, and then pause and listen to it echo around the subtle acoustics in the room before shrieking again a few seconds later. This was no bid for attention, just a self-absorbed fascination, and he would entertain himself with it for upwards of half an hour at a time. It made no difference whether we gently admonished him, or tried to distract him, or ignored him entirely. We could not get him to stop playing this game, especially when we went to a place with tile floors that would reverberate in new and interesting ways, such as every public restroom I ever took him into. I was regularly reminded of how much people do not appreciate unexpected screech-owl impersonations when they are busy in the stall.

At six months old he started crawling, except it wasn't really crawling. He bear-walked on his hands and feet, never letting his knees touch the ground. Amused relatives declared his "downward-facing dog" pose to be in perfect form, but it was no cute trick. If you tried to gently slide his knees to the floor, he would glare and yell as if you were hurting him.

I would eventually learn that all of these behaviors were sensory problems—movement, sound, touch—and were the first warning signs that he wasn't processing the world like a normal child should. It's easy to take our sensory nerves for granted, but they are a critically balanced connection to the rest of the universe. Everyone is familiar with the symptoms of sensory loss, such as deafness or numbness. But sometimes the signals can be improperly magnified, rather than dulled, and this creates havoc in the brain. Consider how it feels to emerge from a movie theater into bright sunlight. Now imagine what life would be like if every light bulb gave you that overwhelming blinding sensation, all the time. What if touching a stuffed animal felt like touching a porcupine? What if the sound of running water were the same as nails on a chalkboard? What if every step you took felt like the first drop on a roller coaster? Our sensory nerves literally define the world for us, and we are wholly at their mercy.

I don't know what it felt like for Paul when his knees touched the floor. But I know he would have done absolutely anything to avoid it.

Yet other major warning signs of autism were conspicuously absent. Paul didn't just make good eye contact; he was in fact outgoing and sociable, and he positively loved being the center of attention. One of his favorite games as a toddler was to get everyone in the room clapping and cheering at the same time, and he would run from person to person like a plate spinner to encourage anyone who showed signs of tiring. Far from being a late talker, he said his first real word at ten months, and his vocabulary grew sharply from there. I kept a list for a while because the pediatrician thought I must be exaggerating. By fifteen months he knew about a hundred words, and by eighteen months he knew the entire alphabet, both upper- and lowercase, and the sounds each letter made. He could accurately count items up to twenty before his second birthday.

He didn't reach his arms out to be picked up like they said he was supposed to, but we didn't notice because he never wanted to be picked up anyway. He didn't point to things at a distance, but we didn't notice because he always took off running for them instead. I knew he was extremely hyperactive, emotionally difficult, and very smart—but autism could not have been further from our thoughts.

Even when things started to go downhill, instead of just along this weird path to the side of every other kid I knew, it was a slow and subtle process. I can clearly remember sitting at the table when Paul was around fifteen months old, and how he insisted on feeding himself with the spoon by shouting, "I do! I do!" at the top of his lungs. He always shouted, even when he wasn't upset. But at some point the pronoun "I" quietly disappeared. That incident at the table is the last time I can remember him using it for sure.

Though the number of nouns he knew continued to soar far ahead of his age group, several were words he'd made up, and these substitutions became more entrenched with age rather than fading. He would say "cue" to mean goldfish crackers, for example, and his name for cheese slices was "kasha cheese." What's more, he seemed to think he was saying exactly what I had, becoming irritated at any attempts to correct his pronunciation.

Meanwhile, verbs lagged. He had a name for every single DVD, book, and toy in the house, but he would never use a word like "want" or "give" before the thing he was asking for. He would never "play," or "put," or "stack," or "drive" anything. He would just name the item he wanted several times for good measure and then continue naming it at increasingly louder intervals until I got the hint.

We didn't notice the language oddities, though, because he did use so many words. At his two-year checkup, the pediatrician asked me if he was putting together phrases and again gave me the skeptical look I was so familiar with when I told her that he'd been doing that for months. Moments later she got a demonstration, however, when I lifted him onto the exam table and he began screaming, "All done! Down! Shoes and socks and go!"

But each of those phrases might as well have been nouns. "All-done" was one word to him, and "down" was not a direction but rather a thing he wanted—a thing I told him regularly to "get," in fact. Even that final triad of demands was a single unit, stolen in its entirety.

"Okay, Paul," I would say to him each day, "let's put on *shoes and socks and go*." Those words weren't steps in a process for him, as evidenced by the fact that the tiny feet kicking against the exam table were already wearing shoes. He just knew that the string of sounds as a whole meant leaving. I didn't know that when it came to speech development, echolalia didn't count. I had never even heard of it before.

Echolalia is a symptom of autism where individuals repeat exactly what they have heard rather than parsing the specific words and reusing them to form their own sentences. My son was the king of it. He knew every lyric to his favorite songs on my iPod, huge chains of syllables that could not have had any meaning for his barely two-year-old brain. He would act out entire scenes from TV shows, dashing back and forth across the room to play all the characters.

He would require us to be involved in certain scripts as well, prompting me for my next line again and again without pause until I said it. This type of broken-record ritual serves the same purpose as other self-stimulatory behaviors commonly found in autism, such as rocking back and forth or hand-flapping, and like all so-called stimming, it is as compulsory as it is comforting. I would sometimes try to break the cycle by going into my bedroom and shutting him out for up to twenty minutes at a time. But when I emerged he would pick right up where he'd left off, midscript or even midsentence.

Some special scripts were non-negotiable parts of the day, such as his drawn-out bedtime routine, which was about ten lines of backand-forth between us, including specific numbers of kisses at specific points in the script. If I made a mistake or tried to change the pattern, he would simply start all over, and if I tried to walk out before it was finished, he would scream indefinitely. If I came back and did it the right way, he would let me leave without complaint. Not that he would go to sleep after I left, of course. Most evenings he would bounce up and down in his crib for at least an hour, loudly reciting various stories and songs to himself before finally passing out.

Many people informed us that his problems were merely a lack of discipline, but he wasn't defiant. He didn't hit, or take toys, or demand bribes. The word "no" simply didn't seem to mean anything to him. If I told him not to pull the DVDs off the shelf, he would begin chanting loudly, "Ah-ah, no touching!" while he did it, as if my words were supposed to be part of the task, or even the name of the task itself. Putting him in time-out just meant he was moved to a new place to script. Physical punishment, the few times we tried it, literally resulted in giggling. Often it seemed as if he didn't feel pain at all.

This lack of reaction to pain is another common symptom of autism. Sometimes I would turn around and Paul would be indifferently bleeding, and I'd have no idea when or how it had happened. He would be more irritated by the fact that his face was wet than by the gash on his forehead, and he could turn a room into a murder scene in minutes as he angrily wiped the blood off on any surface he could find.

My husband, Andrew, and I both believed wholeheartedly in authoritative parenting, and we were ruthless with our consistency. Paul *would* get used to the way we did things, and we were not going to give in. We were willing to run the scripts he needed before any particular event, but in the end, he was going to do what we told him. Yet there were problem behaviors that we just could not crack, like his separation anxiety. We were sure that if we just kept it up, calm and clinical, he would eventually learn that Mommy would come back. Every single week we took him to the children's area at church, and every single week they would page me to come get him after twenty minutes of agonized wailing. I didn't sit through a complete service for a year and a half, but still we kept trying. Everyone assumed he must be this way because we were rushing to his side at the faintest cry, and we repeatedly were given the not-so-helpful suggestion to just ignore it and he would stop. We *were*, and he *wasn't*.

Another nightly battle was tooth brushing, and though it took both of us to gently but firmly pin him down every single night to make even the briefest of brushing happen, we were not deterred. Months and months went by, and still he showed no sign of accepting this basic daily routine.

We soon figured out that the worst punishment we could inflict on him, more horrible than time-outs, or loss of toys, or even spanking, was to hold him snugly in a bear hug. If things escalated to that point, however, it would take a minimum of thirty minutes in this position before he would stop fighting and relax. By the end we would be as exhausted as he was.

In retrospect, his symptoms seem obvious to me now. But at the time no one suspected anything, least of all us. He was quite communicative; he just used his own strange way to do it. He made great eye contact and wanted attention from everyone he met, though he wouldn't actually say the word "hi" or call anyone by their name. It was true that he had undeniable quirks, including walking on his toes and organizing his crayons by color before putting them away without ever drawing anything. But if anything, in my mind that made him a candidate for eccentric genius.

Still, the hyperactivity was becoming worse, and we were starting to see more meltdowns when he couldn't satisfy his compulsions, like when I wouldn't let him dismantle the stacked displays at the grocery store and put them in a neat line along the floor instead. So at the start of the new year, January of 2009, I mentioned my concerns to our pediatrician.

We were actually in her office for a nine-month checkup for my daughter, Marie, but I could not get Paul to understand that the doctor wasn't even going to look at him, and he had been in freak-out mode from the moment we walked in. As I calmly described to the pediatrician why I thought he might have some combination of OCD and ADHD, Paul hung from the locked exam room doorknob by both hands, violently twisting his body back and forth like a screaming wind sock.

I told her that, yes, this type of thing was a typical reaction when he didn't want to be somewhere, and no, it never got him what he wanted. He always did it anyway.

She asked me some questions covering what I now know are sensory issues. Does he refuse to wear long sleeves? Does he hate being touched or hugged? Does he have problems having his teeth brushed, his hair combed, his nails clipped? Does he spin in circles or throw himself on the floor for fun? Does he like staring at bright flashing lights?

Yes to all of the above! I felt a surge of optimism since she clearly seemed to recognize what was going on.

The pediatrician told us he had Sensory Processing Disorder, or SPD, and referred us to an occupational therapist. "I'm not concerned about autism, not at all," she said offhandedly.

I was baffled by this comment. *Of course you're not*, I thought. *This is nothing like autism. What a strange thing to say.*

As soon as we got home I joined an SPD online message board and spent hours reading the recent threads. I learned how to therapeutically extinguish some startlingly familiar behaviors and bookmarked links to various therapy products that could desensitize or resensitize as necessary. I noted all the ways that we could modify his toys and daily activities to create what the therapists called a "sensory diet." Again, I was optimistic since all of this seemed to be something that was well understood, and there were a lot of ways we could help him.

I also came across repeated references to autism. There was apparently a lot of overlap between the two diagnoses, and some people even considered SPD to be a part of the autism spectrum. True enough, there were some unexpected things that struck home—this was when I learned that echolalia and toe-walking were marked traits of autism, even though you never hear about them in the public service announcements. But poor eye contact and delayed speech were also part of autism, everyone knew that, so I felt reassured that ours was clearly a case of plain old SPD.

Chapter 2

The A-Word

THE DAY BEFORE our first appointment with the occupational therapist, we were invited to a birthday party for a child who was turning two. Paul was being his typical hyper self, but things were going relatively well, and it looked like I wouldn't have to make a hasty early exit for once. There was a magnetic alphabet set on the family's refrigerator, and he had been entertaining himself for quite a while, taking the letters down and lining them up on the floor.

"What is he doing?" asked one of the other kids' dads with a frown.

I shrugged. "He's just lining them up. He likes to organize things like that."

The dad seemed extremely put off by this, as if my son had actually been using his third arm to arrange the magnets in a pentagram.

Paul finished his alphabet and proudly declared to me, "ABCs!"

"That's right, great job!" I said, triumphantly hoping the dad noticed that Paul had put them in alphabetical order.

I did have to admit, though, looking around the room, that Paul stuck out more among these other kids than he used to. The last time I'd really seen him in a group of his peers was when we used to go to one of those toddler gymnastics classes. We'd had to quit the group months ago because at the end of every class they would blow exquisitely tiny bubbles everywhere, which stuck to the floor mats instead of popping on contact. Paul would crawl around persistently popping each bubble with his finger and became enraged if I tried to make him leave before his task was finished. This meant that I, as an authoritative parent who wasn't going to acquiesce to a tantrum, had to unapologetically carry him out screaming every single time, since there was no way he could pop hundreds of bubbles before the next class had to start. Eventually I got tired of paying for him to have an extra meltdown each week, and we dropped out.

As Paul flitted from room to room at the party looking for things to catch his attention, I saw the birthday girl whining to her grandmother about a small toy that one of the younger children had grabbed from her. The other toddler lost interest and dropped the toy again, and the little girl picked it up and declared happily to her grandmother, "Okay, now I have it."

This stopped me in my tracks. This girl had just turned two (wouldn't actually turn two until the next day, truth be told, when my two-and-a-half-year-old would be at his first appointment with the occupational therapist), and she had just used a sentence involving an interjection, two pronouns, and an adverb. It didn't even come attached to a request; she had said it purely to update someone else on the situation. Granted, this girl was an especially precocious two-year-old, but the contrast was striking. Paul would not have voluntarily used any word she'd just said, in any order.

Maybe he has a speech delay after all, I thought. That was the first moment that I believed something might be really wrong.

The occupational therapy clinic we had been referred to catered mostly to older patients, and I sat uncomfortably in the waiting room surrounded by grandmothers who clearly thought that my baby girl was adorable and my son needed a good whipping—or three. It was a depressing place, and I knew there was no way the people who worked here could be prepared for my little whirlwind.

Then Melanie came out to greet us, with her baggy cargo pants and her short hair spiked up tall, and she was so unlike the willowy, soft-voiced therapist I had imagined that I couldn't help but grin. This was a woman who knew how to wrestle with little boys, and no one had to tell her that the child currently in high-velocity orbit around the room was her new patient.

She stepped directly into his path, squatted down, and cried, "Hey, I know you! Your name is Paul! Y'all come on this way."

To my surprise he ran after her without hesitation, only looking back at the very end of the hallway to make sure I was indeed following him.

Melanie led us to a giant playroom full of trampolines, bean bag chairs, and large, colorful toys. There was a thick hook hanging from the middle of the ceiling onto which she could attach an assortment of swings, carpeted platforms, and nets. She exuberantly chased Paul around the room, testing his willingness to crash into bean bags (he loved it), let her touch his cheeks (dodged quite skillfully), touch shaving cream with his hands (refused), wear weighted belts (really refused), and sit on different swings (nearly had a meltdown).

At the same time she chatted with me, asking all sorts of questions about his specific behaviors.

"How about toy cars, does he like those?"

"Oh, yes, he loves his cars."

"What does he do with them?"

"He likes to line them up," I said. "It's funny because my stepson did that, too. We definitely have some OCD in the family."

"Uh-huh." She didn't make it sound like she was agreeing with me. "Does he ever spin them?"

"Well, yes . . . " I was hesitant to give this answer because one tidbit I had picked up from my research online was that autistic kids spin cars instead of driving them. "But it's not like he's spinning them just to spin them," I rapidly explained. "There's this scene in the movie *Cars* where Mater is driving backwards, and then he spins in circles and shouts, 'Woo-hoo!' And that's what he's doing; he's acting out the scene from the movie, and he says, 'Woo-hoo,' and all the other lines that Mater says, while he's spinning the car."

Even as I was saying it, I knew my excuse for this behavior was just as weird in its own way, but still I wanted to believe this was different.

"Uh-huh," she replied. Again not agreeing with me, just taking note.

Melanie asked me countless other questions, many of which I answered in the affirmative, but that was the only one I knew for sure I was giving the "wrong" answer to, the one that made it sound like autism. At the end of the hour she explained the various sensory behaviors she had seen and how she could help him work past them. She also told me that she was seeing "a lot of red flags," and that we really needed to go see a neurologist for a definitive answer, but . . . in her professional opinion, he had Pervasive Developmental Disorder.

It was at the very mildest end of the spectrum, she said, though I had thought that was supposed to be SPD. Somehow we'd gotten classified as more delayed, but still mildest. Melanie referred to just "the spectrum" several times, only carefully clarifying several minutes later that she meant the *autism* spectrum and watching me closely for a reaction.

By this point I had my game face on. Though I still viewed "what he had" only as an extension of Sensory Processing Disorder, I had at least settled into the idea that something really was there. There would be time later for consideration, disappointment, frustration, and fear, but in that moment I was safe inside my well-worn social armor.

"I know a lot of parents aren't comfortable with the A-word. . . . " Melanie said delicately.

"Oh, I'm okay with the word 'autism,'" I assured her with a genuine smile. I was still in denial, to be sure, just as most parents are when they hear the news. But my defense mechanism was to turn the whole thing on its face: if my son had autism, then autism must not be that bad. Call it what you wanted; I knew who my son was, and he wasn't any different now just because there was a label on him.

Or to put it another way, I was too ignorant to be devastated. I didn't understand how Paul's future development would continue to deviate more, not less. I could accept these difficult behaviors from a two-and-a-half-year-old because it never occurred to me that he could still be this way as an adolescent, or even as an adult. I did know enough to keep my mouth shut because I'd look like a fool saying it out loud, but in my head I clearly heard myself say, *Well, he may have it now, but soon he won't.*

Remembering it, I am astounded at my own hubris. I certainly had no reason to believe at that time that autism was treatable, but somehow I decided, in my classically pigheaded way, that it would be. I would treat my son, and he would get better. I knew it as clearly as I had ever known anything. It was not some kind of fire welling from within; this was not my Mel Gibson *Braveheart* moment. It was just a simple fact, so obvious to me that it was not even worth questioning.

I spent the next couple of months in a weird dichotomy. Outwardly, I took the diagnosis as a given and freely told people that Paul had high-functioning autism when his strange behaviors were noticed, which was more and more often. But secretly, I felt guilty for telling them what I knew to be lies. It felt like I was garnering sympathy where none was warranted, because I knew I was going to fix this thing.

Don't feel bad for me, I would think. *It'll all be fine soon.*

Chapter 3

Ants, Elephants, and Dinosaurs

THE DAY AFTER our appointment with Melanie, our pediatrician called me at home, which was a little surreal. I'd never had a doctor call us before. It hadn't even occurred to me that she would be receiving notes from the occupational therapy session, though I had of course signed the legal forms allowing it. Dr. Felix's tone was very sympathetic, as you would be with someone who had suffered a family tragedy, and this only confounded me further since I was still of the mindset that it was no big deal.

She recommended a pediatric neurologist and directed me to the Autism Speaks website, which I'd already found on my own way back when I had only been researching Sensory Processing Disorder.

"Of course you're going to want to get as much information as you can. *Good* information," she stressed pointedly.

And again, I was already three steps ahead of her. I'd been tearing through online resources almost nonstop and had come across some of the so-called alternative treatments for autism, especially chelation therapy, where a medication is used to pull out heavy metals that have supposedly built up inside the body. I had rolled my eyes at this hippie mumbo-jumbo and had no intention of pursuing it. But I also rolled my eyes now at the pediatrician's words.

Thanks, but I'll evaluate for myself what is good information and what is not. You weren't even worried about autism, remember?

There was a six-month waiting list for the neurologist she had rec-ommended, so I called around and took the first available appoint-ment with anyone in town, which was still three months away. I really wasn't sure what a neurologist was going to be able to do for us, but we were supposed to make the appointment, so I did.

In the meantime, we had plenty of assignments from Melanie about ways to alter Paul's environment with an eye towards sensory integration. If the sensory signals were muffled, such as when he didn't feel pain or wanted to crash violently into things for fun, then we had to sensitize him to it, to make him more aware of the messages his body was trying to get through to his brain. If the signals were over-amplified, such as when he was nauseated by even the gentlest swing or horrified at the feeling of wet or gooey things on his hands, then we had to desensitize him to the overwhelming flood of sensation.

I pointed out that the signals didn't even seem to be consistent. When he was a baby he had craved high and fast swinging more than anything else, so much so that we'd referred to him as our "little adren-aline junkie." Then one day when he was about eighteen months old he had suddenly just switched. Didn't want to go down the slides any-more, screamed if you tried to put him in a swing.

Melanie said that was common, too, and that his sensory dysfunc-tion might continue to weave about as we tried to bring him back to center. But whatever issue we were addressing, the rule was that if he hated it, we had to make him do it to whatever tiny degree we could, and if he loved it, we had to overdo it until he was sick of it. The recur-ring theme was that I had a lot to do. Regular undirected playtime was no longer going to happen. Every moment and every activity needed to have a purpose.

First, we had to make his toys heavy, to force the sensation of weight and purposeful movement. We drilled a hole in his little scooter car and filled it with ten pounds of dry rice. Paul liked this change and was pleased to demonstrate his triumph over the deadweight car, shoving at it with all his might. But there wasn't a good seal around the car's axles, and grains of rice were constantly leaking onto the carpet.

We drilled smaller holes in his plastic dinosaurs and filled them with copper BB-gun pellets from a sporting-goods store. But he was fascinated with the new rattling sound they made and didn't want to just carry them around like he used to.

I glued a thick layer of BBs into the hollow insides of his jumbo Lego blocks, which didn't seem to add much weight individually, but after stacking a half-dozen together you could really tell the difference. The weight didn't deter him from playing with them, but his game had always been to stack them neatly into one tall tower and then go do something else, so we didn't get a lot out of it.

We were given a special kind of tickling brush to use on his skin, which was supposed to be followed immediately with joint compressions on his arms and legs, the kind of pressure you would feel if you jumped up and down without bending your knees. He hated this activity, and it took me a solid five minutes to hold him still for a few strokes of the brush, plus ten joint compressions, times four limbs . . . and we were supposed to go through this exhausting process every hour! Melanie told me there were kids who instantly calmed at the sensation of brushing, who would even learn to request it when they were getting upset, but my kid definitely wasn't one of them.

Though most of it seemed like a lot of effort for nothing, we did learn one helpful tip that calmed him, and that was riding in the grocery cart. He always stood in the basket, a practice that had gotten me some dirty looks and chastising comments from busybodies who were afraid he would fall. They didn't understand that it was the only way he would tolerate being in the store at all, or that his balance was almost certainly better than theirs, or that even if he did tumble to the floor and break an arm, he would think it was hysterical anyway. Melanie taught me that it was the vestibular motion of the basket that he was craving and said that I should push it faster, turn corners harder, and generally make the trip as much like a go-kart race as I could without getting ourselves kicked out of the store. She even encouraged me to take unnecessary trips to the store if Paul was having a rough day, just to center him with that sensory input.

"Go every day if you can," she said. "Go twice a day. Quiet in the grocery store is better than tantrums at home, right?"

She was right. It didn't matter what kind of day he was having, we could always go ride in the cart at the grocery store and he would be calmer when we left.

During our sessions Melanie spent a lot of time desensitizing his obsessive behaviors as well. If he started lining up toy cars in the therapy room, she would deliberately turn the cars backwards, or bump the line crooked, or switch the order once he'd laid them out. He was allowed to silently fix them, but if he got upset she would make him leave the cars and work on something else. This invariably meant a full meltdown, but that didn't bother her. Nor did it bother me, but only because I was accustomed to listening to it, not because I believed she was going to get anywhere with this purposeful agitation.

Over the course of many months, however, he began to accept error correction as an essential part of the task, and every once in a long while he would not immediately notice a change she had introduced. Even less often, he would glance at the error and actually postpone fixing it for just a few seconds, a few tiny precious moments of tolerance that promised he might someday be able to function in a world that was more chaotic than he wanted it to be.

We had another big breakthrough when we realized that, despite his apparent love of attention and excitement around other people, this behavior was actually a defense mechanism when he was overwhelmed by the presence of too many people. We were at another birthday party several weeks after starting therapy, and a short while into it I noticed the familiar ramp-up in laughing and running, the wild grin that meant he would not be leaving this party on his own two feet. But instead of trying to keep him focused, as I had in the past, I guided him down a hall and into an empty room of the house and shut the door.

I didn't bother turning the lights on, and neither did he.

After a few minutes of exploring the handful of toys on the floor, I asked if he was ready to go back and play. He opened the door, peered down the bright hallway, and instead came back to the toys we'd found. We ended up staying alone in the dark for the rest of the party, with only the light from the cracked doorway angling across the floor.

Eventually, Andrew came and found us, and we casually emerged and said our goodbyes and thank-yous. As we loaded quietly into the car, he and I exchanged raised eyebrows over the ease with which it was all happening.

Suddenly, Paul looked at me and said, "Grocery store."

"You want to go to the grocery store?" I asked.

"Grocery store."

I shrugged. "Okay."

So we did, all four of us. After wandering around for a while, I asked, "Are we all done?"

"All done," Paul repeated with a distinct air of pleased finality. He had figured out what he needed, asked for it, and now felt better.

It turned out my extrovert son was secretly an introvert after all, and was at least partially aware of his own state of mind. He didn't want to throw tantrums. None of his negative behaviors were about what he wanted; they were about what he could and couldn't handle. This was something I had always known but could never prove before to the "needs more discipline" crowd. He was finally developing the tools to discern how he was feeling and help himself work through it.

But these small triumphs only highlighted the size of the problem. Part of me knew it shouldn't be so impressive that my son could occasionally get in the car without being physically forced. When we had been making no progress, it had been possible to believe that the distance between points A and B was not so far, a few steps at most, if only we could figure out how to get moving. Slight progress, on the other hand, was a daunting revelation about how fast we could expect to be moving in the future. Not two or three major steps but ten thousand tiny ones. We were ants following elephant tracks.

As clearly as I remember my thoughts as I was being told my son was autistic, I also remember the moment I actually believed it.

We were at a playground we'd never been to before, recommended by Melanie because it had a gigantic sand pit with life-sized fossils molded into the concrete underneath so kids could dig up dinosaur skeletons just like a real archaeological site. She said they had dozens of plastic shovels and buckets lying around for everyone to use, a rare example of neighbors being neighborly and no one screwing it up for the rest.

What she didn't mention, however, was that the playground was set fairly far back inside the park, more than a quarter-mile hike from the parking lot. She also didn't explain that in addition to shovels and buckets, there were a dozen toy diggers, dump trucks, bulldozers, and excavators, just begging to be lined up across the sand.

As soon as we crested the hill, I knew we were in trouble.

There were only a couple of other kids at first, and they were intent on the main attraction of the dinosaur bones. Paul scampered about gleefully collecting trucks while in my head I was already planning what follow-up activity I would have to promise in order to draw him away from the siren call of vehicles. My usual go-to choice was food—he loved to eat, and I had learned long ago to always go to the park hungry so he would be motivated to leave without a fight.

Normal lunch wasn't going to cut it this time, however. Maybe take him to his favorite place, Thundercloud Subs? No, that wouldn't work, because the new routine we had established was that we went to Thundercloud after therapy each Tuesday, and if we went to that shopping center now, he would see the therapy clinic across the parking lot and be determined to go inside to see Melanie first.

I could take him to a different Thundercloud location, if I could call a friend to look online for me and tell me the next-closest one. That would set the precedent in his mind of always going to *that* Thundercloud after coming to this park, but it didn't matter because I already knew we were never coming back here again. Toy trucks in a public place? Please.

Or maybe swimming, I thought. It was far too cold, but Paul didn't know that. I would use the promise of it to get him home, then inflate the pool in the back yard and let him be the one to tell me swimming was all done after all.

Just as I had settled on this plan, people started streaming into the dinosaur area at an alarming rate. It must have been a regular play-group that had scheduled a date here, because more than twenty kids suddenly descended on the place at the same time, with the moms all chatting as if they knew one another.

I panicked, but it was too late. The first of the swarm had already started grabbing trucks and playing with them, and more were headed towards the other end of Paul's line even as he tried to take back the ones he'd lost.

"It's okay, sweetheart, you can take turns," I cajoled. "Those trucks don't belong to you. First his turn, then Paul's turn. No, not your turn yet . . . "

He heard nothing. The whining escalated to shouting. I chased after him.

"Paul, do you want to go swimming? Hey, let's go swimming! First swimming, then Thundercloud!"

Even if I were willing to let him be a bully and snatch the trucks away from the other children, he could never have kept up with all of them anyway. The random thought crept into my mind that this was why the Roman Empire had fallen. He had spread his troops too thin.

"Ay-yuh-yuh digger! Ay-yuh-yuh excavator! Ay-yuh-yuh dig-ger!" he screeched, twisting in circles and growing more frantic. I picked him up and placed him in front of the few trucks that were still available, quickly putting them in a perfect line and asking him what color they were, and could he count them? But he shook his head back and forth and flung his body sideways with a deep-throated yell, flopping across the sand like a seal towards the nearest group of children.

I blocked his path with my body, holding one truck out desperately. "Oh, Paul, look! Here's your truck. Let's take it swimming with us."

Screw it, I thought, *we'll be the bad neighbors and steal the toy. I can bring it back later.*

But it was no use. We were done, and I knew what was coming. He roared and scrambled to his feet to run around me, and when I put my arms around his waist, he flung himself backwards so hard his legs went vertical and his head almost hit the ground. I caught him and held him tightly in a cradled position, and he gave in to all-out screaming, legs kicking violently out to the side, my arm expertly wrapped around his hips so he couldn't get a good angle to swing round and kick me.

I squatted there in the middle of the sand pit, just holding tightly and waiting for him to breathe between screams so I could take advantage of the pause to stand up without losing my grip on him. I assume everyone was staring at us by this point, but I couldn't see anything except his face as I got in very close and tried one last time to bring him back to me.

"Paul," I said as softly as I could, our noses almost touching. "Paul, swimming or no swimming? Do you want swimming?"

He calmed for just a heartbeat; I saw the connection being made, the pleading in his eyes . . . and then some little boy drove right by us making truck noises, and all hope was lost. I could have kicked that kid myself, but I'm pretty sure Paul got him solidly in the leg as he let out a violent wail and thrashed every muscle in his body at once. I daresay it served that kid right. You don't go playing near wild animals; that's just common sense.

It certainly wasn't the first time I had hauled Paul away from a public place in the throes of a meltdown, not by a long shot. But normally, I was able to leave my daughter within sight in her baby carrier, force Paul into his own five-point harness, and then come back for her. This time the parking lot was too far away. I was much farther from safety than I'd ever been before, alone with both kids.

I shuffled over to Marie's stroller on the edge of the sand pit, where she stared at us curiously. If nothing else I felt incredibly lucky that my second child was an easy one. If I'd had two Pauls, we would have been prisoners in our home.

Still holding his wrenching, screeching body with all my might, I used my elbows to awkwardly turn her stroller around and began slowly trekking back down the walkway, bumping her forward with my hips every couple of steps. Just then, at the peak of my defeat and the start of what promised to be a very long walk of shame back to the car, I heard a little boy's voice nearby over the sound of my son's anguish.

"Mommy, I want to ride on this one!"

I turned my head to see this child climbing eagerly onto a swing. He was at least a year younger than Paul.

And there it was. A normal kid versus my kid. That kid wanted to ride swings, not spend all his time putting trucks in a long, straight line. That kid spoke in sentences and used pronouns. That kid called his mother "Mommy." That kid was barely a toddler.

Paul didn't just have OCD, or ADHD, or a few sensory issues, or a slight speech delay. Paul was autistic.

The two moms at the swings stopped their conversation and stared at us as we shuffled by. For a moment Paul's strength got the better of me; we wrestled for a new position, and he ended up hanging upside down, both my arms around his waist and my head planted jarringly against his thigh to avoid being kicked in the head. I eked out a few more steps this way—any way was fine as long as we were making progress—until I had to stop and squat down again to reclaim a better hold on him.

The two women just kept staring, the pendulums of their children's swings slowly dwindling as their arms hung limply at their sides in shock.

I forced a wry grin that came out more like a grimace and mumbled, "It's fun, isn't it?"

My attempt at motherly solidarity fell flat. They didn't respond, nor did either one come forward to help me push my daughter's stroller.

"I highly recommend not having an autistic child," I tried again, giving a helpless smile, and still got nothing. One of them looked like she might be about to take her child off the swings just to get away from us.

I resumed hobbling forward, step-step-*hip* to the stroller, my biceps aching and my ears ringing. About halfway back I was sure my muscles were going to give out, and I was struck with sudden inspiration. We were over the hill and out of sight of the playground by now, so I spun in a circle several times to disorient him, turning the stroller off-kilter with one foot, and then said, "Okay, Paul, did you want to go back to the playground? Let's go back to the playground!"

Then I set him down in the direction of the parking lot and urged him forward.

He took off running as fast as he could, and I chased him down with the stroller, covering the ground all the way until the cars came into view. He skidded to a confused halt and spun around, but I scooped him up again and continued forward. We'd covered maybe fifty feet with this trick but still had at least fifty more to go.

After another eternity and several new bruises I had him forcibly buckled into his car seat. I shut the door between us and leaned against the car, listening to his muffled screams, my trembling arms too useless to even pick my daughter up out of her stroller.

It wasn't until ten minutes later, after I'd finally gotten her seated, and the stroller folded and shoved in the back, and the radio turned all the way up to drown out the screaming, that I stopped and allowed myself to cry.

Chapter 4

The Color of Spoons

THROUGHOUT ALL THIS, I never stopped scouring the Internet for more answers. I wanted better sensory tools, better techniques to help me get through each difficult day with my son, better explanations for why some autistic children were wild like mine and others were silent and indifferent. Every night I was reading, and reading, knowing it was unhealthy to obsess so much but not caring. I would sacrifice my health for my son's. Every medical page, every charity, every personal blog—all contained more links to more information, and I refused to quit even if much of it was the same information.

There is a novel by Clive Barker that I read many years ago, about a postal worker in the dead-letter office whose job is to sit alone all day, rifling through thousands of undeliverable envelopes, looking for items or cash. As he's reading these endless tidbits of people's lives, each letter a single chapter in a story of love or hate or monotony, filled with the mundanely cruel and cruelly mundane details of life for months on end, it all starts to blur together for him into a singular understanding of the human condition. That was what I felt I was doing with my endless searching on the Internet: pulling everything together, even the bad information, every version of every idea, so that I could try to gain a sense of the *whole thing*, to wrap my brain entirely around this reality that I hadn't known I was living in until now and pull out some kind of meaningful pattern.

One theme I kept picking up, for example, was that highly sensory children like mine seemed to do better in the hours and even days after an occupational therapy session. But that wasn't true for us. We had learned a lot of useful techniques in therapy, and they were helping a little in a general sense, but if anything, Tuesday nights and Wednesdays were consistently the worst time of the whole week for us.

Another thing that came up again and again was the gluten-free/casein-free, or GFCF, diet. Some parents were reporting changes in their children that bordered on ridiculous after they put them on this diet. Others said they had tried it, but it had done nothing. One website called the Autism Network for Dietary Intervention had many hours' worth of reading on the subject, explaining the medical theories behind the diet, and how to do it, and the ancillary role of allergies and other gastrointestinal symptoms. I read through everything published there more than once, adding each new anecdote to my growing collection of data.

As I'd hoped, a pattern started to emerge, though it was not really one I wanted to acknowledge. The more I read about this diet, the more details I found striking too close to home, until I was overcome with the conviction that it couldn't all be hearsay and coincidence.

Children who responded well to the diet were said to be addicted to gluten and casein, with a recognizable display of addictive behaviors. At that point in time Paul's diet was easily 50 percent dairy. He would eat any vegetable I put in front of him as long as I bargained with bites of cheese. He absolutely lived for cheese, and if we accidentally ran out, that was a guaranteed tantrum. We had joked before, in those exact words, that he was a "cheese addict."

These children were also said to suffer from chronic gastrointestinal symptoms, including severe diarrhea and undigested food in the stools. Paul had both problems, no question. At his twelve-month checkup with the pediatrician, I had mentioned his chronically runny, very colorful stools—orange, yellow, emerald green; pretty much every color had come out of him at some point—but the doctor had said that was normal for breastfed stools, even though Paul was eating mostly solids by then. He was still breast-feeding a little, so it was to be expected. I mentioned it again at his fifteen-month checkup, after he had been completely weaned and his stools were still the same, but I was told that if he didn't have a fever, he wasn't sick. That was "just the way his body was." And Paul's demeanor did seem quite happy and healthy, without any recognizable abdominal pain, so back then I had accepted that answer. Only now did I understand that Paul didn't feel pain the same way we did, so it would be impossible for us to really know if his stomach were hurting or not.

There were more symptoms that matched, including red circles under his eyes, known as "allergic shiners," and a voracious appetite without weight gain. Paul could pack away as much food as an adult at every meal, often more. When we went to Thundercloud Subs he would eat an entire ten-inch sub loaded with meat, cheese, and all the veggies, plus a cookie, a large cup of water, and any part of my own sandwich that I didn't happen to finish. It was hard to imagine how that much food could even physically fit inside him.

And when did we binge at Thundercloud Subs? Why, every Tuesday after occupational therapy, shortly to be followed by the worst behavior we were likely to see all week.

I started sharing with Andrew what I had read, and eventually dropped the bombshell that I wanted to try putting Paul on this diet.

He sighed. "I knew you were going to say that."

"I'm the one feeding him," I said. "You won't have to do anything one way or the other."

"Yeah, but long-term? As he gets older, are you going to want to keep cooking separate meals for him?"

I shrugged. "That, or I'll just make all the dinners GFCF for everyone."

There was a long pause. "I don't know," he said. "That would be really hard." His doubts had clearly shifted from my cooking to his eating. After being met with silence, he repeated in a pained voice, "Yeah. That would be really hard."

"Yeah, well. We'll see."

I wasn't convinced yet that Paul had a problem with gluten; it was dairy that seemed to be the real culprit. I knew I was in for one hell of a fight, so I officially cut him off from dairy on a weekend. That way I'd have a second adult around for support as he went through his supposed withdrawal. Saturday morning I poured rice milk on his cereal and held my breath in anticipation. The taste was a little different, but not much, and I had no idea whether he'd notice or not.

Paul climbed into his booster seat and picked up his plastic spoon. "Blue," he said to me expectantly.

"Yes, your spoon is blue."

"Blue."

"Blue," I agreed.

"Blue."

"Yep, that is a blue spoon."

"Blue. Blue. Blue. Blue," he chanted with a manic grin. This was one of his standard scripts, going on and on about the color of his spoon every morning before finally beginning to eat. He had an obsession with colors in general and would insist on calling many things by their color rather than their name. He didn't eat cereal with his spoon, he ate it with his blue, and a blue spoon and an orange spoon were so fundamentally different as to have nothing in common.

I carefully pretended to maintain my disinterest as I saw him finally take his first bite, from the corner of my eye. He tasted the difference immediately, pushed the bowl away, and left the kitchen.

At least he did it without being nasty, I thought. But shortly after he came back requesting cheese, and my refusals were met with screaming.

I held my ground, and so did he. As the hours ticked by in this fashion, I received a few sour looks from Andrew asking if this was really worth it, but I did my best to keep Paul distracted with cars and DVDs, and gave him unrestricted access to the favorite items that he could still eat, like tostadas with refried beans and canned peaches. It was not a pleasant day.

Sunday morning he climbed into his seat and picked up his spoon.

"Green."

"Green," I repeated for him as usual, not looking up.

"Green. Green. Green."

"Yes, that is a green spoon. Do you like your green spoon?"

"Green."

"Uh-huh, green. Can you eat, please?"

"Green. Green. Green. Green. Green." He hesitantly dipped the spoon into his cereal bowl and put it in his mouth. His face flashed with anger. "Yee-yos!"

"Yes, you have Cheerios."

"Yee-yos!" he demanded again.

"I gave you Cheerios. Take a bite, please."

And another day's screaming started.

Monday morning he climbed into his seat and picked up his spoon. There was a long pause.

"This is a red spoon," he said.

"What?" I croaked, choking back the repetition of "red" that had already been on my lips.

He grinned and took a bite of cereal.

"Paul, what did you say?"

He silently took another bite, then another. When he realized I was still staring at him, he dropped the spoon on the floor and ran out of the kitchen squealing with laughter.

"No way," I said to myself.

"No way!" he shouted back at me, diving headfirst onto the couch. "No way, no way, no way!"

I went into the bedroom and woke up Andrew. "Do you know what your son just said to me?"

"Mmmph," he mumbled.

"He said 'This is a red spoon.'"

"Okay."

"Seriously. He said all those words, just like that."

"Well, that's interesting," Andrew said. "Could be something."

"Are you nuts? That's a big freaking deal! Today is his third day off dairy."

"Okay. If you say so." The question *Can I go back to sleep now?* was unspoken but loud.

"Ugh. I'm telling you!" I insisted. "This is a big deal."

"Okay," he mumbled again.

I left the bedroom door open so Paul would come climb on top of him.

Later that afternoon Paul pointed to his toy tools, saying, "This is a wrench. This is a hammer." There was no doubting what I'd heard this time. Fueled by amazement and confidence, I decided right then to jump into gluten-free as well.

That was a mistake. I hadn't done any research into gluten-free products yet, like I had for our first round of casein-free groceries. I had no list of foods and no plan of attack. I foolishly figured I could wing it.

His brand of refried beans had gluten, so they were out. Oats were considered inherently contaminated with gluten due to the manufacturing process, so Cheerios were no good, either. I tried to make my own chicken nuggets, first in the oven, then fried in oil, then breaded with crushed Rice Chex, and he rejected them all. It didn't matter, though, because only after all of them went into the trash did I realize that our ketchup had gluten in it anyway.

We made a rushed trip to the health food store, and I bought $50 worth of GF substitutes, including various cookies, crackers, cereals, waffles, frozen chicken nuggets, and bread. Paul tasted and rejected every last one of them. Frankly, I didn't blame him; they had all the fragrance and texture of drywall.

The tantrums grew much worse. I didn't understand how he could be so angry over losing gluten when he had never seemed especially attached to it compared to dairy, but whatever the reason, the shrieking was one continuous loop now.

Meanwhile, Andrew had gone back to work and I was alone. It took only two days of this before I was completely haggard and demoralized. I could handle the tantrums, but it was my job as a mother to feed my child, and I couldn't figure out what to even give him from one meal to the next. Plus, I didn't know if the added speech improvements we were seeing now were because he'd gone gluten-free or just continuing benefits from the removal of dairy.

The last straw was when I tried to bake my own gluten-free bread from a mix I'd found at the store. The result wasn't just inedible, it stank up the whole house for hours. It was one thing to put real food in front of him and stoically wait for him to be hungry enough to eat it. I certainly had the stamina for that. But I had nothing I could even serve in good conscience. It was all so disgusting!

So I gave him back his gluten with my white flag held high and retreated to ground I knew I could hold. There was no doubt we'd seen a positive reaction when I had taken casein away, and I vowed he would never eat it again.

Over the next couple of weeks the speech continued to pour out of him. During that time he used words like "now," "these," "it's," and "hey" for the first time in his life. Melanie was amazed. When I'd told her before that we were considering trying the diet, she'd told me flat out that she thought it was an old wives' tale. But by the third week she was a believer.

"He's so focused; just look at him," she marveled. "He's never done anything like this before. Just a completely different kid!"

In addition to engaging in unprompted bouts of pretend play with her—real pretend play that had nothing to do with any movie or TV show he'd seen—he was also suddenly quite happy to wear long sleeves for the first time. Prior to this, he had screamed in apparent pain at even a long-sleeved T-shirt, never mind a jacket, and if I did manage to force anything on him, he would rip it off like a miniature Hulk the moment he was out of reach. I had figured surely he would give up and put something on when he got cold enough, but no. His arms were raw and chapped from an entire winter in T-shirts, and I had lost count of the number of strangers in the grocery store who had archly commented on how cold he must be. I always made sure I had his coat in the shopping cart with me, not because I had any hope that he'd put it on, but just so others could see that he did in fact have one. I hoped it would deter them from calling Child Protective Services.

Melanie grinned at me and shook her head as Paul, in his long-sleeved shirt, carefully pointed out the tires and other parts of the vehicles they were playing with. "This stuff is really for real!" she said. She asked me to write down everything I was doing so she could share it with other patients of hers who were interested in going GFCF.

I reminded her that we hadn't stopped gluten; we were just dairy-free.

She shrugged. "Well, clearly, that part's not necessary, then!"

I wanted so much to believe she was right.

Chapter 5

Data Collection

My sister-in-law has a degree in special education, and though she lived too far away to know about resources local to us, she told me about a state program called Early Childhood Intervention. It provided free speech therapy and other services to developmentally delayed children under the age of three. This was a cutoff that Paul wasn't too far away from, but she told me they also handled the transition into the elementary school's program after his third birthday, so I should start the paperwork now.

I harbor no ill will towards the hardworking and underpaid individuals in that program, but to put it as politely as I can, the ECI program in our county was pretty useless. I have heard from parents in other counties who received good services through their local ECI program, where multiple therapists came to the house and actually interacted with their child on a regular basis, but that was not the way it was for us.

Our caseworker, who was not a therapist, described herself as our "brainstorming partner," whose job was to help us figure out solutions to the day-to-day problems of living with a special needs child. Basically, she came to the house once a week and chatted with me, offering casual suggestions the way any friend would, except most of the time she was just passing on ideas that she had seen other clients use with their kids. It wasn't her fault that she'd had no special training in autism, but it didn't provide much benefit to us, either.

They did an official evaluation of his speech skills, as my sister-in-law had said they would, and determined that Paul qualified for thirty minutes of speech services once a month. This limited time was to be spent not with my child but with me.

Our assigned speech therapist was a chipper blonde woman named Nikki who was quite a lot more like I had been expecting Melanie to be. Each month I would give her a rundown on how Paul was doing, and in turn I would receive advice like "Let's keep working on putting 'want' in front of his requests."

Yes, *let's* do that.

It was obvious there was no "us" in this process, only me. Although it would have been illegal on their part, I sincerely hope that they were deliberately skimping on services for us because our household indicated a reasonable income, and they wanted to save their time and funding for the parents who had no medical insurance and no hope of hiring any private therapist. It's true that I wasn't really hampered by their lack of help, only irritated. But if my experience is comparable to what they provided for everyone, then the program ought to be dismantled immediately and the taxpayer funds used for something better.

However, Nikki did do one really important thing for us, which had nothing to do with speech therapy. On her very first visit, she asked, "And what about his diet; what does he eat?"

The caseworker gave her a sidelong glance, and I could tell the two of them disagreed on this topic. But the caseworker had only started seeing us after we'd taken Paul off dairy, so she had no reference point for how much diet had already changed him.

Nikki was supportive when I told her he was off dairy and doing great, but she reiterated the need to get him off gluten as well.

I told her we had tried, but it was just too hard.

"Yeah, it is," she agreed without a trace of sympathy. "But it's worth it. I've seen so many kids who just really turned around. One of my other clients got their son off gluten, a really severe little boy about seven years old, and one month later all of a sudden he started signing all over the place, really communicating all these things he'd never been able to tell them before."

I wasn't that impressed. Paul had responded to dairy within two days, the change was undeniable, but a month later? Who's to say this boy wasn't about to start using his first signs on his own anyway? Then again, maybe others might claim the same about my son's sudden explosion of speech. A closer coincidence, but a coincidence all the same.

I nodded noncommittally at her story, but she persisted a while longer on the importance of getting him off gluten, until the caseworker was glaring and cutting in to change the subject. After they left I was no more convinced of the perils of gluten, but I did decide that I would keep a daily log of what he ate and how he behaved, as many of the GFCF websites had suggested. I am at heart a big nerd with a righteous core of skepticism, and what I wanted more than anything else was hard data. If I couldn't find good studies for this diet one way or the other in the medical literature, I would just have to make my own.

I laid out several thin vertical columns down the middle of a spiral notebook, with larger open areas on either side. These columns were labeled with various parameters I wanted to measure, such as behavior, speech, hyperactivity level, amount of echolalia, and so on. Each day would be broken into five time periods, moving downward along the preprinted lines of the page: before breakfast, after breakfast, after lunch, after snack, and after dinner. I would rank each parameter on a scale of 1–5 during each time period of the day, with a clear mental yardstick of what a ranking meant to me.

In behavior, for example, a 3 meant that we were fundamentally getting things done, even if there was complaining. I might say, "It's time for a bath," and Paul would let out a wail as always, but at a 3, he would generally allow himself to be nudged up the stairs even as he protested. A 2 meant that he bolted away and I had to carry him squirming up the stairs. A 1 meant he had a full meltdown that lasted past the start of the bath itself. A 4 would mean he actually came upstairs cheerfully, which had never once happened in his life, but I left room for it in the ranking because I hoped we might get there someday.

Five was reserved for things that shocked us, such as behaving perfectly in an especially difficult situation or suddenly using a bunch of words he'd never said before. "This is a red spoon" would have been a 5 had I been scoring back then. But I also knew that this would have to be a sliding, relative scale. Now that he was using "This is a" sentences all the time, that had slipped down to a more middling score in speech, and he would have to do something else new in order to shock us and earn a 5.

It was important to score so many different facets of his day because I knew the data could be misleading without a whole picture. A score of 1 in speech (silence) would also be a 5 in echolalia (no stimming at all). He might be off-the-wall hyperactive but using a lot of meaningful speech at the same time. Was that a good day or a bad day? The data had to be precise and thorough so we could see what, if anything, was causing hyperactivity, separate from what might be causing improved speech.

In the open area on the left half of the page, I wrote down everything he ate, with a line inserting each meal between the appropriate numerical scores—breakfast went between the first and second scores of the day; lunch was inserted between the second and third. This way I could see clearly if there was a consistent change in the numbers when he did or didn't eat gluten at a particular meal.

In the open area to the right, I wrote down any bowel movements he had, again laid out where they fell on the day's timeline. The details here were grossly specific, but I knew his GI problems factored into this, and I needed to know to exactly what degree the worse behavior correlated with worse stools. It would take several weeks to really be able to tease out any patterns in the data, but I kept the notebook out on the kitchen counter and made quick notes whenever Paul sat down to eat. Once I got into the habit, it took surprisingly little time.

Another reason I needed data was for my husband. Andrew's always been the type to argue against any assumption that can't be known with absolute pinpoint certainty, and the recent changes in Paul were clearly unsubstantiated in his mind. He didn't try to stop me from doing any of my dietary experiments, but he was indifferent to them at best.

Then one day we arrived to pick up Paul at his Sunday school class—he had finally begun letting me leave him there a few months earlier—but he didn't come to the door as usual. We found him crouched at the edge of a table, spinning a toy car in front of his eyes. He wouldn't look up or acknowledge me, and when he finally heard that it was time to go, he sprang to his feet and bolted out the door ahead of us.

Instead of going towards the front exit, he veered into the main chapel, sprinting down the aisle towards the musical instruments on stage. Andrew caught up and tried to steer him back in the right direction.

Paul began shouting, "Guitars! Guitars!" at the top of his lungs and scrabbling along the floor to get past Andrew's legs. Finally, Andrew had to pick him up and carry him kicking and screaming out of the building.

It was the first meltdown he'd had in over two weeks.

"Something's wrong," I said in the car.

Andrew snorted bitterly. "Yeah, he's autistic."

"No. Something's wrong. He hasn't been like this, not since we took him off dairy."

I peered into the back seat, where Paul was fiercely arching his back against the car seat and screeching through clenched teeth. I frowned and glanced back at the church. "I bet you a million dollars he ate something."

"You said you sent an e-mail to the Sunday school teachers," Andrew pointed out.

"I did. But they volunteer in cycles, and this would be his first day with this teacher since we told everybody. Maybe she forgot—I'm telling you, they fed him."

He shrugged. "Well, call her and ask. Then you'll know."

As soon as we got home, I did.

"Oh, yes," she breathed in wonder. "It was the strangest thing! You know, we gave them all their little Goldfish crackers for snack, and Paul, he just loved them; you know he's always liked those crackers. So we gave him another cup, and he wanted another one, and another one, but after that we said 'Okay, four is enough.' And he got so upset, you know, like he does sometimes. Just laid on the floor crying."

Not crying, I thought. *Screaming. Let's not pretend it was sweet little droplets leaking from the pouting face of an angel.* I knew she could hear Paul still shrieking in the background on my end of the line. Meanwhile, Andrew was watching me with keen interest, as my half of the conversation made it clear that Paul had, in fact, eaten a significant amount of dairy just before this sudden change.

In the end, it turned out that this teacher had an e-mail address only for distant relatives to stay in touch, and rarely checked it. She had never seen my e-mail at all. She was extremely apologetic and promised to never feed him again unless it was a snack he'd brought with him from home.

"You'll know for next time," I assured her. "It's okay." And it really was. Because though I knew we were probably in for at least two days of awful behavior and poor communication while this infraction cleared out of his system, I could tell from Andrew's face that today had served a very important purpose.

"So they really fed him dairy, huh?" he asked after I'd hung up the phone.

"Yep. Four servings of Goldfish."

"Wow," he said flatly. "Good to know."

"Yep."

"I mean, such a great week, nothing but good behavior, and then— bam! Back to crazy." He pursed his lips intently. After a long pause he shrugged and said, "Dairy-free it is, then."

"Dairy-free it is," I agreed.

"But not gluten?" he asked.

"Nah, gluten's too hard."

"Okaaay . . ."

Don't "okay" me, mister. You're not the one who has to do all the cooking. Funny how the argument I had been using to be allowed to try a new diet was now the argument I was using against having to do it.

The important thing was that Andrew was on board. He's an all-or-nothing kind of guy, and now he was my strongest supporter. He offered to pick up rice milk anytime we ran out, since there was a health food store right by his office, and for the next several weeks he was the first to remind the Sunday school teachers that under no circumstances was Paul to share the other kids' snacks.

When my mom came by the house for lunch the next week, she brought me a bag of gluten-free flour. "Just in case you ever wanted to try making your own bread mix," she said lightly. "I read online that you really can't use just one flour. They say you're supposed to mix a bunch of them together in the right proportions to make it taste right. That box mix you tried before is probably just thrown together in some factory somewhere. I bet their recipe isn't as good as the ones posted online, from real people."

"Okay, thanks," I said. *But I'm not going to need it. Because I don't have to do it.*

Then Nikki came back for her second visit, and once again, she spent as much time talking about how I needed to get Paul off gluten as she did about verbs and sentence structure. She was trying to be supportive, I know, but all I could hear was "Other parents are dedicated enough to make their children healthier; why aren't you?"

I was really starting to resent the hell out of it, actually, and I complained to a friend about her. His written reply was short and to the point.

"Jenn . . . You have to try the gluten free thing," he said. "You know it. That's why it makes you feel bad." And he included a link to a recipe for gluten-free waffles.

I banged out a frustrated reply. "I currently have two different kinds of gluten-free waffles, one of which was homemade, and two additional kinds of just-dairy-free waffles in the house. He will eat none of them."

In fact I had spent hours just trying to find a waffle iron in the same circle shape as grocery store waffles, because I knew appearance was at least as important to Paul as flavor. Yet to my surprise, I had found absolutely nothing. All home waffle irons were either square or giant round Belgian waffles separated into quarters. I looked online and even overseas. I would have considered any price, but they were simply nonexistent.

You would think someone would have thought of this before, a way for consumers to make waffles that looked like actual waffles. But I was learning that no, nothing in my life was correlated with what I would think.

Of course I knew my friend was right, much as I hated it. So as I continued to work on making a dairy-free waffle that Paul would eat, I resolved that I would go ahead and make all my experiments gluten-free as well. The kid wasn't eating my waffles anyway, so I wouldn't be facing any more rejection and failure than I was already putting up with. And if I did get lucky and found just one gluten-free thing I could feed him, then maybe I could make another go at it. In the meantime he would just have to keep lying on the floor and wailing "yellow" every time he remembered he couldn't have one of those stupid dairy-containing Eggo waffles anymore.

That was something, I realized. He wanted *yellow* waffles. Right now all I had to offer him were khaki-colored square waffles. But maybe if they were bright freaking canary yellow, like their retail counterparts?

I made yet another batch, this time using my mother's bag of flour and a ridiculous twenty-four drops of yellow food coloring. They were still square, but the color at least looked like the real thing. (As real as an Eggo waffle gets, anyway.)

The next morning I placed one in front of Paul and declared proudly, "Yellow!"

He stared at it for a long time.

Then he ate it.

I didn't even try to act indifferent this time. I squealed and bounced and made big embarrassing *cha-ching* motions with my arms. In an instant Paul had become gluten-free.

For the next three weeks he ate the exact same thing every day: a homemade neon waffle for breakfast, corn tostadas with gluten-free refried beans for both lunch and dinner, and canned peaches and pears whenever he wanted. Within a few days his stools got sometimes brownish and halfway solid for the first time in his life, his speech and focus continued to get better and better, and the tantrums demanding the wrong foods became fewer and fewer.

He did still crave gluten and dairy, even if their absence wasn't driving him into a frothing rage anymore. I tried keeping separate stashes of food for the other members of the family, but Paul proved repeatedly that he could hunt down the smallest molecule of gluten hidden on the highest shelf, like a drug-sniffing dog. He would have gladly eaten foie gras with a side of roasted bugs for dinner if it had had a trace of gluten in it.

I was getting tired of sprinting into the kitchen and slapping errant foods out of his hand moments before they reached his mouth. Andrew wanted to install a baby-gate at the entrance to the kitchen, but I knew Paul would figure out how to climb over it in hours, if not minutes. Finally, I gave up. The last of the illegal foods went in the trash, and I started serving exclusively GFCF meals to the whole family, even though Paul was still eating his tostadas for dinner every night anyway. When he might be willing to branch out and try a bite of our meals was anyone's guess, but I wanted to be ready when he did. Having poison in the house just wasn't an option.

Yet even that wasn't enough. A couple weeks later I caught Paul in the bathroom sucking on the cap of his shampoo bottle and trying (in vain, fortunately) to pry it open. It was hard to believe, but a quick search online revealed that this brand of shampoo actually had dairy proteins in it as a moisturizer.

I was stunned. I had read about other kids hunting for their "fix" this way while they were detoxing. Stories abounded on the GFCF websites about children supposedly eating their mothers' makeup or licking sunscreen off their own bodies, but I'd assumed it was hyperbole. Once again I had to humbly release a piece of skepticism I'd been holding on to and listen to the parents who had forged this path ahead of me. They said it would happen, and it did.

I threw out the shampoo and bought a safe brand, and Paul never again tried to put the bottle in his mouth.

Eventually, I raised my head above the ramparts and realized that the line I'd been tiptoeing back and forth over for so long was far behind me. Paul was GFCF. We were a GFCF family. Andrew ate whatever he wanted while he was out at work, and of course my two step kids ate a standard diet when they weren't at our house, but Marie and I had been exclusively GFCF for almost as long as Paul had been. I was no longer drowning on a day-to-day basis—or at least not in the kitchen.

Yet now that I was moderately comfortable in the present, it was the future that loomed large. This was real, and it was permanent. I had to really cook this way forever, and the handful of dinners I'd had on a short rotation for the last month weren't going to cut it.

Despite being the primary chef in our family for going on six years, I was still fairly inexperienced, a state perpetuated by reluctance. Truth be told, I hated cooking, and having to make everything from scratch for the rest of my life was very close to my personal definition of hell. But I would do what I had to do for my child. This was our life now, so I had to find a way to be motivated about it.

I did some soul-searching. Why, exactly, did I get no enjoyment from cooking? Other people certainly seemed to, yet I saw it as nothing but a chore. The definition of a chore, I reasoned, is something you have to do over and over again. You pick up the toys, only to watch the kids dump them all out again. You wash the laundry just so you can put the clothes right back on. You vacuum the carpet to make room for the new dust to settle. You cook the food, and thirty minutes later it's gone again. There's no proof that you ever did it in the first place.

Sure, you get to bask in the pleasure of your family and their profuse gratitude. Whatever. Verbal praise doesn't motivate me; it never has. Visible accomplishments are what motivate me, and the only meals that stay visible are the ones that no one wanted to eat.

What I needed was a way to make my cooking accomplishments permanent, to turn cooking into a job rather than a chore. A job meant being obligated to people outside my household.

"I need you to get me a website," I told Andrew.

"What kind of website?"

"I want a cooking website. So I can post photos and recipes, and when I don't want to cook I'll have to, because it'll be time to post something new to the site."

"You hate cooking, so you want to run a cooking website?"

"It'll force me to keep trying new things," I explained. "I promise, it will make me hate cooking less. And anyway, people need to know about this diet."

He helped me work out the details. I didn't want one of the standard templates you could get from hosted blog sites. I wanted my own unique domain, with a visual layout I had complete control over and the ability to eventually put up ads and generate revenue. Jobs have to make you money, or they're not jobs, right? But when I told him what domain name I wanted him to register, Andrew balked.

"The GFCF Lady? Ugh, seriously?"

"Yes, I knew you would hate it," I said. "But I don't care. That's the one I want."

"It's just got that whole . . . sassy, power-of-the-woman vibe," he groaned. "It's so irritating. Is that really what you're trying to portray?"

"My readership is going to be 100 percent women," I reminded him.

"But this name makes it about you. I thought it was supposed to be about the cooking."

"It's supposed to be about how regular moms can successfully do this for their kids. It's about the moms feeling like they're not alone. Besides, any successful website, anything successful at all, relies on a cult of personality. You have to be interested in the person behind the message. It's why products have spokespersons; it's why Stephen Colbert has a million viewers every night. There has to be a character in people's minds."

He was not at all convinced. To this day I'm pretty sure he still hates the name. But he did the distasteful deed and registered it for me. Just like that I became a blogger, telling people how to do a diet I had only been doing myself for a month.

Chapter 6

A Gut Reaction

As it happened, my mother was looking into her own nutrition during this time as part of a weight-loss effort, and she attended an informal class taught by a nutritionist named Deirdre. Though the class wasn't specifically geared towards following a gluten-free diet, Deirdre did go into some of the medical problems gluten can cause and mentioned during the lecture that she herself was gluten-free.

Afterwards, my mother asked her if she knew anything about a gluten-free, casein-free diet for autistic children, since her grandson had recently been showing such great success with it. It turned out that Deirdre's primary job was, in fact, working in a medical clinic for autistic children. The main doctor at the clinic, Dr. Bryan Jepson, had written a book called *Changing the Course of Autism*, which went into great detail about the biological processes behind the GFCF diet as well as many other potential medical treatments for children with autism.

My mother recounted this whole conversation to me the next time she came over for lunch, whereupon she also handed me a copy of Dr. Jepson's book.

I read it cover-to-cover in two days. Admittedly, I had to skim a fair portion of the material, as some of it is extremely technical, and the whole book is really written for other physicians, not parents. But

I understood enough. More importantly, it referenced hundreds of medical studies and explanations that I hadn't seen anywhere else. It noted, for example, that the pairing of gluten and casein is not at all random. Both proteins are broken down in the intestines by a single enzyme called dipeptidyl-peptidase IV. If an individual has a problem digesting one protein, they by definition have a problem with the other.

Knowing this simple fact could have saved me so much agonizing. If I had understood in the beginning that gluten was equivalent to dairy in this regard, I would never have waffled over eliminating it. I also learned that the connection between gluten and autistic behaviors in affected children had been noted repeatedly in medical literature since 1980, and digestive disorders in general had been recorded as far back as the very first diagnosed cases of autism in 1943, yet somehow the information was only being passed from parent to parent online, and almost never from doctor to patient.

Dr. Jepson's book further explained how an autistic child's problem with gluten and dairy was not the same as a typical food allergy but rather was a neurological reaction. The addictive behaviors that parents reported were, in fact, due to a literal addiction, as the molecular structure of the two proteins almost precisely mimicked that found in heroin and morphine. If allowed to enter the bloodstream undigested, they would attach to the same opioid receptors in the brain as these narcotics and cause many of the same predictable effects on the body. Imagine giving your infant multiple doses of heroin every day—by the time he reached two or three years old, his resulting developmental problems might look a whole lot like autism.

There were also solid references about the autoimmune symptoms of autism, gut dysbiosis, specific vitamin deficiencies, and the appropriate treatment for all of these. It was more information than I could possibly absorb in one reading. This book would become my bible over the next several years as I thumbed back through its chapters again and again each time we were ready to address some new aspect of Paul's disease.

The footnote citations of medical studies made up almost half the book, so there was no question it was well researched. Why, then, was all of this information so hard to find and so controversial? Why was this detailed medical manual of peer-reviewed studies considered the alternative set of treatments, while the mainstream recommendations consisted solely of nonbiological solutions like skin-brushing and rigorous behavioral training? It was so backwards. In an age when almost every major psychiatric disease had been determined to have a chemical origin in the brain, autism treatment was stuck in the era of Freud. Certainly, there were proponents of biomedical treatment for autism on the Internet—by now I was on at least a dozen different message boards dedicated to these topics and still spent over an hour reading every day—but these parents rarely produced the scientific justification for their actions that was right there to be had, if only they'd looked for it.

I decided to fill out an intake form at Dr. Jepson's clinic, which was called Thoughtful House. This somewhat unusual name was what a founding donor's autistic son had called his quiet hideaway in the back yard. The clinic had a long waiting list and required patients to be on a strict GFCF diet before they could even schedule an appointment.

The initial paperwork included, among other things, extremely detailed questions about the frequency, color, firmness, and smell of Paul's stools. This encouraged me, because although his Technicolor diapers had improved dramatically after we had taken him off gluten and casein, they were still far from ideal. One of the major mantras of parents doing these types of treatments was "It's all about the poop." Until he's having exactly one movement each day, they said, that is fully formed, brown, leaves no tarry residue, contains absolutely no undigested food, no speckles, no mysterious sandy texture, and may smell unpleasant but doesn't fill the room with a nauseating stench that lingers for hours . . . until then, you're not done.

And we clearly weren't done. The GFCF diet had fixed many of Paul's behavioral problems and made him much better at communicating, but his style of communication was still fundamentally the same. Before, he would chant "Yellow-yellow-yellow-yellow" to indicate that he wanted to eat a waffle, whereas now he could say, "Go downstairs, eat yellow waffle-ah-jelly. Open the gate, please." An amazing transformation, no doubt, but the reality was that most of his new speech was still just scripted chunks strung one after the other. He could not have taken that final phrase, for example, and generalized it into "Open the *fridge*, please." As far as he still knew, "openthegate" was one word.

Similarly, he knew that I was identified by the word "Mommy," but only in the same way that he knew his utensil was called a "spoon." He would never have called my name to get my attention, or cried out for me when he was hurt, or yelled it joyously when he saw me return. He couldn't comment on something funny he saw, or refer to anything that had happened in the past, or use speech for any purpose except requesting what he wanted in that exact moment.

He also still spent large portions of his time scripting for fun, and if anything, he had become more obsessive about lining items up, not less. The diet had merely increased his attention span for these activities, not lessened the compulsions. Yet at the same time, he no longer threw a fit if the script was interrupted or if the line of toys was moved. Life was immeasurably better for all of us with Paul on his new diet, but it was still very much life with an autistic child.

Different relatives came to accept the diagnosis at different rates. My mother had been on board from the very beginning, and she had the most open and accepting response of anyone, including me. While most relatives were still having their feelings hurt that Paul wouldn't hug them, she was happy to accept a quick high five as the sincerest form of intimacy he could offer. My mom's always been more politically active than I, and just a few weeks after we began seeing Melanie, she informed me that she had officially changed her monthly charity donations from an anti-coal-mining nonprofit to the National Autism Association.

"It's my new cause," she said matter-of-factly, pointing out the autism awareness car magnet she'd received as part of the membership package. There honestly seemed to be no grieving period for her— she wanted recovery just like I did, and would get me every tool and article she could find that might help, but I got the feeling that she wouldn't be disappointed if we achieved less. She was very zen about the whole thing.

My father, on the other hand, cheerfully maintained a more confident version of my own stubborn denial. He glossed over the diagnosis itself and heard only the part about how his brilliant daughter was going to buck the medical establishment and fix it. This narrative fit all too well with his lifelong distrust of doctors and his assumption that *of course* I was smarter than they were, so there was nothing to worry about. He only barely acknowledged that our struggles were greater than any other family's.

"Having children changes everything! I told you it would. No one is ever prepared for it," he would pronounce sagely, as if this really all fell under the aegis of new-parent jitters. I loaned him my copy of Dr. Jepson's book, and that helped to sober him up a bit as far as the medical seriousness of Paul's condition, but it also reinforced his belief that we had the information we needed and everything was under control.

"You know what they're going to say, don't you, after you finish everything you're doing?" he said. "They're going to tell you he never had it to begin with."

"Good," I said with a defiant shrug. "As long as they get the chance to say that, I don't care."

He ignored my implied fear that we might not get that far. In his eyes I was a righteous avenger who would change the way the world looked at autism. In reality I was more like a cornered animal: willing to take any measure to escape and not exactly interested in forming a predator-prey United Nations after the fact. Later he would have the chance to see a few older autistic children in public and would gain a greater appreciation for how hard things might be for us on a daily basis. But for now he was just bemused with his own prediction, patiently awaiting the day when I got around to "finishing everything" so he could be proven right.

"Have you thought about writing a book about all this stuff you're learning?" he asked. "Something from the parent's perspective. You have the doctor's book, that's great; now we need the other side of it. That's your job. Or maybe work together with him on a sequel. You could alternate chapters, you talking about what you did and then him talking about why it worked." My protests that I had no time for sleep, let alone writing a book, might as well have been directed at Paul for all they were heard. (And clearly, I lost that argument in the end.)

My mother-in-law was resistant to the diagnosis, partly because Paul knew more colors, numbers, and letters than most of the children in the low-income preschool class she taught. Autistic children often excel well beyond their peers in these academic subjects, though, and many are reading as young as three years old, as Paul was showing signs he might do. The fact that he had mastered the alphabet by eighteen months was actually a strike against him in the diagnostic balance, a common symptom known as hyperlexia. At any rate, her process of acceptance seemed to take longer than most. Every time she saw us she would ask, "So, do you really think? . . ." The question always trailed off in a tone indicating she didn't really believe it herself but was too polite to openly disagree with us—too polite to even say the word.

"Yes, he is definitely autistic," I told her firmly during one family get-together as we watched Paul bouncing around the room reciting snippets of television monologues. "I mean, when you see him next to real kids, it's so obvious—"

"He's a real kid!" my own mother interrupted, horrified. "He's certainly not a fake kid."

"I know," I said with an embarrassed laugh. "That's not what I meant."

But it was what I meant. Other people had kids, and I had something else. Something I loved dearly, and understood better than anyone else, and was ferociously dedicated to, but an entirely different creature nonetheless. It was like having a pet dog and suddenly finding out it's a cat instead. *Oh,* you think, *that's why it would never sit or play fetch.* A cat is not a smaller, shorter-haired dog, nor is it a dog that "sees the world in a different way." A cat is different on a more fundamental level, and someone who knows all about dogs still knows nothing about cats. None of this made my son any less mine, or any less loved, but the dog costume had been unexpectedly yanked off my cat, and I couldn't shake the bitter feeling that I had been tricked.

That feeling of loss was painful, as any parent of a special needs child can identify with, but it also strengthened my resolve to reclaim what I felt was rightfully mine. I admit that this wasn't the most tranquil attitude to take, but it was how I felt, and still feel today. Autism parents often share inspirational messages with each other about marathons-not-sprints, or appreciating Holland, or the famous verse "Life isn't about waiting for the storm to pass; it's about learning how to dance in the rain." But that mindset just wasn't for me. I reject both dancing and waiting. I would rather invent an umbrella or, more likely, be so arrogant as to stand firm in the gale and command the clouds out of the sky. I am not a silver-lining kind of person, and I have never been able to view life's setbacks as gifts. Setbacks are setbacks, and the only option, as far as I'm concerned, is to simply work harder to overcome them.

"Well, when the school district evaluates him," my mother-in-law would say diplomatically, "they'll be able to tell you where he is in relation to other children his age."

"Yes, they will," I would agree, just as diplomatically.

The evaluation she was referring to was known as the Transdisciplinary Play-Based Assessment, or TPBA, and it was the next in a long line of bureaucratic acronyms that would come after ECI. The TPBA would score his developmental delays and thus confirm his eligibility for PPCD, or the Preschool Program for Children with Disabilities. After identifying and enumerating his specific deficits, this information would be used to write his IEP, or Individualized Education Plan, which was a list of goals that the PPCD teacher would be aiming to teach him over the course of the school year.

An IEP is an official acknowledgment that the standard curriculum (kindergarteners learn the alphabet, first graders learn addition, etc.) isn't realistic due to a student's disability, so a new scale is devised, unique to each child who has one. Sometimes the accommodations are minimal; for example, an IEP may hold the student to the normal curriculum, but with modifications such as more time to complete tests or additional help like speech therapy. In other cases, depending on the severity of the disability, an IEP goal can be as basic as learning to press a button on command by the end of the year.

The next acronym up the chain is the ARD (Admission, Review, and Dismissal) committee, a group of individuals who craft the IEP and who will ideally, but not always, have some knowledge of the child whose future they are deciding. At a minimum this ad hoc group includes either a principal or vice principal, the child's teacher and therapists, and the parents. Other common attendees are an ARD coordinator, a lead special education coordinator, any private therapists the parents have hired, social workers, language interpreters, and sometimes even a random general ed teacher who has never taught the child and likely never will, but is invited in order to provide "perspective." In short, anyone deemed by anyone else to be pertinent to the discussion can attend.

In theory an ARD meeting is a collaborative process, with everyone having the student's best interests in mind. In reality it is a highly legalistic procedure, and the adversarial relationship between the family and the school is taken as a given. The school is the one footing the bill, after all, so all staff members have a strong incentive to find that a child doesn't need as many services as the parents think he does, and many parents hire legal advocates to attend meetings and fight on their behalf.

Even before our first interaction with the school district, my mother had given me a book called *Wrightslaw*, the widely acknowledged bible on navigating the special education system and protecting your child's legal rights. Initial browsing of the book had left me disgusted. It was thorough and excellent advice, to be sure, but the basic assumption throughout was that the school would be out to screw you every step of the way. It was not *if* the school blocks your request for an evaluation but *when*, followed not by "Here are the people at the school who can help you" but rather "Here is the notarized form letter you will deliver, containing the most effectively threatening legalese."

I am not a confrontational person, and I didn't want that kind of relationship with our school. It didn't have to be that way; I was sure of it. Certainly, everyone at our school seemed to be taking the evaluation process seriously so far. I was told to block out no less than three hours for our TPBA and to bring any favorite toys or snacks that might keep Paul's enthusiasm up during the barrage of standardized tests he would be undergoing. Upon arrival I learned that "play-based" meant that the evaluations would take place in a fully stocked preschool classroom that had been reserved for our exclusive use. They were serious about getting a thorough picture of him.

Our evaluation team included a lead PPCD teacher, an educational assistant, a school district psychologist, and a speech language pathologist, none of whom I'd ever met before or ever saw again. All four kept their attention on Paul over the next several hours, each one taking their turn trying to engage him in activities and administer tests while the others took detailed notes.

A few weeks later they mailed us an eleven-page report with their findings.

> During the TPBA, Paul was observed to engage in limited age-appropriate social interaction skills and play behaviors. . . . Throughout the assessment he either responded no-no-no when questions were asked or he made no attempt to respond. . . . While walking around the room, Paul commented Superhands, uh-uh-uh Superhands, etc. His mother noted that these were lines from a favorite TV show. When the play facilitator commented that she wanted to see Paul's hands, he loudly protested no-no-no-no-no. Play with the birthday cakes was then introduced. Paul labeled the numbers on the cakes. When the play facilitator began to sing the Happy Birthday song, Paul put his hand out and said uh-uh-NO! Paul showed pleasure when the bubbles were introduced. He commented bubble and pop the bubble as he popped bubbles with his hands and feet. When the play facilitator tightened the lid of the bubble container and put it on the floor, Paul picked up the container and attempted to open it. After a couple of unsuccessful attempts to open the container, he handed it to the play facilitator and verbally requested bubbles . . . please. Before the play facilitator could open the container, Paul walked away. He briefly played with a keyboard

toy and then returned to lining up vehicles. He again repeated a series of rote, repetitive phrases.

It went on and on. The report's lengthy descriptions of his behavior were no surprise, as I'd been there in the room and had provided a lot of information about things they hadn't been able to see demonstrated in person. What startled me was the scoring.

First were the percentile scores from the standardized tests. In the test for autistic behaviors, such as repetitive movements and echolalia, he was between the 55th and 75th percentiles, "Very Likely Autistic." In general social awareness, compared to normally developing children on the cusp of their third birthday, he was in the 1st percentile—that is, the poorest rank he could have.

Worse than that, though, were the descriptions of what age his behaviors did match up with. In academic skills such as reading and math, he was already equal to a four-year-old; that much was no surprise. But his overall speech score was commensurate with that of an eighteen-month-old, and on the social/emotional scale he was only a nine-month-old.

An infant. Less developed than his baby sister. I thought I had accepted the reality of this diagnosis, but that number hurt. Especially since I knew how much worse he'd been just two months ago, before we'd put him on his diet.

At the time of the evaluation we still hadn't gotten to our appointment with the pediatric neurologist—it was the day immediately after, as it happened—but the assessment leader reassured me that they didn't need a formal diagnosis to enter him into the PPCD program. They had a generic designation they could use called NCEC, which stood for noncategorical early childhood delay. She presented this as a great boon in our favor.

I later learned that the district will push to use that designation even when a formal diagnosis is available, because once the word "autism" is on the record, they are assumed to be responsible for more services than they have money to provide. Better to remain undeclared and hope the parents don't learn about the state-mandated autism rider for special education services. *Wrightslaw*, it would turn out, had been completely right.

I hadn't yet learned how the system worked, however, so I thought it was great news that they could admit him to the program without a diagnosis. Besides, I had no interest in loading up on special education services for the next fifteen years anyway. I couldn't wait for the day Paul no longer qualified, under any designation.

Chapter 7

Thoughtful House

I STILL WASN'T sure what we were supposed to be doing at our first appointment with the neurologist, since we were already well aware that Paul was autistic, but I thought perhaps the doctor might want to check for seizure activity, since as many as 30 percent of autistic children also experience some form of epileptic seizures. I suffer from partial temporal lobe seizures myself (yet another risk factor for having an autistic child, for those keeping count), so it was reasonably likely that Paul might as well. Ultimately, the appointment would turn out to be even more pointless than I'd feared, and it was the first big step in my rapid disillusionment with the medical establishment.

After waiting for over an hour, we were first seen by a physician's assistant, who had me list all of the symptoms and behaviors that had led us to schedule this visit. I knew the jargon by now—he's *a runner*, communicates mostly by *echolalia*, engages in both physical and verbal *stimming*—but she insisted on thorough details.

"Describe what you mean when you say 'echolalia,'" she said, to which I responded with a textbook list of examples, as if anyone might accidentally use the word "echolalia" without knowing what it meant.

"Okay. Tell me about the daily spinning you mentioned."

"He spins," I repeated. "Every day."

"Ah . . . so, on his feet, spinning in circles?"

"Yes. Just like he's doing right now."

She glanced at him. "Ah."

And so on, for every symptom. Even without the patronizing clarifications, I had just gone through all these same symptoms the day before with the school district and was really quite tired of it. Eventually, she left, and we waited for another half hour before the doctor finally came in.

He, in turn, looked over the information the assistant had written on the chart and then went down the list asking us to review each bullet point for him again.

"So, lots of echolalia?"

"Yes."

"And he'll use that, both to sort of communicate in his own way as well as say things to no one in particular?"

"Yes."

"Okay . . . hmm . . . "

The truth was the neurologist looked extremely uncomfortable, as if he didn't want to be in the room at all. He kept glancing furtively at Paul and seemed to be going slower and slower as he approached the end of the chart.

"So . . . it says here you've got him on a dairy-free diet?"

"Gluten-free and dairy-free, yes."

He made a face. "Yeah, that's really only for patients who have severe digestive problems."

"Oh, yes, he's had terrible digestive problems for years."

"Ah . . . yes . . . I see that here. Okay, well, a couple separate problems going on at once, then."

"But it's not really separate," I pushed back. "The diet made a huge difference in his behavior and speech."

"Yeah, that's what some patients say," he muttered, not the least bit interested. Another long pause as he stared at the paperwork. "And the occupational therapist, she told you it might be PDD-NOS?" This extended version of the acronym accounted for the unwieldy subtitle "Not Otherwise Specified," which was sometimes used to separate

PDD on an emotional—if not medical—technicality from "real" autism. The joke among parents was that PDD actually stood for "Pediatrician Didn't Decide," while NOS was assigned a variety of meanings, not all of them polite.

"Yes," I said.

He continued scanning and nodding to himself. His silence was made all the more obvious by Paul's steady chatter. Finally, the doctor narrowed his eyes and leaned back uneasily.

"So . . . do *you* think he has PDD?" he asked.

I was stunned. "Yeah," I blurted out, only barely stopping myself from finishing with "duh!" Instead I managed to declare, only slightly less disdainfully, "I think he has autism."

The doctor's face visibly melted in relief. "Yes, yes, I would definitely say high-functioning autism, not PDD," he said. He began scribbling rapidly in the chart, all tension gone.

And I suddenly understood. He had thought he would be breaking the news to me and was terrified to have to do it. For a moment I felt bad for him; he must spend every day destroying the dreams of parents, watching them either break down in tears or storm out in angry denial.

But then my contempt returned. He was a doctor, and that was his job. Medical students have to take whole classes on how to break bad news to patients. Oncologists tell people they are going to die from cancer every single day. Yet this man had effectively asked me what diagnosis I wanted to hear, which was pathetic, not to mention unethical. I am certain that if I'd said, "No, I really think the occupational therapist has it wrong," he would have eagerly agreed that it was too soon to know for sure.

Apparently, there wasn't much left to say after that. The neurologist noted that there were medications available for obsessive-compulsive tendencies and antipsychotic drugs for the kids who just couldn't calm down, and he'd be willing to consider either type for Paul after his third birthday. He did think the PPCD class might help with some of the behaviors, so he instructed us to come back for a follow-up in the fall to evaluate which prescriptions would be most appropriate.

I asked if we should do an electroencephalogram (EEG) for potential seizure activity, but he said it wasn't warranted since Paul had never had a visible muscular seizure, and he would have to lie still to get a good reading anyway. I had to admit that Paul wouldn't be able to do that. This being agreed, we were ushered out, our formerly anxious doctor now striking up pleasant conversation and apologizing for the initial wait.

Never mind the three months we waited to get in, I thought, *just so you could be too chicken to tell me what I already knew.* I hadn't even told him what I thought about his suggestion of putting a three-year-old on antipsychotics. As one final insult, when the benefits statement came in the mail a few months later, it showed that his office had billed our insurance $500 for that whole fifteen minutes of useless quivering.

I scratched neurologists off my list of people who might be able to help us. Or at least I scratched that particular doctor off the list and moved the rest of the neurology profession to the very back of the line, to wait for a day when Paul might be able to undergo an EEG.

Though we were still only four months past our initial diagnosis with Melanie, I felt like time was rushing by. Everyone agrees that there is a critical window for treatment with autism, and Paul's upcoming birthday was no longer a celebratory milestone but a dire warning about how little time we had left.

Usually, this need for "early intervention" is said in the context of therapy rather than medical treatments, but the simple fact was we couldn't afford therapy. It's all well and good to trumpet the notion that an autistic child needs therapy to make progress, but most people, including our pediatrician, were unaware that this therapy costs literally thousands of dollars a month and usually isn't covered by insurance. We were already paying $260 a month just for one hour a week with Melanie, and some studies showed that a minimum of twenty hours a week is needed to make any long-term difference. Autism therapy costs more than college, and people usually spend over a decade saving up for that. Ironically, many autism parents use their children's college funds to pay for treatment because, as one mother told me bitterly,

"Hey, not going to need that anymore, right?" Other parents choose to go $100,000 into debt, figuring they will just pay it off over the next fifteen years rather than saving up for it, but most banks won't accept a functioning child as loan collateral.

The only money available to me was medical insurance to see medical doctors, and I was going to use that to the fullest extent that I could. We had managed to get our intake with Thoughtful House scheduled less than two weeks after our appointment with the neurologist, but still I felt that time was hurtling away from us. My impatience was compounded by the fact that the initial appointment wasn't going to be with the doctor at all but with a nutritionist. This seemed unnecessary to me since we already had Paul on a GFCF diet, but it was part of the process and apparently couldn't be skipped.

Our nutritionist at Thoughtful House was a young woman named Kirsten, and based on a detailed three-day food diary that we gave her, she gave us a complete breakdown of his average nutrients and deficiencies. My guard was raised as she began naming brands of vitamins and minerals that were better than others, in the sense that they were gluten-free and used no artificial colors or sweeteners. This was something I'd been warned about by our ECI caseworker, who was as dismissive of Thoughtful House as she had been about the GFCF diet, though she was definitely coming around on that latter question as she saw Paul making steady improvements each week. The caseworker had told me a story about another client of hers who had gone to Thoughtful House but wanted to keep using some of the supplements their child was already on. Supposedly, this family had been told that they must use only approved supplements, purchased directly from the Thoughtful House office, or the clinic would refuse treatment altogether.

That was obviously unacceptable—if it were true. Knowing that I could no longer trust everything the doctors said did not turn parental anecdote into the Oracle at Delphi, especially not second-hand anecdotes like this one. Autism is above all an epidemic of misinformation, and I felt that I had no choice but to investigate every single thing myself. So I had resisted the urge to simply cancel our appointment after hearing this story, but I had also come in with an even more distrustful attitude than usual.

"This is what the bottle looks like, just so you know," Kirsten continued, holding one out to me. "Natural Calm is the brand, but the mineral you're looking for is called magnesium citrate."

"So I should buy that here?" I asked, my face a mask of calm curiosity.

"Oh, no! Don't do that," she replied.

"I . . . can't?"

"Well, you can if you really want to," she said, "but it's cheaper at People's Pharmacy. I just wanted to show you what it looks like so you could find it on the shelves. We only have some in the office here because many of our patients are from out of state, or even out of the country, and they can't get it where they are. So for them, we'll ship it to them at cost, but we have to pay the shipping to get it here from the manufacturer in the first place, so it's going to be maybe a buck or two more expensive than you'll find in person at the store."

Then she named one or two other brands I could use if the Natural Calm were out of stock or Paul didn't like the flavor. It seemed this place was on the level after all. There was no proprietary line of supplements, no display for sale in the waiting room, no smarmy doctor's face plastered on anything. It was just a normal medical office, albeit one very well designed to accommodate autistic children. Each exam room, if it could even be called that, was carpeted, furnished with chairs and couches instead of a paper-covered table, and stocked with piles and piles of toys. And when Kirsten had entered the room, she had quickly appraised just what type of autistic child I had brought with me and expertly moved her chair to block the door handle without a second thought.

Actually, it was amazing. This was the first place I had ever been where other people *got it*. The information they were giving me made sense, not just scientifically but based on my personal experiences with my son's symptoms and reactions. I felt that they already knew my story before I came in, and everything they said resonated with things I had seen myself or corroborated research I had found online.

The magnesium citrate, for example, was meant not just as a nutritional supplement because the dietary analysis had shown that Paul was deficient in magnesium, but also to increase bowel motility. I reminded Kirsten that he struggled with diarrhea, not constipation, but she explained that it was possible, in a way, to have both at the same time.

"You've seen food come out undigested in his stools, right?" she asked.

"Yeah, all the time," I said.

"So, using the food bits as a kind of marker, how many days happen between when he eats a certain food and when it comes out again?"

"Oh, could be anywhere from two to five days, usually."

"See, that's too slow," she said. "The whole digestive process should be about twenty-four hours. The fact that his stool isn't solid is totally separate from how fast it's moving through him. When his food just sits inside him for days at a time like that, especially undigested, it's going to ferment, and cause all that bloating, and lead to major problems with his gut flora."

I told her that I had stopped letting Paul have certain foods that always came out undigested no matter what, like tomatoes and oranges.

She nodded. "That's a good idea, for now. Something else you might consider adding is a digestive enzyme with meals, which will help break down his food." She made a quick note on her clipboard, muttering a reminder to herself to ask so-and-so before we left. Seeing the question on my face, she explained, "That's the woman you talked to at the desk before you came in. Her son has done really well with digestive enzymes. I know there are a couple different ones that are good, but she was telling me the other day that she had really liked one of them better than the others, and I can't remember which one it was."

"So she has an autistic son, too?" I asked, surprised.

"Oh, yeah, they all do," she said, gesturing in a circle to indicate the entire office. "I mean, the ones who have kids anyway. There are a couple who don't, but usually that's the only way anyone gets into this business."

They all do. I remembered reading in the introduction to Dr. Jepson's book how he had radically altered his career as an ER physician after his own son had been diagnosed with autism. His distraught wife had been reading about all these crazy treatments on the Internet, and he, being trained in sound scientific rigor, had set out to prove to her that there was no medical basis for these theories. Of course, having delved into it, he had discovered that there actually was a significant basis for it, and had ultimately left his prominent and successful position in the ER to pursue biomedical treatment of autistic children.

Everyone gets it here, I thought, *because they live this every day just like I do. And they're telling me what works, not just in a study a researcher did somewhere, but what is working, today, in their own homes.*

The thought occurred to me that maybe I would work here someday, too.

"As we heal his inflammation," Kirsten went on, "he'll be able to digest more. But ideally, he really shouldn't be eating anything that he can't digest properly. Not until he's ready."

This was a familiar sentiment. One quotation I had run across several times in my research was by a prominent gastroenterologist named Dr. Samuel Gee, who said, "We must never forget that what the patient takes beyond his ability to digest does harm." Hippocrates, the father of modern medicine, even went so far as to declare that "all disease begins in the gut."

I believed it to be true. *Until his digestion is perfect*, I reiterated silently, *we're not done.*

"So you're saying anything that comes out undigested—after we start giving him these enzymes, I mean—anything after that that's still coming out, we have to take it away from him?"

She gave a sympathetic smile. "It would be better for him, if you can manage it."

Oh, I could manage it, all right. I'm the one who once allowed my picky stepson to starve himself for a day and a half until he finally decided that eating anything other than crackers would be a good idea. I'm the one who already took away dairy and gluten from an autistic child who could throw a better tantrum than any I'd ever seen.

And gave it back once, a voice said.

Shut up, I told it.

If this was what my son needed to get better, then I would rip the Band-Aid off and not apologize for it. I would take away all food and put him on an IV if that was the medical treatment necessary to cure this medical disease.

We took in all of Kirsten's nutritional recommendations, adjusting his diet accordingly and adding one new supplement a week while watching for changes. The supplements he took each day got written in my notebook along with the other data, which Kirsten had praised for being very thorough, even though I had been embarrassed by the scrawl of notes filling each page from top to bottom. They were actually quite organized, I knew, but it was all shorthand and made sense only to me.

With these notes it had become clear, for example, that every time he ate peaches, Paul would have a significant spike in hyperactivity just a few minutes later. Had he always been reacting to peaches? Or had he developed this new sensitivity only after eating peaches two to three times a day for months on end? It was impossible to know, since prior to going gluten- and dairy-free, the hyperactivity had been at a constant maximum. But when we took peaches out of his diet, we were rewarded with another lowering of that threshold and a little more meaningful speech. Step by step, we isolated more foods he couldn't tolerate, and day by day, he improved.

Chapter 8

Be the Change

ONE OTHER THING struck me powerfully about the Thoughtful House waiting room, besides the autism-friendly design and complete lack of product placement. Delicately lettered across one entire wall was the Mahatma Gandhi quotation "Be the change you want to see in the world." This philosophy seemed to genuinely drive the office, since for most of the employees this was not going to be a particularly career-advancing job, and in some ways it could be quite detrimental, given the controversy currently surrounding autism treatment. I was moved by their dedication and felt that I had an obligation to fight this battle as well. My cooking website wasn't enough; I needed to show the world my evidence that this was real.

So I got out my camera and began filming. I imagined that I'd need to film a lot and edit several clips together in order to capture all the new things Paul could do now. But as it happened, I got everything I needed in just one take.

He was sitting in the office chair with Marie, watching an animated version of "Green Grow the Rushes, Oh!" on YouTube. He noticed my camera and said, "Ayuh-yuh-yuh taye a pitch-i-ker." He loved the flash in his eyes.

"I will take a picture, just a minute," I said, continuing to record.

He squirmed a bit but didn't fuss at being put off, which he most certainly would have done prior to his dietary change. Then he decided to hug his sister.

"Ahh, squeesh," he mumbled.

"Are you giving her good hugs?" I asked.

"Ah-yuh, squeesh."

This was good, I thought. Now I could check off "showing affection" from the list of things I wanted to demonstrate.

A moment later he squinted his eyes tightly, then rolled them back in his head and smacked himself hard in the face with both hands. He would usually do this tic only a couple of times a day, so catching it on camera had been very lucky. I definitely wanted to include evidence of the negative symptoms we were still seeing, because this was going to be a long-term project. I envisioned posting progress videos every few months, all the way from now until recovery. If I wanted to prove them wrong when they said, "He must have never really been autistic to begin with," then I needed evidence from the very beginning, good and bad.

I was just about to turn the camera off when the YouTube video ended. *"One is one and all alone and evermore shall be so!"* sang the chorus of children.

There was a long pause while Paul visibly collected his thoughts.

"Use your words," I prompted. "What do you want?"

"Ayuh-yuh-yuh-yuh number one," he said.

"Use your words," I insisted. "Say . . . "

It clicked. He sat up straight and pronounced clearly, "I want—watch again—please."

"Okay! Good job!" I said while he dropped focus from this great effort and stimmed on the phrase "number one" a little more.

I shut the camera off. This was everything I needed. I decided I wouldn't do a montage after all; I would just upload this whole interaction and let it stand on its own. Better that no one could claim I had used editing techniques to make it look like he could do things he couldn't.

Now I needed a "before" video. What had been the last thing I'd recorded of him? I had only recently learned how to use the video function on my camera, so there wasn't much. I searched backwards through a couple of my daughter crawling around, one of her eating . . . and finally found one with Paul in it.

Oh, yeah, I recalled. That *video*.

In it Paul was running back and forth on his toes, screaming at the television while it showed the movie *Cars*. The funny thing was, he wasn't actually having a meltdown. In his mind his screams sounded like the revving of the engines in the movie, and he often did this (correction: used to do this) while watching the opening race scene. He was half-naked, having yanked off his shirt in agitation, and only occasionally paused his screaming in order to spin in circles.

This was Paul's old stimming behavior at its finest. I had actually already uploaded the video to YouTube back in October, several months before the word "diagnosis" was even on our minds, in order to humorously show a friend just how much she was missing by not having kids.

I switched that video from private to public and revamped the description. This wasn't a video of "my crazy two-year-old" but rather "my autistic son at the age of two years, five months." The moral of the story was no longer "Keep your girl babies and give the boys to the wolves," *ha ha ha*. God, how unfunny that was to me now. Instead I changed it to "He was verbal, but it was 100% echolalic, and 85% meaningless echolalia."

It was painful to see the video with new eyes, to remember how ignorant I'd been. And yet it was also incredibly encouraging, because we hadn't seen anything close to this behavior in two months, and already we'd begun to forget how bad it had been. If he'd come this far in such a short time, our goal of mainstreaming by kindergarten didn't seem like such a challenge after all.

I put a link to the two videos on the "About Me" section of my website, with the classic Internet promise of "More Coming Soon!" I would put our story out there and "be the change" at every available opportunity. I would tell every parent I met, and especially every doctor, about biomedical treatment for autism. It wasn't enough to just ignore the doctors who were telling me I was wrong; I had to step up and tell them they were wrong.

When my first big chance came, though, I wilted.

Having gotten through the nutritional rounds at Thoughtful House, we had now seen the nurse practitioner there, a tall man with dark, curly hair and wire-rimmed glasses named Lucas. He had ordered some comprehensive urine and stool tests as a starting point, and the results of those revealed some metabolic problems that might or might not be indicative of mitochondrial dysfunction.

This was one of the major conditions that Hannah Poling, the first autistic child whose family won damages from the Vaccine Injury Compensation Program, suffered from. The ruling denied that the vaccinations had caused her autism but acknowledged instead that the shots had indeed caused her seizures, encephalopathy, and ensuing mitochondrial dysfunction, as these were known side effects of the vaccines she had received—rare, but possible, and printed right on the insert if anyone cared to look. The official percentage of autistic children suffering from mitochondrial dysfunction had not been tallied in a large study at that time, but anecdotally, Lucas said it seemed to be about 10 to 15 percent of their patients. Paul had some of the potential markers, so we would need a blood test to rule it out.

At the same time, we were due for Marie's fifteen-month checkup with our regular pediatrician, and the lab was in the same building, so I foolishly thought I should kill two birds with one stone and get Paul's blood draw done just before the appointment. Having not dealt with a full-on kicking meltdown in months, I had forgotten how strong Paul could be when he wanted to, and my own strength had atrophied without those daily wrestling matches.

That's one thing you should know about autism moms: many of us are built like we live at the gym because we have to heft, restrain, and chase our children at full speed long after they get too large for that sort of thing. Though he wouldn't be violent over a disrupted line of cars anymore, I did expect that a needle in the arm would be what the therapists refer to as a "nonpreferred activity." So I sat Paul on my lap in the lab chair and preemptively assumed the bear-hug position.

It wasn't nearly enough. At the first needle prick he convulsed so hard that the metal-frame chair literally hopped off the floor, and the previous confused whimpering turned to classic Paul rage. I fought to regain control while the nurse fumbled with her equipment. Paul began kicking, not the spasming back-and-forth of a toddler's tantrum but the aimed, deliberate attacks of a prisoner fighting for his life. I wrapped each of my legs around his shins, then locked my ankles together to keep them trapped. This, however, gave him leverage to try to rise up vertically at the hips, and I had to move my arms up and over the tops of his shoulders to immobilize his torso.

"Someone else is going to have to hold his arms still," I said through clenched teeth. "It's all I can do to keep him here." Another nurse came to help. Then a third one piled on, and finally they got a needle back in his arm and began getting a few drops of blood here and there. But the needle had to be resituated every few seconds as he kept jolting it out of the vein.

When we'd gotten a little over half a vial of blood, one nurse said, "We may need to finish this another time. . . . "

"We are *not* doing this again," I growled at her rudely. "Get it done."

Eventually, they did, though it took about twenty minutes in all. Paul easily switched back to happy mode once it was over, but I felt as if I'd run a marathon. I was red-faced and sweaty, with my ears still ringing from the screaming. There were bruises already forming on my shins and large red marks on my ankles where they had been grinding into each other. My leg muscles quivered and threatened to give way as we shuffled across the hall to the pediatrician's office.

The doctor noticed my obvious exhaustion, and I apologized and explained that we'd just been at the lab getting a blood draw done for Paul.

"Who ordered a blood draw for him?" she asked, not quite casually.

"Thoughtful House," I muttered, knowing this conversation was becoming important but too tired to care. "His labs showed extremely high levels of lactic acid, so they want to rule out mitochondrial dysfunction."

"Oh, that's just—no," she sputtered. "Listen, he does not fit the profile of mitochondrial dysfunction. I can look at him and see that."

I nodded dully and said, "I researched it. Not all patients have the typical low muscle tone. The lactic acid was there, so they're following up on it."

"Look," she said firmly, "if they find mitochondrial dysfunction, you call me." She said this as if I should do so even in the middle of the night. "I will refer you to someone, a *real doctor*, who knows about mitochondrial dysfunction and will take care of him."

I stared at her, indifferent. Inside, a voice was telling me to rise to the occasion, to calmly explain to her that everyone at Thoughtful House was, in fact, a licensed medical doctor. I wanted to ask her how she could be so sure my son did not have mitochondrial dysfunction and yet be so afraid that Thoughtful House would mishandle it if he did. But I had no fight left in me that day. I stared as if she'd said nothing.

"Is he still going to the occupational therapist?" she asked finally.

"Melanie, yes."

"Wonderful." She smiled. "Melanie's great, isn't she? We really like her. She's really just great. You know, I can't stress enough how important early intervention is; you absolutely have to intervene as early as possible."

"Mm-hmm," I grunted. *You don't even know what that means*, the voice inside me shouted at her. *You can't name one type of behavioral therapy for autism, and there are a dozen. Never mind how much this "early intervention" costs! Try $3,000 a month. Maybe you can afford that on your doctor's salary, but not us.*

I said nothing.

Her focus turned back to my daughter for a while, since it was supposed to be her appointment after all. But towards the end of the visit—during which Paul played quietly on the floor the whole time, in stark contrast to our previous experiences there—she again brought up autism treatment.

"Listen, I just really want you to be careful of those guys at Thoughtful House," she pleaded. "I have some other patients who are seeing them, and they're treating for things we just don't see the symptoms for at all, like yeast infections." She rolled her eyes.

Again I just nodded. The voice was telling me to respond, to point at Paul and ask if the other autistic patients were improving as much as he had, to ask her if she even remembered what Paul had been like just three months ago. But all my systems had shut down.

I wandered out of the office in a daze, thinking only about how I could maybe put on a DVD for the kids and sneak in a nap. It wasn't until hours later that I began to let some of her comments sink in. "Be careful of those guys"? How dare she! This was not some magic healer operating out of the back of a van. In the process of insulting the incredible people at Thoughtful House, she had belittled my own judgment and intelligence as well.

What help had this pediatrician ever offered me at all, in fact? First, she had told me when Paul was a year old that chronic, foul diarrhea was no big deal. Then she had been sure he didn't have autism, and now she spent all her time telling me what not to do about it. She didn't even know anything about the things she was supposedly in favor of, like therapy or ECI or PPCD; I'd had to learn about those from my sister-in-law.

Of course I was also furious with myself. I was supposed to be standing up to the widespread ignorance about my son's medical condition, and here I had just let it wash over me. I felt the bitter frustration of someone who has thought of the perfect comeback long after the affront has passed. I wanted to go back to her office, to schedule another appointment just so I could sit her down and tell her all the ways in which she was wrong. In the end I opted for a 44-cent stamp over a $40 co-pay and wrote her a letter instead. Here is just some of what I wrote:

Dear Dr. Felix,

I have a lot of lingering frustration over things I didn't say at our recent appointment, because I was too tired from the earlier lab work with Paul. Let me start off by saying I completely understand your skepticism of the biomedical treatments for autism, and skepticism is an excellent trait in a doctor. You do not want to be treating your patients on hunches and faith. But at the same time, it's hard not to take it personally when you effectively insinuate that the things I am *telling you* I see in my son must be either coincidence or imaginary. I assure you, I am giving every treatment offered by Thoughtful House the same careful consideration I would give to any medical treatment, weighing the risks and evidence available. I am being rigorously objective in my daily documentation of Paul's symptoms, and whether each one improves or not with any given treatment. What's more, I am taking videos, so that others can judge the difference for themselves.

Here I included links to the videos I had begun posting on You-Tube. Which was silly because she would have had to type in those long URL codes by hand if she'd wanted to see the videos, but still I hoped there was a chance she might.

I know that when you repeatedly say, "We really like Melanie" (his occupational therapist), what you are really telling me is "I approve of occupational therapy as a treatment, and it has studies to back up its effectiveness," and the implication is that you don't approve of the biomedical protocol (despite the fact that it, too, has many recent studies to back up its effectiveness). I know that you are not actually endorsing Melanie herself, because the truth is you don't know Melanie—if you did, you'd know that she strongly supports the biomedical treatments, she knows that they make her own sensory integration treatments far more effective, and she has been particularly blown away by the *immediate and complete* change Paul showed when I implemented the diet as strictly as I have (he is not just gluten-free and casein-free, by the way, but also following the Feingold rules of no artificial colors/flavors/sweeteners or preservatives). In fact, Paul's sensory issues, which improved only very slightly with therapy from January through March, completely disappeared after going on the diet.

In addition, everyone involved in Paul's PPCD program was also in favor of biomedical treatments before they ever met us, including the school psychologist and all four professionals who performed his assessment. When I told Paul's teacher that he is on the GFCF diet, she said, "Oh, wonderful, that means he'll be one of my good kids." They *all know* this stuff works because they work with autistic children every single day, and they know who is getting better and who isn't. Paul is not just "a lot calmer," as you have acknowledged—he leaped straight from gestures and echolalia to 3–4 word spontaneous manding, with no learning curve in between; his physical and visual stimming are way down; his tantrumming is down to the level of a normal three-year-old, and the causes of those tantrums are now logical (because I have told him "no," for example, rather than because he can't get his cars to line up exactly right).

I know that you have particular distaste for the idea that a yeast infection is somehow the root of autism, and rightly so—there is no one root of autism for even a single autistic child, let alone all autistic children. Yeast infections are championed by dirty hippies as the cause of everything from toe pain to cancer, and they clearly are not. But that doesn't mean there is no such thing as a fungal infection— vaginal yeast infections and infant thrush are very real maladies. The truth is, fungal infections are just one common comorbid condition of autism, along with many other gastrointestinal problems. Not all autistic children have chronic digestion issues, but mine does, as I have mentioned many times. And as it turns out, Paul's stool and urine samples didn't show a significant yeast infection, so the doctors at Thoughtful House obviously did not recommend that we treat for one. What they did show is a strong Clostridium bacterial infection (another common comorbid condition, but one that doesn't happen to have been picked up as a battle cry by dirty hippies, so it doesn't get the same negative association).

Perhaps your position on this information will be (1) the test re- sults were inaccurate or falsified (they came from your own preferred lab down the hall), or (2) the infection is real, but it has no associa- tion with his autistic symptoms. But even if that were the case, why wouldn't I want to treat an infection in its own right? I'd like my son to stop having chronic loose stools even if his autistic symptoms don't improve one bit. However, at every step of the way, when we have adjusted *any* aspect of his food intake or digestion, his autistic symptoms have changed as well (either for better or for worse; it is often a case of trial and error, not steady improvement), so I am personally quite confident that treating his intestinal infection with an antibiotic will be no different. I know you once suggested *Lactobacillus acidophilus* as a first step for Paul's digestive problems—and that is also part of the treatment recommended by the doctors at Thoughtful House—but he has been taking multiple doses daily for months, yet his lab work showed zero colonization of beneficial bacteria.

The party line is that "early intervention" is the key, but what does that actually mean? It's early, I'm ready to intervene—what specifically do you suggest I *do*? We had to wait three months to see the pediatric neurologist, and his assessment was "Yes, Paul is autistic. Come back when he's older, and I can put him on antipsychotics." How is that early intervention? Meanwhile, the waiting list for ABA therapy is over a year long, and I cannot afford $40,000 a year regardless. Occupational therapy has almost outlived its usefulness for Paul. So what other options does that leave me? So far, not a single treatment advocated by Thoughtful House has had any risk at all—and so far, we have seen extremely positive results with every step. I'm not sure what it is that you want me to "be careful" of. If you think I am being given false hope, all I can say is the results have been quite real so far, and I have the behavior logs and the videos to prove it. If you are afraid I will be scammed out of money, you should know that insurance is reimbursing me at the standard out-of-network percentage. What's more, their pricing is at a fair, up-front hourly rate, which equates to an actual hour of face time with the doctor and is quite a bit less than, say, the pediatric neurologist, who billed my insurance $500 for less than 15 minutes of time, 90 percent of which was me redescribing the same symptoms I had just given in great detail to his nurse. If you are afraid we will end up agreeing to something more risky like chelation drugs, I will admit that it is a possibility in the future, after careful consideration of the prerequisite lab test results, and whether Thoughtful House has continued to earn our trust with successful treatments. But a quick search of antipsychotic drugs shows there are far more known side effects and risks for those treatments, especially in children, and the neurologist was apparently ready to dole them out like candy to my son without any additional information or examination of him. So who should I be more careful of, again?

It is a travesty that legitimate medical work has gotten tied up by the inherent politics of the situation. In fact, I have volunteered to participate in several of Thoughtful House's currently running medical studies, even though it means Paul may sometimes receive a placebo at first and delay his treatment by a few weeks, because I know published studies are the only way to prove what everyone in that office, everyone in the PPCD program, and all the occupational therapists at Redford Rehab already know to be true. In twenty years, the biomedical protocol (the genuine set of proven treatments—gastrointestinal, immunological, and toxicological—not the silly anti-yeast, cranial-sacral, balance-your-chi nonsense that people mistakenly associate it with) is going to be the standard accepted treatment for autism. As the evidence accumulates, things necessarily change. Medical knowledge is a constantly evolving thing: we laugh at what we thought was true thirty years ago, and it is utterly foolish to think we won't still be laughing at many of today's assumptions in another thirty years.

Please understand I'm not angry—you are a good doctor, and I have no intention of leaving your practice in search of someone who already agrees with me, because that would defeat the purpose. Instead I plan to demonstrate to you that I'm right about this, however long that may take. I look forward to sharing my child's continued improvement with you.

Sincerely,
Jennifer Noonan

Embarrassingly enough, the version above was shortened to remove redundant references and some extra information about my daughter. The copy I actually sent to the doctor was quite a bit longer. I half expected her to ask me to leave her practice after all, with a tirade like that in her hands, but she didn't.

She never responded at all.

Chapter 9

All in the Family

JUST BEFORE SUMMER a startling thing happened.

For almost a year we had been planning a small family reunion involving several of my cousins and their children. When we had initially offered to host this event, we'd had no idea of Paul's diagnosis and had in fact been counting on him to grow out of what we thought were "terrible two" behaviors before then. Now we were just grateful to have organized it on home turf. Traveling with Paul had never been easy, but at this point in our lives it was impossible, even with his recent improvements. The car had made him antsy even as a baby, and any trip lasting longer than forty-five minutes was cause for wailing.

True, we could take breaks on the road, but Paul was not stupid. Thirty minutes on a playscape was not enough to reset the clock and make him forget how much he hated being in the car, nor was food or any other distraction. The previous Christmas had been our last valiant attempt to visit my in-laws in Fort Worth, with the not-so-brilliant plan that this time we would take the Amtrak train. It would stretch the trip from three and a half hours into five, but we thought that with the ability to move around and the novelty of being on a train, he might manage.

Instead the center aisle had become an obsession, and he was compelled to run up and down the entire length of the train again and again. I had to follow close behind him because at any moment he might decide to climb on top of another passenger, or grab their belongings, or start a loud echolalia chain that could not be stopped unless I was there to provide the right responses. He was not at all interested in the scenic car with its panoramic walls of Plexiglas, nor did he even want to sit in the dining car and eat all the bread and cheese he was still allowed to eat back then. He just ran, and yelled, and had a meltdown every single time he got to the door of the quiet car and was denied entrance.

Five hours there, five hours back, plus a general refusal to sleep in an unfamiliar place for all the days in between. After the Christmas train fiasco we didn't leave the city limits for two years.

Fortunately, he was more reliable at home, especially now that he knew how to retreat to his room when he needed a break, so we decided the summer family reunion could still take place. I e-mailed my extended family to let them know about the major changes our household had been going through over the past few months. They were all supportive of our situation, and whatever initial misgivings they may have had about my GFCF kitchen, their praise for the meals I cooked that weekend seemed genuine enough. I did my best to make concessions where I could, including allowing myself to purchase a bag of regular hamburger buns alongside our standard gluten-free brand.

This was the first time any gluten had crossed our threshold since clearing the house three months earlier, but I felt safe with the decision. Paul's cravings had finally subsided, and though there was still some jealous whining when he saw others eating forbidden foods, he was usually happy as long as he had a reasonably equivalent substitute. On a whim I decided on the afternoon of the cookout to eat a regular hamburger bun along with the other adults, even though I didn't mind the gluten-free ones. GF buns were expensive, and any wheat-based buns that didn't get eaten that day would go in the trash, so I chose the practical route.

Moments after I swallowed the first bite, my stomach clenched in pain. After the third bite I had to stop eating, and though I managed not to vomit, my body tried for the rest of the afternoon to convince me it was the best course of action. Later I was treated to even more unspeakable symptoms that kept me awake most of the night.

Andrew was unconcerned. "It's just because you haven't eaten gluten in so long," he reassured me. "I think it would happen to anyone."

"I don't know about that. How long has it been since you ate, say, a mango?" I asked. "But if you ate a mango right now, you wouldn't get horribly sick. Not eating something for a long time doesn't inherently make your body freak out about it."

Indeed, I was profoundly affected by what had happened on more than just a physical level. The instant I'd felt that first cramp, it was as if an abstract mural I'd been staring at had been rotated, and suddenly I saw with clarity the picture that had been right in front of me the whole time: I had celiac disease. Or some type of autoimmune reaction to gluten, at any rate.

This was not as great a logical leap as it would seem. First, I had already come across research showing that women with any autoimmune disease have a greater risk of having an autistic child, and women with celiac disease in particular are four times more likely. What's more, I had two immediate relatives, an uncle and a grandmother, who had both been stricken with colon cancer at a young age. They hadn't known to look for root causes at the time, but doctors now knew that if left untreated, celiac disease can eventually result in appendicitis, liver damage, and cancer, most often of the pancreas or colon.

Even more interestingly, after being diagnosed with the same cancer he had watched his mother die from, my uncle had decided that he wasn't going to suffer through the radiation and chemotherapy that she'd had. Instead he had delved into alternative cancer treatments, and it was an oft-repeated family story how he had gone to "some place out in California" and radically changed his diet, among other treatments. Instead of dying within the six-month time frame his original doctors had given him, he had gone into complete remission and lived another four years before succumbing to an unrelated illness.

I had known all of this, but somehow I had been viewing everything through the narrow lens of autism, and had not put together the obvious family history.

Most of all, though, I was haunted by a particular childhood memory.

When I was about eight or nine years old, I found my grand-mother's high school yearbook on the large built-in bookcase in our dining room. It was the only memento my father had left of her after all his possessions had been stolen at one point during college. As I gently turned past photos of 1930s teenagers in their suits and horn-rimmed glasses, he squatted beside me, telling me about my grand-mother for the first time, and about the illness that had claimed her when he was only twelve years old. Her appearance was typical of the time, with a dark dress, primly curled hair, and a pleasant smile that was careful not to be overdone. She didn't look much like me, and her "best known for" and "most likely to" bylines indicated a personality far different from my own, but for reasons I didn't understand, I felt a strange connection to this woman in the yearbook.

As my father began explaining to me in simple terms how she had died from something called colon cancer, I turned to him and said calmly, "I think I will, too, someday."

Only now did this memory come back to me, this creepy thing I had once said to my poor dad. At the time this vision of my own death wasn't a fear, just a fact in my mind. I don't remember what he said in return, but I hope he wrote it off as some kind of paternal idolatry on my part, a misplaced desire to be just like this woman whom he clearly loved and missed. Nonetheless, my unshakeable belief that I was des-tined for colon cancer persisted for years, long past the point when I grew out of wanting to please my father in every way. It was never something I dreaded, just something that I was sure would inevitably happen to me, a genetic time bomb waiting to go off. I had heard that diseases often skip generations, and somehow I just felt sure that I was due for it.

And whether it had been just a childish pretension or a subcon-scious awareness of a disease that was already damaging my intestines even then, I knew that it was relevant now. Many people with gluten intolerance have minimal or even nonexistent gastrointestinal prob-lems, but there are always symptoms manifesting somewhere. I had been so focused on the state of Paul for the past three months that I hadn't even noticed how good I'd felt myself. Fantastic, in fact. A lifetime of fatigue, insomnia, allergies . . . all of it had disappeared since I'd gone gluten- and dairy-free with my son.

It was only because of Paul, I realized, that I had been alerted to my own gluten intolerance at all. Perhaps I had been destined to die of colon cancer before my children were grown, and this horrible thing called autism had saved my life.

This led to another realization that had been fomenting in my head for a while: I am on the mild end of the autism spectrum myself. Those who have known me only as an adult might find it unlikely, but that's because I spent years conscientiously modeling certain peers who clearly understood better than I did how this whole human interaction thing was supposed to work. Those who knew me as a child, including my own mother, have smiled and nodded knowingly when I've brought it up.

For one thing, I never look people in the eyes, even now. Eyes are, for lack of a better explanation, entirely distracting to me. Unlike some autistic individuals who have described eye contact as being painful, I am able to do it without particular discomfort, but I absolutely cannot focus on what is being said or happening around me if I am looking at the speaker's eyes. Call it tunnel vision, deer in the headlights, or whatever metaphor you like. I hear and see nothing except those eyes, and if I persist for too long I also start to get overwhelmed with the indecision of which eye I'm supposed to be looking at.

Instead I have always instinctively looked at people's mouths when they speak. It makes so much more sense to me. Why wouldn't you naturally look at the source of the sound rather than trying to listen to one thing while looking at another? I can even remember becoming aware as a child that other people didn't do this. "What color eyes does he have?" someone would ask, and I would scoff at the question, as if anyone would know the answer to that. Might as well ask me to notice how many freckles he had on his right arm. But others would answer the question confidently, and I slowly came to realize that I was the only one who didn't pay attention to people's eye color as a regular habit.

Not such a big deal, though; I figured I just wasn't very observant. But the point was driven home at summer camp one year when one of the counselors had a condition known as heterochromia iridum. This meant that one of his eyes was actually two different colors, bright blue and brown in a striking asymmetrical pattern. After two months of interacting with this counselor on a daily basis, I learned about his unusual eye only when another camper referred to it, and then I adamantly accused her of lying until confirming it for myself.

Now I knew I was weird. How could I not have noticed something so obvious? Evidently, I had not even indirectly glanced at my counselor's eyes once during the whole time I'd known him. After some reflection I concluded that it must be because I didn't hear well, and thus I needed to look at people's mouths for the extra lip-reading cues. Yet later experiences proved that, if anything, my hearing was more sensitive than most people's.

I wanted desperately to be like my peers at that age, so for a while I made a conscious effort to look at people's eyes instead. But I simply could not keep track of conversations that way, and after looking like a spaced-out idiot several times, I gave up. People must not be able to tell whether I was looking at their eyes or their mouths, I decided, since no one had ever commented on it, so I could just follow my preference and pretend I was the same as everyone else.

In addition to avoiding eye contact, I was horrible at social interaction. Not shy or anxious; I loved people and wanted nothing more than to be the center of attention, just like Paul. But I couldn't understand how people made up casual conversation on the fly. Why would people say, "Nice to see you" sometimes and "How are you?" other times? There seemed to be an infinite number of small-talk options and no way to choose the best one among them. The world was very black-and-white to me back then, and above all I was competitive. There always had to be one best answer for every situation, just like on multiple-choice tests.

I tried to tease out the rules on my own, like a puzzle, but the only guaranteed truth I could come up with was that you had to choose something different than whatever the other person said because people thought it was strange if you just parroted them. But this seemed to me to be a distinct disadvantage to the person who spoke second. If I let the other person say something first, then they would surely choose the best phrase for themselves, and I'd be stuck having to choose something marginally less appropriate. But if I went first, I ran the risk of choosing something completely off base because I still could not figure out how they knew which phrase to choose in which scenarios. I didn't want to be last place *or* second place; I wanted to win. For if all social interaction weren't some kind of subtle alpha-dog competition, why would anyone bother with it? That was only logical.

So I looked for stock scenarios to learn from, mostly from TV. This turned out even worse for me, as I felt strongly compelled to complete certain scenes I had applied, even when they did not match up to reality.

In sixth grade, for example, we were being forced to play a loose round of softball in gym class, and the girl who regularly bullied me had been placed in the pitcher's position. She was doing a fairly poor job of it, and a couple of the other children began making fun of her. One of them declared that I should be pitching instead, since it was known that I had played on a real baseball team with the boys. This was true, though it wasn't because I was any good. I just liked playing with boys better than girls, and gender equality meant Little League was technically open to anyone, even though I was the only girl in the whole organization.

As bullies do, she turned her anger on me instead of the ones who had actually been mocking her and sneered, "Oh, really? What position did you play—benchwarmer?"

I knew this scene. She was the bully; I was the nerdy one. She was supposed to be mean, and I was supposed to be cowed. That was how this interaction always got played on TV.

"No," I replied, mustering as much dignity as I could. As in, I literally thought that phrase silently, *mustering as much dignity as I could*, novelizing my life and giving myself acting notes in the middle of my delivery. I had to play my part. "I was the substitute," I finished lamely.

They all laughed, she went back to lobbing balls over the catcher's head, and I blushed furiously. Like I was supposed to.

The thing is, it wasn't true. I wasn't the substitute. There was no such position on the team, not in the heyday of "everyone plays; everyone gets a trophy." I played outfield, because I was a slow runner but decent at catching pop flies, and occasionally second base. I was no doubt in the bottom half of the team talentwise, but even as the only girl I wasn't the worst player we had. Yet I didn't say that. I lied and said something more demeaning than the truth because I didn't know how to create my own scenes. All I knew how to do was imitate modeled behavior and place myself in the roles I had seen played out before.

My competitive nature overcame this problem eventually, as I ruthlessly gathered more data and began to craft more nuanced roles for myself. I was eventually exposed to, for example, scenes in which the bullied kid stands up for himself, so I could add that to my repertoire. This process was sped along by my best friend in high school, Tara, a consummate social butterfly who took me on as a project, not knowing that she was passing on more than just fashion sense to me. It was also helped by participating in community and high school theater, where I did well at believable portrayals because every moment of my life was already a portrayal of someone else. Nothing was natural for me, so in the end anything could be natural.

Another telltale spectrum trait for me is sensory dysfunction. My excellent hearing, which I eventually parlayed into a career in audio engineering, crosses the line into hyperacusis in many cases. The sound of sloshing water used to be so grating that I would beg Andrew to give the kids their baths when they were young because I couldn't stand even being in the bathroom with a tub full of water. Interestingly, my aversion to water sounds has improved somewhat as I've gotten older, but my tactile aversions have gotten worse. Firm touch is fine, but a feather-light touch on my skin causes me to yell out and writhe away in discomfort. It doesn't tickle; it *hurts*. Like Paul, I also hate jackets, though my problem is less with the sleeves on my forearms and more with a perceived constriction around my shoulders. There are days when even my usual shirts are intolerable on my shoulders, and I will change clothes repeatedly until I find one I can deal with, much to Andrew's amusement. More than half of my wardrobe is sleeveless. I also hate shoes and will wear sandals for as many months of the year as I can possibly get away with. The closed-toe shoes I do own are all one size too big so I have room to move my whole foot around inside. If my feet start bothering me while I'm driving, I won't hesitate to take my shoes off and drive barefoot.

I realize that all of this seems to imply that I favor a genetic causality for autism when I've just spent half a dozen chapters arguing the opposite. But the world is not as black-and-white as the adolescent me would ever have believed. The medical consensus now is that the manifestation of autistic traits is a combination of genetic susceptibility and environmental triggers, just as it is for most diseases, and studies comparing the autism rates among identical twins (same genes) and fraternal twins (different genes but same environment all the way back to the womb) have confirmed this. The very fact that there are any sets of identical twins in which one has autism and the other doesn't proves that it cannot be an exclusively genetic disease.

Such a complex picture of causation is common in human biology. A person can have, for example, a strong genetic predisposition towards diabetes yet still avoid it as long as he or she adheres to a diet-and-exercise regimen that is perhaps more stringent than the rest of us require. In the same way, a person can have a genetic predisposition towards autism yet remain mostly symptom-free, like me, when not exposed to whatever environmental triggers are causing this generation's tsunami of sick children.

Of course it would be impossible to be ignorant of the controversies surrounding environmental triggers of autism, and I do have my own opinion on the question of vaccines. However, the most shameful and tragic thing to me is that the furious debate over causes has stalled the search for treatments for so long. At that point in our journey one could not even indirectly reference dietary, autoimmune, metabolic, or any other type of biomedical treatment for this disease without being dismissed as an "antivaccine nut." This was because Dr. Andrew Wakefield, the UK researcher who first suggested a connection between autism and the measles-mumps-rubella (MMR) vaccine, was a pediatric gastroenterologist by training, and the bulk of his research was actually not on vaccines but rather on the GI disease of his autistic patients, which he was the first to identify by the name *autistic enterocolitis*. The medical community was so determined to thoroughly discredit his statements about vaccines that they threw out the baby with the bathwater and rejected everything he'd ever said about autism. From that moment forward you could no longer say that autistic patients had GI disease, which hadn't been so revolutionary before, because that was what He Who Shall Not Be Named had said, and absolutely no one wanted to be tarred with the wrong causation brush.

Meanwhile, parents who were convinced that a vaccine had caused their child's autism were more likely to aggressively investigate GI treatments, vocally claiming them for their own as part of a cause-and-treatment package that neither they nor mainstream doctors were willing to separate. Rather than focusing on their potential common ground for the benefit of children who were already sick, the two sides had become further and further entrenched, and no doctor wanted to stand in the crossfire by even acknowledging the possibility that autism had medically treatable components, regardless of what its cause might be. They would freely admit that they didn't know anything about your child's disease—except they knew for sure that the only, only, *only* treatment for it was therapy.

On the one hand, having my own spectrum mindset was helpful in figuring out how to communicate with Paul. Often I knew what small thing was bothering him when no one else did because I could reach back into my youth and consider what I would have felt at the time. But this also had the side effect of breaking down my ingrained coping mechanisms. The more I tapped into that old way of viewing the world, the more I found it creeping up when I wasn't expecting it. Paying close attention to the sensory overload Paul might be experiencing also allowed it to start bothering me again.

I was deteriorating in other ways as well. Since Paul's diagnosis I had lost twenty pounds. This was aided by going gluten-free, no doubt, but it was too much. I had been fit before and was now unhealthily thin. I had reignited my childhood habit of grinding my teeth at night, clenching so tight that I woke up with a sore jaw every morning and undoing thousands of dollars of teenaged orthodontic work as the unrelenting muscle tension pulled my jaw back into an overbite that had been corrected for over a decade.

These and other physical manifestations of stress were probably part of the reason why I hadn't noticed right away how much better I felt being gluten-free. I was tuning out all signals from my body, both good and bad, in order to focus every neuron I had on behavior, diet, and supplement patterns. It was a massively multivariable experiment, and I had to constantly keep track of the data, tease apart the causation from the correlation, and mentally line up treatment plans based on my theories. Paul's future was on the line, and nothing else mattered.

I had also finally grasped the uncertainty of that future. He was getting better, but was it enough? I believed we had a chance at recovery, but I also understood now that the odds were against us. For every story of recovery I found, there were a hundred of those who weren't quite there yet or, worse, who had been exhausting themselves for years with only moderate gains in return. The vast majority of these parents still agreed it was worth it, even those who saw only an improvement in health with no change in cognitive ability at all, but their tone of defeat was unmistakable. The unfortunate side effect of believing that your child's disease is inherently treatable is that you also believe, on some level, that it's your fault if he isn't making progress.

How much easier it would be to believe there was nothing I could do about it! Emily Perl Kingsley, who wrote the famous essay "Welcome to Holland," was the mother to a Down syndrome child. Her bad news was a fierce kick in the chest on the day her son was born, but after that his future was laid out with relative predictability. Part of the torture of autism is that the future is so impossibly unsure. Your child might become a fully functioning member of society, go to MIT, and appear no different than anyone else, even if he does have to look at mouths instead of eyes and can't stand to give his own kids a bath. Or he might smear poop on the walls for the rest of his life and be so violent that he requires institutionalization before he's a teenager. Either way you're expected to work your ass off for it.

One autism mother named Susan Rzucidlo wrote a counteressay called "Welcome to Beirut." In it she presents autism as a war zone instead of a mellow, unexpected vacation in Holland. It is not for autism parents to catch their breath and look around, she wrote, but to armor up, because "this is war and it's awful. There are no discharges, and when you are gone someone else will have to fight in your place."

Though I still wanted very badly to be in Italy, part of me understood that even Holland was better than Beirut. There is no question that parents who make peace with their child's limitations are happier, and for my own sake I did try to make myself embrace the silver-linings worldview rather than the one of eternal battle. But my attempt to rebrand this bunker in the rubble as a windmill surrounded by tulips failed like the quixotic endeavor that it was. I was still bitterly determined to get out of this place, regardless of what country it was in.

The only phrase in Kingsley's essay that really spoke to me at all was "everyone you know is busy coming and going from Italy . . . and they're all bragging about what a wonderful time they had there." My fear for the future was often outstripped by jealousy in the present, slowly layering itself into a deep resentment of others who still had their perfect lives. On bad days I would walk through the grocery store glaring at the other mothers with their talkative, engaged children, mentally jabbing a finger at each one.

I hate you . . . and I hate you . . . and I hope your *kid gets a horrible disease so you know what it's like.* . . . I knew it wasn't healthy, but I did it anyway, because in some ways it was this very unhappiness that kept me striving for a better outcome for Paul. Acceptance meant giving up; hating autism meant fighting on.

When I'd first shared our diagnosis with friends, one had said, "I think you'll get the same joy from his progress and growth, maybe even more, if the steps are smaller."

At the time I thought, *I hope so . . . but I bet not.* And I was right. All along the way, whenever we've accomplished a new goal or conquered some difficult behavior, the only emotion I've ever felt was relief. Relief that we were one step closer to recovery, one step farther away from permanent dependency. I never doubted that this thing could be fixed, but I sometimes doubted whether I could accomplish it. The adage "We're only human" was no consolation—sometimes our best isn't good enough, and I still didn't want second place.

Chapter 10

Thank God for the Internet

I WAS SO wrapped up in researching, experimenting, planning, and coping that I mostly gave up noticing what was going on outside my bubble. Sometimes I deliberately avoided it, in fact. I had never been a big user of Facebook, but not too long after our diagnosis I had to remove myself entirely because I couldn't handle the bitter monotony of all my contemporaries reporting on their young, happy families.

The final photo that broke me was innocuous, from a distant high school acquaintance I barely remembered. His four-year-old son had passed the gold-belt test in his preschool karate class, and he had received a paper certificate with a foil seal on it and everything. I stared at the proud little boy on my screen and tried to put Paul's face on his, to believe that we could even hope to be there by the age of four, just one year away. My imagination wasn't up to the task. Never mind the uniform he would have refused to wear, or the certificate he would have torn up for fun, or his inability to follow instructions and actually participate in a karate class at all . . . no, Paul didn't even understand that he was supposed to hold still for a camera and smile. I couldn't have faked that photo even if I'd tried.

I looked at the little ninja before me and realized that I hated him. It was one thing to be casually resentful of strangers as an emotional outlet, but this stain was spreading to my actual friends, and I couldn't let that happen. The only way to keep myself from despising my friends and their children was to withdraw.

Other social outlets were shrinking away, too. Shortly after we had implemented the diet, Melanie had encouraged us to take Paul to some large regular playgroups in the hope that he might be ready to imitate another child once in a while. I did try a few times, but again my own despair made it too difficult. I wanted nothing more than to blend in, but the older his peers got, the more his behaviors stood out enough to require an explanation, and before long I would always find myself admitting that he had autism.

Their next question was inevitably "How did you know?" Of course what they really meant was "Reassure me that my child is nothing like yours." So I would have to tell our story, and then they would ask more questions, or want to tell me about their friend/neighbor/relative who had a child with autism, and before long the play date was over and I was exhausted.

It was all interesting and fresh to them, but for me it was the same conversation with every new parent we met. Oh, sometimes there were variations: maybe their friend/neighbor/relative had tried that diet stuff, too, and it hadn't worked, and I'd get to feel like they were calling me a liar. Or maybe they wanted to talk about vaccines, and I would have to try to feel out where they already stood on the matter so I could avoid a confrontation. (This is usually the first question asked by other autism parents, incidentally: not "How did you know?" but "What do you think caused it?" We all know there are two camps, and we all want to segregate each other from the outset so we know what we can and cannot talk about.)

Or worst of all, maybe their child did actually have a suspicious number of similarities to my "How I Knew" list, and then I'd be treated to condescending reassurances that my son must be normal after all because their kid did all the same things. I tried to avoid these parents completely, which wasn't too hard since by now I could pick out the other spectrum kid in a crowd within seconds. Part of me felt like I should say something to them, help them get started before their window of opportunity closed any further, but if people don't even want to hear it from a neurologist, they're certainly not going to listen to some whack-job mom they met on the playground.

Aside from the growing dread on my part, we had to skip a large number of the play dates anyway, because they were held at parks we couldn't go to. The road had to be at least fifty feet from the playscape, preferably with a fence; otherwise I couldn't keep Paul out of traffic. He would still unexpectedly make a break for it every so often, and I could catch up to him in time only if I had a reasonable buffer. Some of the best playgrounds in town were off-limits to us because they had used their land to the fullest extent, pushing the equipment right up to the sidewalk, or worse, to the edge of a creek or pond. Water was an even bigger attraction for him than speeding cars, and the fact that he didn't know how to swim just made it more fun. *Look how the adults chase and yell when I jump in the deep end!*

Eventually, I gave up and withdrew from the playgroups as well.

I knew I needed to seek out others who were going through what I was, if only so I wouldn't have to give a primer on autistic behaviors all the time, but this was problematic as well. All the other autism parents I'd met so far were not like me. They were either blissfully at peace with the "gift" God had given their family, or they were just defeated.

The clearest example of the latter was a monthly coffee hosted by our school district's special education department, which I attended only once. It was held in a creaky wood-paneled portable school building, with mismatched 1970s office furniture and flickering fluorescent lights. Melancholy seemed to hemorrhage directly out of the dingy walls and rattling window unit. My hesitant entrance was acknowledged with several pitying nods and the stark instruction "There's zucchini bread."

Since I had to politely decline the snack in front of everyone, I felt obliged to take some coffee instead, though I don't actually drink coffee and could tell that this was a terrible brew even with my unsophisticated nose. Everyone watched me silently as I filled my cup and dumped in some sugar to make it look as if I actually planned to drink it. Finally I located an empty metal folding chair and sat awkwardly, holding my lukewarm Styrofoam cup in both hands, before the group's conversation resumed.

For the next half hour, I listened to these dead-eyed parents of mostly older children share their desperation. One told the group that yet another attendant had just quit, and she thought she would have to leave her job because no one else would take care of her son in the afternoons. Another was angry because the local work program had told her that her child was not competent enough to bag groceries. The worst was an Indian mother whose son was actually pretty high-functioning, but he would laugh hysterically whenever she injured herself in some small way. She kept choking up and repeating, "He doesn't love me, you know? It's like, why doesn't he love me?"

This was not support. This was torture. I was not going to be one of those parents, not ever. The moment the meeting was scheduled to end, I mumbled something about another appointment and ducked out the door, dumping my coffee in the bushes outside.

Thank God for the Internet. If I didn't have that, I don't know where we'd be today. It's embarrassing that it took this long for me to look for a local biomedical support group, but in my defense I had been hunting for the most information possible and was only now realizing that I might need more than just hard data to sustain me. Sure enough, I found one immediately, and though there wasn't a high volume of posts on the message board, the members met in person at a restaurant once a month. As soon as I saw the first message referring to a gluten-free diet as a given, not something to be debated, I decided to go.

There was no way I could get there by the appointed 7:00 start time, though, because Paul's current bedtime script required both parents to say their lines, and it took two people to administer his nightly supplement concoction anyway. As with tooth brushing, negotiation and cajoling over his meds was futile. We had learned to just mix all the powders together with a little fruit juice and have one parent hold him still while the other syringed the whole mess into the back of his throat with a quick water chaser.

I posted a message asking if it would be okay if I came an hour late, and I was assured that if there was one thing this group understood, it was that autism needed flexibility. Lots of moms came and went as they needed, they said, and some number of them would be there at least until the restaurant closed. Often the conversations went on even longer, just standing outside in the parking lot.

When I did arrive I was surprised to see how many people were there. I had counted maybe half a dozen active posters during my short time on the board, but there were at least three times that many crowded around several shoved-together tables. They were so boisterous and engaged that my approach was barely noticed. I took a chair at the end and just listened at first, the smile growing wider on my face.

"Can you post that recipe to the board?"

"When we started the methyl B12 shots—"

"Bringing an advocate to our ARD was one of the smartest things we ever did."

"Which brand of 5-HTP do you use?"

"Have you tried the Epsom salt lotion instead of the baths? We order it online; I can post the link."

Someone finally figured out I was new, and quick introductions were made, but the pace never slowed.

"I need some new lunch box ideas, GFCF and soy-free. What are your kids' favorites?"

"Have you seen the new research on right-brain, left-brain connectivity?"

"He had to do a round of antibiotics, but I upped his probiotics, and our doctor called in an antifungal prescription as well. We'll see how it goes."

I thought I knew a lot about biomedical treatments, but there were real veterans here, and defeat was the last thing on any of their minds. Many of them were patients at Thoughtful House, like we were, but I learned that there were a few other low-profile biomedical doctors in town as well. All of these women had their kids on some kind of special diet, and several were more advanced than ours. There was the

Specific Carbohydrate Diet (SCD), the Body Ecology Diet, the Gut and Psychology Syndrome (GAPS) Diet, and even more that I had never heard of. Being gluten- and dairy-free was the minimum in this group rather than the extreme.

To my surprise, I also learned that many of the moms here were gluten-free themselves, having followed the same path of inadvertent discovery that I had. The restaurant we were meeting at, in fact, had been chosen because there were several gluten-free options on the menu. And just in case the dichotomy of my two experiences had not been staked out clearly enough to me already, someone even happened to mention that they had found a great recipe for gluten-free zucchini bread.

I was inundated with so much new information, not only about treatment but also about schools, compounding pharmacies, therapies, tutors, restaurants, recipes . . . and, as promised, we did continue in the parking lot well past closing. I didn't want to let these women get in their cars for fear I'd never find them again. After months of savage isolation in Beirut, I had stumbled upon a giant enclave of compatriots. They not only spoke English, they had a map of the territory and an escape route. Joy and disbelief battled for my attention, but joy won out. I had found my people, and they welcomed me.

Chapter 11

A Special Education

WHEN I DID have contact with my old world, the real world, it was always startling to see that it had just been sitting there, unchanged. It felt like we were traveling at light speed back and forth while mere moments were passing for everyone else I knew. When my friend Tara happened to message me with a generic "How are things?" I found the question almost impossible to answer. I tried to summarize the therapy progress, and the doctors' appointments, and the school evaluations, and the dietary changes, but even skimming the surface of each one left me typing several paragraphs of information.

Before I'd finished she interjected, "So, I mean, they really think he's autistic? Did they actually use that word?"

Oh, *wow*. Was she really that far behind? Was everyone outside our immediate family? It was my fault if they were, since I had set myself furiously digging in this mine tunnel and hadn't come up for air yet. But I just didn't have the time to send lengthy memos on a weekly or even daily basis, which was what would have been necessary to keep anyone else up to date. This whole adventure was less than six months old to begin with, and it hadn't been that long since I had last talked to Tara, a couple of months at most. But time passes differently inside a mine tunnel. It felt like I would need a month just to explain everything that had happened in the past month.

I was too tired to give any more backstory, so I gave up.

"Yes, he's autistic," I replied bluntly. "In a couple days we go to the school to visit his special ed classroom for next year."

I knew the phrase "special ed" would sting her, almost as much as if I'd flippantly declared he was going to ride the short bus (which he was, to tell the truth). My abruptness was perhaps cruel; after all, she cared about him, too, and hadn't been prepared for this any more than we had. But I needed her to be where I was, not miles back. I was busy forging ahead, and I didn't have time to hold anyone else's hand. If I could face the facts without sugarcoating, she'd have to as well. It didn't occur to me that I might simply be cutting her off rather than forcing her to catch up faster.

There was a long pause before she wrote, "What will he do at school?"

That was something I couldn't answer. PPCD was another one of those things we were doing because we were supposed to. I couldn't imagine how it would actually work. To begin with, he'd scream indefinitely every morning about being left with someone new. And it wasn't like he'd sit down for story time, or glue together a craft, or play a game of Duck-Duck-Goose. The very idea was a joke, just like the whole social portion of his school evaluation had been. Being in a room full of toys and having recess on a playground would be fun for him, sure, but was there a point?

Frankly, I didn't care. It was, if nothing else, four hours a day of free respite care when I could just sit down for once and take care of my daughter without Paul needing constant attention.

"I honestly don't know," I replied. "I figure that's their problem."

When we arrived for our scheduled visit a few days later, class was in session, and there were a dozen children engaged in various activities. The whole room had been divided into a tight, primary-colored cubicle farm. There was a kitchen play area, as one might expect to see in any preschool classroom, but tall cloth partitions had been arranged completely around it so that there was only one narrow entrance. When you were playing kitchen, it was not possible to do or look at anything else in the room.

Some cubicles had just a small table with one or two chairs and no other decorations or distractions. One had a single fine-motor toy laid out on the table, the kind of thing Melanie would have used. Another had an array of baskets on a small shelf, each with a child's name on it along with a simple picture that was repeated in other places that child's name appeared. If Tony couldn't recognize the letters of his name, he could at least hunt for the big blue sun shape.

The setup was as impressive as it was intimidating. Everywhere I looked, cordoned-off children were focused on their tasks, and though it wasn't quiet, it certainly wasn't chaos, either. It was not, as I'd expected, a room full of Pauls. Put him at the desk with the fine-motor toy, and he wouldn't move the little pegs in and out like he was supposed to; he would just line them up by color and walk away. Melanie could usually get him to participate, but Melanie also never left his side during their sessions and had to prompt him with instructions every few seconds. This classroom had only one teacher and two aides.

Did that mean that Paul was worse off than most of the kids even in this special ed classroom? Again the social assessment of "nine-month-old" swirled in my head.

Then it got worse. One of the aides saw me and indicated she'd be with me in a moment. She reached up to a shelf above her head—all the shelves were high, I noticed, beyond the reach of children standing on chairs or even tables—and rang a small xylophone. Suddenly, all the children were in motion, and I saw poker chips, of all things, flashing out of the aides' pockets and into their expectant little hands.

"Here's your chip, Jacob," they said pleasantly but firmly. "Go check your schedule, Mia."

Most of the kids didn't even need these small instructions; they just took the chip and headed towards a short hallway connecting this room to the next. I heard a chorus of tinny *clangs* and short Velcro rips. Then, one by one, each child returned and headed to a new station, placing a small laminated square on a waiting piece of Velcro at the entrance to their area.

Just like that they had rotated centers and were down to business again. There were three children playing in the kitchen area now, and three matching squares stuck to the Velcro at the entrance, each with a small picture of a kitchen on it. The landing pad they were attached to had a larger version of the same kitchen picture printed on it.

"Caleb, we have a visitor with us today," the aide said to one of the boys in the kitchen area. She took my son by the shoulders and guided him in. "This is Paul."

"Hi, Paul!" Caleb waved enthusiastically. "Come play with me!"

This display made me feel awful until I remembered that the class had some neurotypical students mixed in, children of school staff who received a discounted daycare rate in exchange for allowing their children to serve as role models.

Caleb must be a staff kid, I thought. *Surely. Even so . . .*

"That was amazing," I said to the aide, who introduced herself as Laurie. "I mean, the transition, with the pictures and everything."

She smiled. "Oh, yeah, the kids love to use the cues."

"But Paul . . . can't do that," I said sheepishly. "Not even close."

"You'd be surprised. The first week of school is pretty tough," she admitted. "Getting everyone used to things. We pretty much spend all day just guiding little bodies around until they get it. But they see the older students doing it, so that helps, and most of them just love how regimented it all is."

She pulled a poker chip from her pocket to show me. "We break it down into steps, and each step automatically leads to the next one so they don't have to remember the whole process. Whenever we give them one of these, it means they go check their schedule. We say it all day, and it just becomes completely ingrained. 'Here's your chip; check your schedule. Here's your chip; check your schedule.' If there's a chip in your hand, you *have* to go put it in the can."

Laurie led me over to the hallway between classrooms, where a large coffee can sat on the floor with a slot cut into the plastic lid. Lined up along the entire length of the wall were three-foot-high Velcro columns, each one topped with a child's photograph. They were currently filled about halfway up with different laminated square pictures.

"Chip goes in the can," she said, popping it in with a clank. "Just the sound is enough to excite some of our kids; they love getting a chip.

And now they're here in front of the schedules, where they needed to be. They find their photo, pull the next cue off, and it tells them where to go. Everything's top to bottom, since it takes a long time for some kids to learn that reading goes left to right."

My mouth might very well have been hanging open as I stared in awe. So this was how a picture schedule was supposed to function! You can't spend more than ten minutes learning about autism without hearing about picture schedules, but no one had ever been able to explain them to me effectively. Our ECI caseworker had even brought laminating supplies and bits of Velcro so we could make one together early on, except she hadn't really understood how they were supposed to work, either. She told me I was just supposed to lay it out each morning—left to right, of course—and show it to Paul, and this would somehow give him security about what was going to happen during the day. It was true that he preferred routine, but the important thing to him was that it was *his* routine. If he didn't feel like going to the store that day, he wasn't going to feel relieved to know where it was on his schedule; he was just going to be irritated for hours before it happened. Or worse, he might see the picture and decide that he needed to go there right now, never mind how early it was or who was still in pajamas—and God help us all if he chose a place that wasn't open yet. There are indeed many autistic children who get upset if something unexpected comes along, but Paul loved spontaneity and unpredictable results, as long as they entertained him.

This process in front of me, though, this beautiful machine, could really work for him. The cues weren't supposed to be detachable just so I could rearrange them each day, as our ECI lady had thought. They were intended to be mobile, to almost trick the child into going where he needed to be. Coin goes in the can, always. Picture goes to matching picture, always.

"This is really cool," I told her.

"The only ones it doesn't do much for are the kids who just don't have the processing speed yet. You know, there are a few who just can't remember where the can is, no matter how hard they try, or can't understand that the smaller picture matches the larger picture even though they're different sizes. But for the ones who get it, they just don't want to comply . . . " She glanced wryly towards Paul. "It works really great for them."

"And it's emotionally detached," I said, still marveling. "It's like, 'Hey, I'm not telling you what to do, the card is. Nothing I can do about it.'"

"Exactly!"

"So at the end of the day? . . ." I began, and Laurie gave a tired smile.

"Yes, once the kids go home, the three of us have to pull all the used cues from all over the room and sit here on the floor putting together every schedule for the next day. But it's not bad; most of it is pretty similar from day to day. When a child is potty-training there will be like fifteen restroom cues inserted all over their schedule, but the major parts of everyone's day are the same. We all go to lunch together; we all go to recess together," she said, pointing at the appropriate lines of cues running horizontally across the wall, in the same spot on everyone's schedule.

"Yeah, Paul's not potty-trained at all," I told her apologetically.

"We change diapers," she said. "Not a problem."

"Also, he has to be on this restricted diet. . . . "

"Gluten-free, right?" she asked. "We have a lot of kids on it. We even have the special play dough, and all that."

I couldn't get over how amazing this place was. "So I can just send his lunch and all his snacks, no big deal?"

Laurie waved a hand. "Almost all the kids bring their own food, because even the ones that aren't on a special diet are real picky about what they'll eat." Then she pointed past me to the other end of the hallway. "Mrs. Allison's about finished with her small group if you want to go in there and meet her."

I approached the door to the second classroom, which apparently belonged to them as well. Through the narrow window I could see her, squatting in front of four small chairs in a semicircle. Every few seconds one of the boys would turn his head and act like he was about to get up and wander, but Mrs. Allison was attuned to his body language and would gently trap him with her outer arm and urge him back to the front while never missing a beat on the large white notepad she was gesturing at with the other hand. I dared to hope that maybe that boy could be Paul someday. The least attentive one in the group for sure, but still successfully corralled in his seat without fussing about it. Maybe by the end of the school year—who knew?

I was surprised to see how young she was. Later I would learn that this was only Mrs. Allison's second year of teaching. I had assumed that someone who ran a ship this tight must have decades of experience under her belt, but over time I came to learn that running a special needs classroom is a lot like caring for newborns: it's usually best left to those who still have the energy to do it. Burnout is high in the teaching profession and much more so in special education. Plus, having graduated recently meant Mrs. Allison was up-to-date on the very latest behavioral therapy programs. She was using techniques in her classroom that hadn't even existed ten years ago.

I didn't know it at the time, but we were extremely lucky to have her. Since then I have talked to many parents about their child's PPCD class, and none of them came close to ours. Some were actively bad for the children's progress—nothing more than a lawless day care turned up to eleven. Screamers allowed to scream, runners tearing apart the room, teachers shouting at the kids and handing out cookies and candy all day long just to keep mouths silent for a few moments.

But Mrs. Allison's class was truly a therapy setting, the kind parents paid thousands of dollars for. Her small group filed out, poker chips in hand, and I got a chance to ask her a few more questions about how everything worked before the next group came in. She explained one of the more cryptic cues I'd seen on some kids' schedules, labeled "PRT." It stood for Pivotal Response Training, which was basically a fine-tuned version of Applied Behavioral Analysis, or ABA, yet another acronym that autism parents toss around freely.

Applied Behavioral Analysis is the granddaddy of all behavioral therapy for autism. In ABA, very specific goals are chosen, and they are broken down into small steps that are taught one at a time, sometimes in a way that initially doesn't even relate to the skill that is being taught. For example, if an ABA therapist is trying to teach a child to use eye contact, she might create an activity where the child has no choice but to look to the therapist's eyes for information. The therapist might hold out two toys and say, "You can have that one," but only indicate which toy she means by glancing at it. If the child isn't even aware that she should be looking to the face for clues, the therapist may have to begin by ridiculously pointing down to the toy with her entire head, then slowly scaling back to just nodding towards the allowed toy, and eventually just twitching her eyes, as the child eventually forms the habit of always looking to the therapist's face when she starts speaking.

ABA is also heavily rewards-based, but on a small and frequent scale. So in the previous example, the two toys might both be cars, and if the child takes the correct car, he would be allowed to drop it in the track and watch it race to the bottom before another two cars are shown to him. Reach for the wrong car, and the therapist won't hand it over.

This type of progress may take months of lengthy one-on-one time, depending on the child, and of course these goals can come only after the child has first learned to cooperatively sit in a chair and "attend" to whatever activity the therapist has prepared, which may take several months of intense therapy just in itself. Needless to say, ABA is tedious and takes a special type of personality to implement it, but it is a proven method for teaching skills.

In the classroom PRT time was mostly focused on academics, since the school was simply not responsible for teaching things like eye contact. A student might be completely nonverbal and constantly stimming, but if he or she could follow most instructions, complete age-appropriate written work, and not disrupt the class, then the school had fulfilled its duties to the letter of the law. Not surprisingly, Mrs. Allison went well beyond the legal requirements. She told me that she used all periods of the day for practicing skills, even recess. She might make a student go down the slide five times before allowing them to obsessively pace the perimeter of the playground, or go say "Hi" to three friends before being allowed to play.

"Of course if I do that," she said, "I make sure to send them to the staff kids or someone really high-functioning so I know they'll say 'Hi' back, and get that positive feedback."

We returned to the main half of the classroom, and Mrs. Allison invited Paul to sit and have a snack with the class. He eagerly sat in a chair with the promise of food, but when she held out a red plastic cup and asked if he wanted some water, he shouted, "Red and blue makes a purple one!"

"It's from a show," I sighed, but she already knew that.

One by one the other children at the table indicated to her which cup they wanted, either verbally, with crude gestures, or, in a few cases, clear sign language. I wanted to be optimistic, because I couldn't imagine a better place for Paul, yet I was still worried that they were not going to be able to get the same results out of him that they were used to. He talked, which not all of the kids did, but he didn't *answer.* Even with his mouth crammed full of gluten-free pretzels, he was still scripting.

"Would it be okay if I took a few pictures for a social story?" I asked. "Just to try to get him ready for the first day. They really help him."

Social stories are another thing everyone talks about for autism, and our ECI caseworker had suggested early on that we try them. But once again, she was just repeating what she'd been told and didn't really have any idea how they were supposed to work. She brought me an example of a "good one" from the home office, and I was even less impressed than I had been by her description. It was nothing more than four stick-figure drawings accompanied by sparse sentences such as "I don't run away from Mommy in the parking lot. I don't run away from Mommy at the store. Running away is dangerous." I marveled at how stupid this thing was. If my child understood the phrase "running away is dangerous," we wouldn't be having problems in the first place. Yet every book and online resource kept talking about what a great tool social stories were and how helpful they could be.

A good social story was in first person, they said—but that seemed wrong to me because most autistic children have a difficult time with pronouns. Paul always referred to himself by his own name, and usually we were stuck speaking about ourselves in the third person as well if we wanted him to understand. A good social story used actual photos rather than illustrations, they said, because autistic children are so literal. That made sense, yet every example of a social story I found online used bad clip art at best, hand-drawn stick figures at worst. So, like everything else, I had quickly decided that I was going to toss out the rules and start making my own social stories the way I knew my son would connect with them.

Paul and Mommy are going to the store today. Paul is so calm! He holds Mommy's hand and walks. I took a photo of the entrance to our grocery store to illustrate this page and even tricked him into holding my hand for a few moments on the kitchen table so that I could take a picture of it and put it in the book. He wouldn't follow instructions, but he would imitate a book or movie in a heartbeat, and I was hoping that if I could create scripts for him to follow, he would do it even if he didn't understand why.

It had indeed helped a little, and soon I was making longer books for bigger events. For one special trip to an Imagination Movers concert, I had woven a fifteen-page narrative whose only real purpose was to illustrate that at some point it would be time to leave. As expected, Paul had begun screaming as soon as we had tried to exit the theater, but then I had said, in the exact lilting tone I had used as we'd read the book each night leading up to the big day, "Now it's time for lunch!" He had miraculously snapped into scripting mode midtantrum and finished reciting the page for me. It told the reader that Paul climbed into our vehicle and buckled his seat belt, so he did. A minute later he remembered that he hadn't actually wanted to leave and started screaming again, but by then we were on the road.

So I had come to the PPCD classroom that morning with my camera, knowing I would want to make him a social story for the first day of school. We would have ten weeks to drill it into him because Paul's third birthday, the day he became instantly eligible to join the class, happened to fall just a couple of days after school let out for the summer. If we read this book every night between now and August, maybe he'd be ready.

It's Paul's first day of school! On this opening page I put a random photo of him with a big grin on his face.

First, Paul gets his backpack and his lunch box. Here we ran into a snag. Halfway through the summer I received the PPCD school supply list, which included the specific request that all students use a full-size backpack that could hold a standard folder, not one of the smaller novelty ones made for preschoolers. I'd gotten his backpack well in advance so I could include it in the social story, and of course I'd bought the wrong kind. So I had to go out and find a new one, still emblazoned with Lightning McQueen but clearly not the original. I took a new photo of this backpack and his lunch box by the front door, then reprinted and reassembled the entire book and switched them out. That night before bed, I held my breath while he stared at the new picture that had appeared in his book as if by magic, but eventually he let me continue reading without complaint. Whatever rationalization he came up with, I'm sure he never once believed that he was mistaken about the change.

Here comes the school bus! Mommy helps Paul get into his seat. I was particularly proud of this page, as there was no way I could have photographed an actual school bus in front of our house. Instead I found a nice picture online of an approaching bus and took a photo of the street from our driveway at what I guessed was approximately the same angle. I cut out the image of the bus using the basic Paint program on my computer and pasted it into the shot of our street. Not exactly professional graphics design, but it got the job done.

Mommy waves bye-bye. Paul says, "Wait for me, Mommy. I'll be right back!" This part was important. If I included dialogue in the story, he was more likely to script it. On the first day of school I would say, "Mommy waves bye-bye. Paul says . . . " and he would hopefully finish the line and believe that it was okay because the story said he was leaving me, not the other way around. He would eventually figure out what had happened, no doubt, but by then he'd be screaming at the bus driver and not me.

Paul is happy to see his friends. Look at all those friendly kids in the stock photo. He totally gives a flying hoot about them.

Riding the bus is lots of fun. I swear.

I had pages talking about his cubby, and the play kitchen area, and the dress-up mirror, and the snack table. School cafeterias look remarkably similar, and I found a picture of one online that was almost identical to the one at his school. I took a photo of his new lunch box, open and filled with food, and of course planned to send those same foods on his first day.

At the end of the day, the bus comes to take Paul home. Look, there's Mommy waiting for him! I used the same photo of me waving goodbye in our driveway. If he thought I stood right there, waving in an endless loop until he returned, so much the better.

Today was a fun day of school. Unlikely, but I could dream. He was as ready as he could be. There were going to be some tantrums on the first day, and perhaps every day after it. I was used to it, and I knew the school staff had to be used to it, too, but I couldn't help but feel guilty inflicting him upon them.

Chapter 12

Formula for Success

As THE SUMMER went on we continued to make great progress in many areas, yet in others we were frustratingly stuck. Paul's stools were only moderately improved during this time, and sometimes just as bad as they had been before we'd started altering his diet at all. This was strangely encouraging because it suggested there was more room for progress, that the opportunity for even bigger cognitive and behavioral advances was within our grasp if we could only solve the ongoing GI problems. But the data was overwhelming. My diligent note-taking was isolating more and more foods that were giving him distinctly worse behavior, and every time we removed one, another soon became apparent. Lucas suggested that we run a comprehensive immunoglobulin G food sensitivity test, so that I could skip all this detective work and just have the results on paper in front of me.

There are five types of antibodies created by the immune system. One of these is IgE, which is responsible for what we consider a typical allergic response: itchy eyes, congestion, hives, and, in the most severe cases, anaphylaxis. An IgE reaction is what doctors refer to as a "true allergy," and once you've developed one, it is expected to be with you for life. Another type is IgG, and the bodily response to these antibodies is gastrointestinal upset and inflammation. This response is sometimes referred to as a food "sensitivity" rather than an allergy, though it is an inappropriate reaction of the immune system all the same. IgG reactions are thought by many physicians to be harmless because they're never life-threatening, like an inability to breathe is, and they are also notoriously impermanent. Over time a patient's IgG reactions can shift and change, and what is causing distress now might be perfectly fine to eat six months later. Or it might not. But generally speaking, they are considered by most doctors to be more trouble than they're worth.

For us, however, GI inflammation was everything. The law of diminishing returns says that you have to put in more work for smaller gains closer to the top, while farther down the bell curve even a small increase in work can lead to very big results. For an average child near the peak of his potential, the comparison with and without his IgG-reactive foods might be "I feel fine" versus "I guess I feel a little better; I never really thought about it." But for a child with autism, even a small amount of GI improvement might mean the difference between severe symptoms and minimal ones. For us, any digestive relief was worth the trouble.

I would have run the IgG test sooner, if I'd known there was such a thing. But the unplanned benefit of delaying this long was that I had another opportunity to cross-check my work. I had my own list of foods that I was sure Paul was reacting badly to and was no longer feeding him. If all of those items showed up as strongly IgG positive, and the foods that I felt he was eating without reaction showed up as negative, then I could have greater faith in both my own observation skills and the future reliability of the IgG test results. I wanted data, data, and more data.

I got more than I bargained for. When the results came in, Paul was indeed highly reactive to all of his suspect foods, with scores in almost perfect alignment with what I had personally noted as being more or less severe. The range of the lab results went from 0 to 3, and we'd been told even before taking the test that we should probably ignore everything except the 3s. Midrange scores were more likely to be false positives and more likely to fluctuate over relatively short periods of time, so we were better off focusing our efforts on removing just the top offenders from his diet. We were warned that even this could be a lot of work, since for an autistic child with severe GI symptoms, there could be as many as ten or twelve foods scoring this high.

Paul had twenty-seven. Cantaloupe, carrot, cashew, coconut . . . the page was full of alarming red ink. And many of them were surprisingly inconvenient. Garlic and flaxseed were his two highest sensitivities, almost off the charts. This wouldn't seem so impossible to deal with except that his rice bread used flaxseed, and most gluten-free lunch meats and chips included garlic. There was another brand of rice bread that didn't contain flaxseed, but it still involved eggs, which turned out to be one of his "true" IgE allergies. One brand of chips didn't have garlic, but they were cooked in safflower oil, another of his highest sensitivities. And on and on.

I was overwhelmed and demoralized at the mountain of work I had just been presented with, yet I was still glad to have the information. Most of my note-taking had been focused on the main ingredient, and who knows how long it would have taken me to figure out why he was reacting to this brand of turkey lunch meat but not that one, especially when both were likely to have been served with egg-based mayonnaise on the sandwich.

One by one, I began to find an acceptable replacement for each food he could no longer have, just as I had when we'd first gone gluten-free. I gave up trying to find a commercial bread that left out all the ingredients we needed to avoid and started baking my own. Before long we had successfully eliminated all of his most reactive foods, and while this left him with a capriciously short list of things to eat, Kirsten signed off on it as being perfectly balanced and healthy.

As expected, his baseline behavior improved in tandem with each removal. We started seeing days with straight 3s in the behavioral column of my notebook and even the occasional 4. Everyone who saw his lunch box marveled at all the vegetables he ate, and usually I just accepted the praise without explaining that he ate them only because the alternative was starvation. Then one day I went to change his diaper, and it was full of undigested pinto beans. That was worrisome. He'd never had a problem with pinto beans before. We gave it some time, tried giving him smaller servings and more digestive enzymes to help him break them down, but it only got worse. Soon we started to see behavioral spikes after he ate pinto beans, too. It was not really surprising that he'd developed a new sensitivity, since that was how he'd ended up with so many after all. We hoped that maybe this meant he'd lost a few of his old ones, but there didn't seem to be anything we could safely reintroduce from the forbidden list without a reaction.

Then bananas showed up. And pickles. And pears. Each time we removed a food, a new food became a problem. Kirsten told us that his immune system was still in turmoil, and until things settled down he was probably going to keep developing sensitivities to whatever happened to be in his system at the time. She said one thing that might help, however, was rotation—to have Paul eat a particular food only once every four days. Supposedly, this would minimize the chances of anything being in circulation long enough to get picked up by his immune system.

Dividing the remaining foods by four meant that each day effectively got one item from each food group. In the grains category, it was amaranth on day one, corn on day two, sorghum on day three, and chickpea on day four. I baked one kind of sandwich bread made from sorghum flour and another made from chickpea flour. Amaranth got baked into pumpkin bars to hide the strong flavor, since a loaf of bread made from amaranth was a deal-killer as far as Paul was concerned. At least on corn day I was able to fall back on packaged items, like Kix cereal and a dairy-free Cheetos substitute called Tings.

Meats were then arranged so that he could have turkey and ham lunch meat (both still garlic-free) on the two respective sandwich bread days, beef hot dogs on corn days, and homemade chicken nuggets on amaranth days. Fruits were similarly down to one kind per day, and the remaining veggies he would eat were split up as evenly as they could be. I found myself buying bags of Terra chips, which are made from a variety of colorful root vegetables, and sorting them by hand so that I could give him the yucca chips one day, and the taro chips the next day, and the weird purple chips I didn't even know the name of on the day after that.

It was ridiculous. And it didn't work. Strawberries started coming out undigested, then almonds, then all the corn products. Meanwhile, his stools had regressed back to being as liquid and colorful as they'd ever been. This was not a static condition but an active disease that we were fighting, and we were being steadily boxed in.

Another option had come up a few times on my biomedical message boards, though I was loath to consider it. Each time I'd read about friends taking this unreasonably drastic path, I had assured myself that at least we'd never have to go *that* far. This has been an important, painful lesson that I've had to learn more than once: I must never draw a line in the sand, because in that very moment the tide is called in. Declare something to be beyond my ability, and it is guaranteed that I will have to do it.

The nuclear option I'd been hiding from was something called an elemental formula, which would replace all food. The amino acids and nutrients it contained were in perfect balance for the needs of the human body and already broken down into their purely absorbable, "elemental" state, thus making digestion unnecessary. Unlike standard baby formulas, which are stewed in a base of cow's milk, soy, or occasionally some other protein like hemp, an elemental formula is completely hypoallergenic. It would be literally impossible for Paul to have an immune reaction to it.

We were on the fence. Would he be miserable, having the last of all food taken away from him? Or would it be no worse, after all, than having to eat things like sorghum bread with pureed cucumber spread? Besides, since when did medical treatment ever get to be enjoyable, anyway? Kids with diabetes don't enjoy getting stuck with needles, but they have to do it all the same. That's just life.

Based on medical advice and the experience of other families who had gone this route, we knew there was a very real chance that spending a few months on this formula would allow dramatic healing. His digestive tract could take a complete break, and his immune system would stop getting challenged with food proteins all day long and have a chance to finally settle down. We decided to go for it.

The formula was prohibitively expensive, over $1,000 per month, but some families reported that they'd been able to get insurance coverage with a doctor's prescription. Thoughtful House obliged. Our MD argued at length with an MD working for the insurance company over the definition of "medically necessary," and we had to file forms, fax over Paul's complete medical records, and launch multiple appeals. Their representative read sections of Texas insurance law to me over the phone, and I responded with sections of Connecticut law after reminding him that the governing force in this case depended on where their business was headquartered, not where the policyholder lived. In the end we were successful, and not even by a percentage. Just as with any standard prescription, we would pay a monthly co-pay of $40 for all the food Paul would eat. This would turn out to be the only treatment we ever tried that actually saved us money.

So on November 24, two days before Thanksgiving, I handed him his first sippy cup of Elecare, the brand of elemental formula that was rumored to taste the least awful. Paul tried it but wasn't impressed, and fussed halfheartedly for his real breakfast. A few hours of distraction and occasional encouragement made no difference, so I brought out the big guns: bubbles. The first and greatest of all ABA rewards. For each tiny sip he took, I would blow the bubble wand. He would spend thirty seconds obsessively popping them all, ask for more, see that I was serious about putting the bubbles away, and finally take another minuscule sip. About thirty minutes into this process, he seemed to realize that his hunger pains were abating and that the formula didn't taste so bad after all. He started taking larger sips.

He drank eagerly the next day. He was also surprisingly calm and alert.

On Thursday, Thanksgiving, we went to my aunt's house for the family gathering, bringing along Paul's can of powdered formula to mix for him as needed. During the main meal we stationed ourselves at a table on the back deck so that Paul would have the yard to play in while we were eating. He gave one curious glance at my plate of food, pausing with his head tilted and eyes narrowed, as if he'd just now realized we weren't all drinking the same stuff he was. Then he emptied his cup quickly and ran off to play.

Eventually, he became impatient for the other children to join him and came back over to us. Peering at my stepson's plate, he saw an old favorite, and I tensed.

"Fritos," Paul said.

"Yeah," I confirmed apologetically. "Did you want some Fritos?" My tone made it clear I wasn't offering them to him, just commiserating—letting him know that I recognized his frustrations and this wasn't some sort of elaborate punishment.

"No," he said firmly, almost scandalized. Then he ran off again.

There was a long pause as we all watched him go.

"Did Paul just say he didn't want Fritos?" my stepson asked.

"Yep, looks like it."

"Weird," he said.

It was indeed very weird. But sure enough, Paul took to the elemental formula better than any other dietary restriction we'd had to impose on him. He loved his formula and didn't seem to miss food in the slightest. He couldn't communicate well enough for us to know, but it seemed to me that he was not in pain anymore, and that he understood why.

I had deliberately started this intervention over the holiday break in order to give us a few extra days to get him settled. When he returned to school on Monday, Mrs. Allison reported that Paul had suddenly started greeting his friends by name throughout the day. It may not seem like much to a parent of a neurotypical child, but for an autistic child, a spontaneous "Hi, John!" is a huge deal. He'd certainly never done it before.

Though she couldn't help but know about the formula, in general I kept Mrs. Allison in the dark about his various supplement and medication changes, by agreement. I had told her at the beginning of the year that I wanted her to be an objective observer on Paul's behavior, to help me know if I was really seeing what I thought I was with any given treatment. There were many occasions where we tried something new, or accidentally ran out of something, and Mrs. Allison would e-mail me that same day, telling me that he'd had an especially good or bad day, depending on the change.

In general school was going well. He had even let me leave him at the door without a single complaint on the first day—after all my work creating layered school bus art for his social story, the driver had been unfamiliar with the new route and never arrived—and Mrs. Allison had commented on what a completely different kid he was since she'd last seen him at the class visit in May.

"When you first brought him in, you know, I thought okay, this is going to be . . . " She struggled to find a polite phrasing. "Not necessarily the most severe kid in the world, you know, but just, he's—"

"A lot of work," I offered.

"Yes, a lot of work. Very intense. But then he walks in here on the first day and doesn't make a peep! Well, unless he needed his diaper changed, anyway."

Paul had also taken quickly to the picture schedule, just as they had predicted he would. One weekend shortly after school started, I had opened a bag over his lunch plate and said absentmindedly, "Here's your chips."

"Check your schedule!" Paul had finished gleefully. I had to look twice at his mischievous grin to be sure, but I swear he wasn't just finishing the script; he had actually understood that he was making a joke.

And now, with the introduction of the formula, he had made another big leap forward, just in time to go back and see the neurologist at age three and a half, to in theory revisit the question of psychiatric medication. I proudly described to the physician's assistant the various treatments we were doing and the astounding progress we'd seen. This time I didn't mind the prospect of having to tell my whole story twice, as she listened with genuine interest and asked relevant questions.

"Well," she said finally, after we'd made our way through the standard evaluation checklists, "I have to tell you, unless something changes, you don't have to come back here. He's no longer a candidate for anything we would prescribe. I can't say I know much about what you're doing, but whatever it is, it's obviously working, so I'd say just keep doing it."

And with that we were checked out. She didn't even bother sending the neurologist into the exam room after her. I was elated, vindicated, thrilled to have a medical professional outside Thoughtful House actually speak to me with respect and trust. She saw that Paul was a completely different child from the one she had seen six months earlier, and she hadn't written it off or pretended that he hadn't been so bad to begin with. She had to know her acceptance was a little revolutionary, not to mention her advice to keep doing what we were doing, and it's possible she didn't really pass on any of the details about our appointment to her boss. Then again, maybe not—I have recently learned that a different doctor in that practice has switched sides, so to speak, and become extremely interested in particular biomedical treatments for autism, so maybe the world was starting to change behind the scenes even then. Regardless, we knew where we were going whether anyone followed us or not. I was feeling more and more confident each day that we were going to beat this thing.

It's easy to see now that this confidence was premature, but it was also necessary. I know that we have been extremely lucky, as I have close friends who have taken the same steps we have, with the same level of tenacity, and not yet reached full recovery. But fighting anything this hard takes a sizable ego, to believe that you can, in fact, be David against Goliath. You have to believe wholeheartedly that you can prevail, because that confidence is the only thing that will give you the strength to keep going when things get tough.

And they were about to get very, very tough.

Chapter 13

Eats Shoots and Leaves

IT BEGAN JUST before Christmas with the startling discovery that Paul had lined up all his toy cars in one long, winding path across the living room floor, just like in the old days.

"Oh, no! Paul, what is this?" I cried, unable to hide my dismay. It had been at least four months since I'd had to watch my feet for trip lines of vehicles.

"Cars," he answered matter-of-factly.

I wondered whether he had been exposed to a forbidden food somewhere, but that kind of reaction should have faded within a week at most, and the lines persisted. Then behavioral issues started to creep in as well, mostly connected to routines. His expectations were becoming increasingly rigid, and before long he was reintroducing verbal scripts that he had abandoned months ago.

I knew something was wrong, but I couldn't figure out what. It certainly wasn't a new food sensitivity; the formula was as invariable as you could get. So the next step was to do trials with various antimicrobial supplements in case he'd picked up a fungal or bacterial infection, which always affected his behavior. Some seemed to help a little, but their effectiveness wore off after a week or two, and he would start sliding downhill again.

I scanned my notebook for clues. Cognitively, he was fine, still steadily improving. It was only his obsessive-compulsive tendencies that were spiking out of proportion to everything else. Lines of toys snaked through every room of the house, and soon he was having routine-based meltdowns again, the kind we hadn't seen since before taking him off gluten.

By March we were having at least one major meltdown a day and lots of general fighting over daily events like bath time or getting the mail. This short trek down the street to the mailbox cluster was something we used to do every day after school, but I was skipping it more and more frequently. Chief among his new issues was an obsession with opening and closing doors, and Paul simply didn't understand why he couldn't break into every house we passed and slam the front door a few times. I gave up on the walks entirely after I had to carry him kicking and screaming all the way back home for the second time. Not only was it as exhausting and frustrating as it had ever been, now I got to add being demoralized to the list, since I'd thought we were past this sort of thing.

I reminded myself that at least he was still screaming great sentences like "I want to open that door! Put me down now!" It was no consolation.

The answer came by random chance, as they often have. We were on the large trampoline in our back yard one afternoon, and Paul was in a borderline-meltdown state. He was flinging himself around in a half-bouncing, half-crashing kind of way, landing on head or feet or back, like a one-person mosh pit. His voice wavered back and forth between twitchy overexcitement and irritable screeching. He wanted me to bounce with him, to bounce harder, *harder*, to chase him at top speed, to tackle him like a linebacker . . . I was worn out, but this excuse did not satisfy him. When I dared to sit down on the mat to rest for a moment, the insult was too great for him to bear. He flung himself backwards towards me, his head landing in my lap so he could furiously glare up at me as he let out a long, frustrated scream.

From this angle, I could see all the way into the back of his throat. His tonsils were huge.

He had no fever, but that was not surprising. He hadn't had a single real fever since he'd gotten roseola, a mostly harmless viral infection that causes a few days of elevated temperature and a skin rash, at eighteen months. (It's possible, in fact, that this infection was a key trigger in worsening his autism, but at the time we weren't on the lookout for such things.) Lucas had told us that Paul's lack of fevers was another sign of his immune dysfunction. A fever was a normal response to pathogenic infection, he said, not caused by the germs but by the body itself, to intentionally roast these foreign organisms that couldn't survive at higher temperatures. As long as it stayed below the threshold that was dangerous to our own cells, around 105 degrees Fahrenheit, then a fever was actually a good thing, and medicines that artificially lowered it only prolonged illness. The average child should expect at least two to three moderate fevers per year as their bodies appropriately recognized and killed off the various diseases that we all get exposed to, and without fevers, Paul would be at a significant disadvantage in fighting off, say, strep throat.

Based on when the behavioral regression started, it was my guess that he'd had strep throat for almost three months now. I immediately called for an appointment.

"You know, it might even be PANDAS," Lucas mused, as I detailed the door obsessions and reappearance of toy lines. This really unfortunate acronym stands for Pediatric Autoimmune Neuropsychiatric Disorders Associated with Streptococcus. It's a complicated autoimmune disease, but in short, it means that strep causes obsessive-compulsive behaviors in certain children. When they are given antibiotics for the strep, the OCD goes away, too.

"Constant throat pain is likely to cause general bad behavior, of course," he went on, "but aside from that, PANDAS could potentially be responsible for the spike in OCD behaviors that you're seeing."

He gave us a prescription for azithromycin and also ordered a blood test for DNase and ASO titers, a measure of the amount of strep antibodies in his system. Current theory says that when a child has PANDAS, the autoimmune reaction is not to the bacteria itself but to the body's own antibodies against the infection. It is the immune system being allergic to itself, in a way. If he had PANDAS, Lucas told us, Paul's strep titers would be very high.

Instead they came back at zero. This was quite strange in its own way. We had been concerned about the possibility of off-the-charts numbers, but it had been an underlying assumption that there would at least be the normal, moderate level of antibodies that one would expect with any current strep infection. The bacteria were definitely there; a physical swab in his throat had cultured positive and confirmed it. Yet his immune system had generated no antibodies to strep at all, as if it weren't even aware that there was an infection. When a normal substance is misidentified as a bad guy, we call it an allergy, but it seemed that in this case the opposite had occurred. A pathogen had been misidentified as a good guy and was being left completely alone.

Whether this might still qualify for a diagnosis of PANDAS depended on which research source you read. Some claimed that the presence of high DNase antibody titers was a de facto requirement for the diagnosis, whereas others said that a certain percentage of PANDAS patients showed no elevated titers yet still saw elimination of their OCD with antibiotic treatment.

Frankly, I didn't care what they called it. What I needed was for Paul to get better, and he did. Within hours of the first antibiotic dose, we saw major behavioral improvement. By the second day, he was back to normal; that is, where he'd been in early December. No tantrums, no car lines, no door obsessions. Meanwhile, his tonsils were visibly returning to normal size as the days passed.

I was overjoyed. We had finally identified and fought past another setback! Whether the problem had truly been PANDAS or just Paul's inability to verbalize the fact that he was in severe throat pain, I didn't care. My emotional roller coaster was up again, and when it's up, I always foolishly assume that we'll stay there forever.

A couple of days after the last antibiotic dose, the behaviors started to creep back in, and the roller coaster plummeted down once more. I stuck a flashlight in his mouth, and sure enough, his tonsils were getting bigger.

Okay, I thought, *so it was a persistent infection.* That wasn't terribly surprising since it had had three months to entrench itself. Another course of azithromycin once again brought immediate relief.

And again the symptoms came back within days of finishing it. We continued this pattern, with Lucas steadily increasing the strength and length of the antibiotics, for two months. Yet the symptoms doggedly returned every time, and what was worse, the effects of the medication were starting to wane even when he was on them. I was terrified of the day when the antibiotics were going to give him no relief at all and we would be trapped in OCD hell.

Before that could happen I took him to an Ear, Nose, and Throat specialist. After listening to our history and examining Paul's throat and nasal passages, Dr. Shikari said, "Well, it sounds like the problem is primarily in his adenoids, since the tonsils are only moderately enlarged right now."

I admitted that Paul had just finished another round of antibiotics two days ago. "They're on the way up," I assured him. "First the behavior comes back, then the tonsils get large a day or two after that." I cursed myself for not delaying the appointment by a few days so the doctor could actually see what we were there to show him.

Dr. Shikari said that it would be reasonable at this point to remove Paul's adenoids altogether, which was the answer I'd been hoping for. We had already done a second test for strep titers, and again the results had returned no presence of antibodies whatsoever. Plainly, his body was not going to fight this infection itself. Even if we did manage to conquer it with drugs, he would inevitably be exposed again in the future, and we had to assume he wouldn't be able to fight it next time, either.

"What about the tonsils?" I asked. "I don't want to go through an operation and then find out we have to come back and take them out later."

"If the tonsils are enlarged on the day of the surgery, I will take them out, too," he conceded.

"Oh, they will be," I promised.

And they were. I deliberately didn't give Paul any more antibiotics, even though we had one refill still available. This meant two weeks of OCD frustrations, but I happily—well, willingly—put up with them, knowing that there was a light at the end of the tunnel. During this time I also repeatedly checked his tonsils to assure myself that they were getting bigger, as expected. As I had said to the doctor, I had no intention of committing to an operation unless everything was getting taken care of at once.

We made a social story for the trip to the hospital, but given the state of his illness at that point, Paul was still uncooperative on the day of the procedure. We agreed to let the pre-op nurses dose him with a drug called Versed, which they promised would make him calm enough to put on his hospital pajamas and go to the operating room without a fight. I wasn't convinced anything could do that, but it began working within minutes, and soon I was able to easily coax him into opening his mouth for Dr. Shikari, who had come to check on us before scrubbing in for the procedure.

"I told you they'd be big by now," I said with a rueful smile.

"Yes, I see." He frowned. "A tonsillectomy is a bigger procedure, though. It requires an overnight stay."

"Oh, yes, we came packed for it," I said, indicating our bag.

He nodded. "Okay."

By then Paul was too loopy to stand, and he allowed a nurse to casually lift him into her arms and carry him away.

"We need to get some of that Versed for home use," Andrew joked.

The next part was nerve-wracking tedium, as hospital waiting rooms tend to be. Andrew had to leave for work, and I played with my phone, occasionally letting my parents and in-laws know that he was still back there.

Finally, Dr. Shikari came out to give me an update. "Everything went beautifully," he said. "No problems at all. The adenoids were blocking about 50 percent of his airway, so aside from the infection they were no doubt interfering with his sleep as well."

"Did he take the anesthesia okay?" I asked.

"Yes, he let them put the mask on, and then he was already asleep for the IV insertion. Everything was very easy. Now, waking up may be a different story," he warned. "He will be disoriented, and it's not unusual for children to be pretty upset as the anesthesia wears off. The nurses will give him something additional for the pain as soon as it's safe."

"He's not awake yet, though, right?" I asked nervously.

"He was still asleep in the recovery room when I last saw him, but don't be worried. It can take a while to wake up; that's normal."

I gave a short laugh. "I'm not worried that it will take too long, I'm worried that he'll wake up before I get back there. He's going to rip the IV out as soon as he opens his eyes and try to throw himself out of the bed. Do they know that?"

"I'm sure they can handle it," he said with mild amusement. But it was no exaggeration, and I could tell that he had not warned them at all. I started gathering our bags. I needed to get to the recovery room right away.

"We went ahead and just took out the adenoids," Dr. Shikari added casually, waving his hand as if this fact were no more important to me than what he'd ordered for lunch. "You know, tonsil surgery is really much more intense and results in a lot more pain. I just couldn't justify putting a child through that when it's not completely necessary, especially not a child with, you know, special needs."

"You didn't take out the tonsils," I repeated in disbelief. *What? Get back there and do it, before he wakes up!*

"It's really very traumatic," he said.

Oh, really? How does it compare to three straight months of throat pain? And how dare you try to play the special needs card, to model for me how much compassion you have? As if you have any idea what our lives are like.

"Postsurgery care includes a strong round of antibiotics," he continued quickly, "so I'm sure that will clear up any leftover infection that might have spread from the adenoids."

We talked about his tonsils in pre-op, and you said, "Okay." This was not what we agreed to!

But there was nothing I could do about it now. "Fine," I said tersely. I had to cut my losses in this conversation and get back to see my son. He could be running around the room, screaming and pulling out other patients' IVs as we spoke. All I could do was pray that Dr. Shikari was right about the new round of antibiotics. If we had to come back again and get his tonsils out in a couple of years, well, I guess that was something I would have to worry about later.

Fortunately, Paul was still asleep when I got to his bed in the recovery room. I also saw with great relief that the arm containing his IV line had been thickly wrapped from elbow to fingertips with a splint inside, as solidly as a full forearm cast.

"This is perfect," I said to the nurse monitoring him, nodding towards the IV line. "It's exactly what he needs."

She smiled at me with pity. "We don't usually go this far, but the pre-op nurse made a note."

"I was worried. Dr. Shikari said he hadn't mentioned anything to you."

She rolled her eyes. "The doctors never do."

It turned out that I needn't have worried about rushing to his bedside, as we waited longer and longer for the anesthesia to wear off. There are studies indicating that autistic individuals have a harder time metabolizing substances out of their bodies than other people, and it certainly seemed to be the case here. Paul was still deeply asleep after a full hour, even with the nurse shaking him, so she resorted to rubbing a cold washcloth over his face.

After several swipes he finally leaped upwards in a confused rage. He was still heavily drugged, though, open eyes notwithstanding. His head lolled to the side, drooling profusely and with one pupil more dilated than the other. I only barely caught his dead weight as he tried to throw himself out of bed with drunken limbs. If I'd been smart, I would have just climbed up into the bed with him before he woke up, never mind what the nurses thought, but it was too late for me to do anything other than bear-hug him. It was harder than usual, though, because even as he was attacking me with some limbs, other parts of him would unexpectedly go limp and threaten to slip to the floor. The moment I shifted my position into one of support instead of restraint, I'd be given a painfully unmitigated kick as my reward.

I was glad when Dr. Shikari passed through the recovery room with another patient and I got to flash him a bitter look that said, *See? Not exaggerating.* He quickly scurried away.

After another thirty minutes the anesthesia truly wore off, and Paul was in the state I had been prepared for—furious, but at least alert. Purposeful instead of delusional. It was at this point that he finally became aware of the IV in his arm, and he unleashed a melee of clawing fingers, all the while yelling, "Take it off, take it off, take it off!" at the top of his lungs.

Eventually, the nurses realized he wasn't going to get any more clearheaded than this and moved us to a real room with a door that I could block with minimal effort. Things got a little better once they did remove the IV line, but hours later I still had to restrain him on my lap in a wheelchair as the discharge nurse rolled us all the way out to our car in the parking lot. She helped me force him into his car seat and apologized that she couldn't come home with me to help.

Halfway home he vomited all over himself, and suddenly he was fine. He rode the rest of the way in relative quiet, calmly let me clean him up, ate a normal lunch, and played on the computer for the rest of the day. Mr. Hyde had miraculously transformed back into Dr. Jekyll.

Dr. Shikari called that evening to see how he was doing and was baffled to hear that things were great. Perhaps he didn't even believe me. True, Paul was also on the postsurgery antibiotics, which were more powerful than the azithromycin he'd been on before, but things stayed level even in the days after he finished them, and I started to believe that we might really be past this after all.

I was wrong, of course. About three weeks after the surgery everything suddenly came back with a vengeance. Big tonsils, OCD, tantrums, and all. Now, however, there was less irritation and helplessness in Paul's tantrums and more anger. I know how frustrating it was for me to have precious relief snatched away from us again, and it was surely even worse for him.

We were lucky that school had just let out for the summer, because by the time we were able to get back in to see Dr. Shikari, things were worse than they'd ever been. Paul was having a lengthy, uncontrollable meltdown at least two to three times a day, and he was in fact right in the middle of a screaming fit in the car, straining against his seat belt with his back arched as far upwards as it would go, on the day I told him that next we would be going to Dr. Shikari's office.

Instantly, the scream cut off, and he dropped back into a normal seated position. "Okay," he said calmly. "Go see Dr. Shikari. Go see Dr. Shikari now."

I began crying. Paul had many struggles, but he most definitely was not stupid. He understood what was wrong with him; he just couldn't communicate it. Paul knew that Dr. Shikari had fixed the stabbing pain in his throat once before and trusted that he could do it again. He had been screaming to try to get through to me, and now he knew for sure he had, so he could stop. How awful it must be to never be able to tell anyone what hurts or how to fix it. It crushed me to see the hope in his eyes now, as if my ignorance had been the only roadblock to getting him help, and now everything would be fine.

"Paul gets an IV to help him take some special medicine," he recited pointedly. "It is like a shot. He is nice and calm and does not fuss." This was a page from the social story we had made for his trip to the hospital. He was using echolalia to request an IV needle.

Echolalia is not hard to translate once you understand the psychology behind it. Imagine that you are trapped on an alien planet with no chance of understanding the language. Assume as well that this species has completely different appendages than we do, so pointing and gesturing are useless. You are starving, but you have no way to communicate this. All you know is that the last time they fed you, one of them said, "Oogly boogly, nama nama shin!" So you keep approaching various aliens, repeating this phrase in the hope that one of them will feed you again.

Trouble is, it turns out that "Oogly boogly, nama nama shin" means "I hope you like this!" A useless social phrase that has nothing to do with food. You'd look like a lunatic saying it over and over, and you'd still go hungry. The aliens might even get mad at you, since you keep bothering them with nonsense. At some point you might start to scream in hunger and frustration, and there you'd be, a perfectly intelligent person, having an autistic tantrum on the floor.

For Paul, language was easy to memorize, but difficult to attach meaning to. What mattered for him was the overall scene the phrases came from. When he was upset, he would shout lines that characters on TV said when they were upset, even if the actual words were about how much he hated washing the car, or something equally irrelevant. Or he would pull an "oogly boogly" and recite whatever words I usually said to him during an event. Any time he hurt himself, for example, he would wail, "It's okay, honey," because that was what I always said to him when he was hurt. If he was hungry, he would prompt me with my line, "Do you want something to eat?" and then wait for me to repeat it so that he could answer in the affirmative, because he knew the script was supposed to go that way.

So when he recited his social story about going to the hospital, it was his way of telling me that he wanted that scene to occur. "It is like a shot," Paul pleaded with me again. "He is nice and calm and does not fuss!"

Translation: *I promise I will not fuss about the needle. Please let me go back to the hospital*.

"I know, sweetheart," I said, attempting to hide my tears from him. "I'm trying as hard as I can to get you there, I swear."

But Dr. Shikari was very skeptical to see us back in his office so soon. He gave a short peer into Paul's mouth and pronounced the tonsils to be "close enough" to normal.

"Will you please swab him?" I asked. "I'm a hundred percent certain he has strep again."

"I don't feel that's necessary. There's no fever. He seems fine to me."

I gestured helplessly at Paul, who was pacing and fidgeting around the room, frantically trying to open drawers and take apart medical models. "Do you remember what he was like the last time we were here? The post-op appointment?"

"Sure."

"That was him being fine. This is him not being fine."

"I don't see anything wrong with him that he couldn't stop on his own—with the right guidance," he sighed.

Oh, hell no. He did not just say that. But I am a coward, so the righteous fury stayed right inside me where it was, and the diplomat kept trying.

"Please, you don't understand. For two weeks I had my son back; for two weeks he was nothing like this. Then I lost him again. This is not bad behavior; this is a reaction to the throat pain coming back." I wasn't even going to try to explain PANDAS. If Dr. Shikari would only culture his throat!

He grunted. "Paul? Paul, come here."

Paul didn't exactly come, but he adjusted his orbit so that his pacing and hopping were nearer.

"Paul, how does your throat feel right now?"

"It's okay, honey," he whimpered.

He closed the folder with a satisfied smile. "Good."

"No!" I cried. "Listen, that's—do you know what echolalia is? When he says, 'It's okay,' that actually means it's not okay—"

Now I really did sound insane, and Dr. Shikari wasn't buying it in the least. And why should he? I was telling him up was down, and black was white.

"Paul, look at me," he interrupted me sternly. "I want you to stop this. I want you to behave for your mother. You can behave if you really want to. I know you can."

This was the closest I've ever come to punching another person. Somehow his horrific accusation was far worse now that he was daring to say it to Paul's face.

"All right, we're done," I said. "We're leaving."

"Today, Paul is going to go visit the hospital!" Paul said happily.

"No, honey, not today," I snapped. "Dr. Shikari says he won't help you."

It was not my best parenting moment, I know, but I honestly hoped Paul would have a meltdown in the middle of the office. I was so furious with this so-called medical professional, this complete jerkwad who thought my son could stop being so autistic "if he really wanted to," that I would have just stood there and smugly watched it happen. *Please, feel free to discipline him back out of it. Good luck with that. I'll be right over here.*

But Paul thought all was well and was too excited to listen. He skipped easily out to the car and helped me do his buckles.

"He walks right by Mommy in the hospital parking lot," he continued, oblivious as always to the fact that something was very wrong with Mommy right now. "First, we check in at the desk, and then Paul can play in the waiting room."

I sat in the driver's seat, listening to the rest of his social story and glaring at Dr. Shikari's ugly brown office building in mindless desperation. What now? I was so lost, I couldn't even start the engine. Going home seemed pointless. Worse than pointless; home was the polar opposite of where I wanted to be. Returning home was a defeat too painful to bear right now, so I just sat there, dead in the water.

I briefly allowed myself to indulge in the fantasy of driving up to the hospital entrance and flagging down some willing doctor. "Sure," she'd say, "I still have a few minutes left in my lunch break; just follow me back to the OR and we'll have those tonsils out in a jiffy." What I wouldn't give for life to be so easy. This stupid daydream was realistic on one account, though. We needed a new doctor, and I meant to get started on that process immediately.

I have never been good at reaching out for emotional support when I should, but sometimes I think I trick myself into getting it when the rabidly independent part of me would have refused to burden others with my troubles. I dialed my friend Tara on the rationale that one of her daughters had had a tonsillectomy a year or two ago, and maybe she could remember the name of their doctor. I could have texted or e-mailed the same question, or delayed the phone call by an hour or two without consequence, but somehow I ignored the fact that

I was already near tears and convinced myself that this was a logical, information-seeking phone call.

Within just a few sentences I was openly sobbing at her, something she had never witnessed before or since. I know I had every right to ask for support in that moment—my life was a nightmare, and this doctor had not only refused to help, he'd had the nerve to tell me I was a bad mother to boot—but I'd be lying if I didn't admit that some small part of me is still a little embarrassed about that call. Coming out of the blue like that, when she hadn't heard my voice in months, the whole thing must have been baffling to her.

But she did comfort me, for which I was grateful. She also explained that their own experience had been straightforward because her daughter had had three positive strep cultures within a six-month period. This was, she had been told, the gold standard for tonsillectomies, and their ENT had signed off on the surgery immediately after looking at the records from their pediatrician.

Three positive cultures in six months. That was all I needed. Forget trying to explain behaviors, forget debating with anyone exactly how large his tonsils were or were not on a given day. I needed to make a fresh start with a doctor who didn't already think I was insane and get three positive cultures from that one office. Then I could get his tonsils taken out by any ENT in the city, no questions asked.

Now, finally, I had the strength to start the car. Emotional support is great, but a plan of action is so much better.

Chapter 14

The Summer from Hell

JUST HOURS AFTER we stormed out of Dr. Shikari's office, we sat in the waiting room of my own general practitioner. I chose him primarily because he made same-day appointments, but also because he had never seen my son and didn't know he had autism.

What brings us in today? Well, the pediatrician was all booked up, you see, and Paul had been complaining about a very bad sore throat. *Never mind what language he'd been complaining in.*

Did he have a fever? No, because the Tylenol had brought it down, but he'd had one earlier. *You know, earlier in his lifetime. But it's not a valid question, since Paul never gets fevers.*

Was his appetite down? Yes, it was. *No, it wasn't. But again, not a valid question, since nothing in the world could diminish this child's appetite.*

I had crossed the line into outright lying, but frankly, it was necessary. All of these questions really only meant "Does he show other general signs of illness?" And the answer to that was a resounding yes, if you knew Paul well enough to know what to look for. I was done trying to explain our special circumstances. I would do whatever it took to get the labs done and let the positive throat cultures speak for themselves.

So my doctor swabbed his throat without a second thought, as any reasonable doctor would, assuming they hadn't already decided that my son was a destructive, attention-seeking delinquent.

Of course it came back positive for strep. One down, two to go.

At that moment I wanted nothing more in the world than to fax those results straight over to Dr. Shikari's office, just to prove to him that I was right. But that would only clue my doctor in to the fact that there was a bigger drama going on here, and the backstory could taint his opinion of us. Besides, even if Dr. Shikari had reconsidered the issue, I no longer wanted him to operate on Paul ever again. It's just not a good idea for the man wielding a scalpel over your child to hold a grudge against you. Of course he would never deliberately harm him, but I believe the subconscious always factors in. Would he be as patient or as thorough as he would be with an adorable child who reminded him of his own, no doubt perfect progeny? He would not, and it's silly to pretend the world works any other way. My only objective was to walk into a brand new ENT's office with three positive cultures on the books, so I had to keep my triumph to myself and march unrelentingly forward.

My doctor gave us a prescription for antibiotics, and I was sorely tempted to simply not give them to Paul so that we could come back in two weeks and be absolutely certain to get our second positive culture. I wasn't bothered by the medical ethics of such a stunt, but it was too cruel for me to pull off as a mother. My child was in very real pain, and I had something in my hands that would make it go away, at least for a little while. There was no way I could deny it to him, with everything he'd been through. I had to wait out the two weeks anyway, and I had complete confidence the problem would come back as soon as the pills were done, so I might as well give him some relief during that time.

This was a stupid, stupid decision. Since I had been forced to keep him ignorant about our history with strep, my doctor had given us a standard, first-line-of-treatment prescription, and it barely made a dent in Paul's symptoms. But when we came back to the office two weeks later, the culture was somehow negative. I had not counted on this.

"Is it possible that it's coming back," I asked carefully, trying to sound curious and not desperate, "and just not strong enough yet to trigger the five-minute test? He has definitely been complaining that his throat still hurts."

My doctor shrugged. "It's possible. Or it could be that his throat is sore from something like allergy drainage, for example."

He suggested several allergy treatments to try, which I dutifully pretended to be interested in, and he told us to come back if Paul's throat was still hurting after that. I agreed that we would, but I knew I was walking a thin line—the next time we came back, Paul *must* culture positive, or this doctor would be lost to me as well.

It was a gamble as to how long I could stand to wait, though, because things were getting rapidly worse at home. The meltdowns were longer and more violent every day. What's more, they served as a legitimate form of exercise for him, and it was during this time that Paul's fight-or-flight strength finally surpassed my own. Never mind that he was barely four and I had the biceps of a soldier; his frenzied brain was tapping into a primal stamina I could not compete with. The only way to prevent him from hurting both of us was to move him to the bed and lie half on top of him, pinning his hips with the weight of my leg and his chest with my top arm, the other arm cradled snugly under his neck to prevent him from smashing his head into me. Meanwhile, two-year-old Marie would just stand there and solemnly watch me pin her raging, screaming brother to the bed for at least half an hour at a time until he wore himself out again. Who knows what tortures she thought I was inflicting on him, but it could not have been good for her emotional development. Even now I worry that this time in our lives permanently affected her on some level.

It was at the point now that any door, anywhere, would cause a complete meltdown for Paul, and we literally couldn't leave the house. He wouldn't even try to run over and open them anymore—he knew he wasn't supposed to, and underneath it all he did still want to make the right choice even when he couldn't, so just seeing a door would trigger the internal struggle and send him into a rage. The only time my prison sentence was lifted was when I would go grocery shopping alone at night, after Andrew came home and the kids went to bed, which happened the other way around more often than not these days.

We were halfway through the summer now, and I had no idea what would happen if Paul were still like this when school started again. I desperately wanted to go back to my doctor and try another throat swab, but I was terrified that it would be too soon, and if it came up negative, we'd have to start all over.

Finally, I pulled the trigger, and thank sweet merciful Jesus, it came back positive. Two down. My doctor shrugged at this "unexpected" return of the infection, agreed that there must be some "small amount" of strep still remaining from the first round, and gave us the same entry-level antibiotic prescription as before.

This time I threw it in the trash. I understood now that to give it to him would be to prolong the suffering, not relieve it. Just two more weeks, and we'd be on our way.

But those two weeks were a living hell. Even without leaving the house anymore, Paul was up to five or six meltdowns each day. He was hoarse from the hours of routine screaming, and Marie was still passively watching every moment of it, which was even scarier. Andrew would come home from work just in time to kiss the kids goodnight, or not in time at all, and when he'd ask about my day, I was often unable to recall anything about the previous twelve hours. I couldn't tell him what day it was, or what I'd eaten for lunch, or even if I'd eaten at all. The horrible truth was that I was hard-pressed to even muster pity for Paul anymore. I knew intellectually that none of this was his fault, but daily emotional abuse will break anyone eventually. The rational side of me insisted that there was still a kind, desperate little boy trapped inside the monster, but both he and my rationality were being crushed to oblivion. If I had thought my life was a nightmare before, now it was so bad that I couldn't even be bothered to care what it was.

Studies have shown that mothers of special needs children have as much cortisol in their brains as active-duty military members, and that 80 percent of them suffer from significant symptoms of post-traumatic stress disorder. That summer there is no doubt I qualified.

The day he was supposed to have taken his last dose of antibiotics, I dragged Paul back to my doctor one last time. He was a mess, and so was I, and the nurse was shocked when I unapologetically hefted my screaming child up onto the exam table and wrestled his limbs underneath me in order to hold him still for a throat swab. She was hesitant to do anything to this thrashing creature before her, and from my vantage point right next to his head, I could see that the Q-tip barely brushed the roof of his mouth and definitely did not get all the way to the back of his throat. I suggested she try again, but she assured me she'd gotten it and fled the room.

The minutes ticked by. The doctor came in.

The test was negative.

I wanted to shriek as loudly as Paul was already doing.

He was very kind to me about it and said that we could certainly come back in another week if I was really sure the infection was still around. But he also tentatively asked if Paul had ever had any behavioral therapy, and I knew it was over. We'd lost his confidence. I might force one more swab out of him if I were very lucky, but after that this office would be dead to us.

We trudged home, as near to rock bottom as I've ever been. When the next tantrum came I didn't even get up to protect him. I just sat on the couch and stared, wondering if he was going to hit his head on the corner of something, examining how I would feel if that happened. To my relief, the answer was still yes, I would feel terrible. But that light was getting smaller, and I still couldn't force myself to go pick him up.

I glanced back at my laptop, having already forgotten what I'd been looking at just moments before. In my browser I had several windows open, apparently researching what it would take to travel to Mexico and have a doctor there take out his tonsils. American cash could be a powerful motivator, and less scrupulous didn't necessarily mean less talented.

Was that how bad off we were? I considered the question with clinical sincerity—not despairing that it might be so, just objectively curious about the level we'd sunk to. I made a detached assessment of this woman on the couch, unable to *be* her anymore, just estimating how much more she could take. Going to Mexico was a terrible idea, but sometimes terrible ideas are all you have left.

I put that thought on hold for further review and clicked over to my mail program instead, occasionally glancing at Paul from the corner of my eye. A few message board posts had come in while we'd been at the doctor's office, and I numbly skimmed through them.

Someone was asking about having a therapist shadow their child in the classroom. (Answer: It's at the principal's sole discretion, and most of them say no.)

Someone was thinking of moving to Austin and wanted to know what the "good" autism schools were. (Answer: None, really, but here are some worse ones to avoid.)

Same old, same old . . .

But here was something new. Someone was asking about a doctor to treat their child's allergies. And someone else had replied with the name of an ENT who was, by their account, the most wonderful doctor they'd ever seen. She had lots of experience with autistic children. She understood that they communicated differently and that pain could affect their behavior in ways it didn't affect neurotypical children. She had even been known to remove tonsils based on a whole picture of the medical history, not just strict numbers of strep cultures.

Her name was Dr. Melba Lewis. She had no website and no listing with our insurance company, and didn't even seem to be in the phone book, yet apparently she ran a thriving business based solely on referrals. I pulled my phone out of my pocket and called. If she turned us down for a tonsillectomy, at least we'd be no worse off than we already were.

Ten minutes into our first appointment Dr. Lewis asked me, "Have you ever heard of something called PANDAS?"

"Oh, my God, yes," I croaked, unable to hide my astonishment. "I know exactly what it is."

She had asked *me*. She was prepared to convince me it was a real disease. I was finally, finally in the right place. We talked a little bit more about Paul's medical history, and suddenly Dr. Lewis had a calendar out and was discussing hospital dates.

"How soon do we want to try to fit this in?" she asked.

I took a deep breath and blinked back a few tears. This was really happening!

"As soon as possible," I said. "Honestly, if you said you could do it tomorrow, we would be there."

She laughed. "Well, tomorrow is booked. Two weeks is about as fast as we can get you in."

"Two weeks would be fantastic. Two weeks is . . . just amazing. Thank you so much."

After we'd settled the details, she pulled out a swab kit, and my heart stopped for a moment, even though I already had our surgery paperwork in hand.

"I don't know if . . . " I began weakly. "I mean, he doesn't always culture positive, and . . . "

"Oh, we're taking his tonsils out either way," she assured me. "I just want to find out if I can give him some antibiotics before the surgery."

"You would do that?" I asked. "I mean, he's been on some pretty strong stuff; basic Zithromax doesn't cut it anymore."

"As long as this comes back positive, we can give him the good stuff." She smiled. "No reason for him to suffer while we're waiting."

The swab was indeed positive for strep, and she wrote the prescription. I could have kissed her.

As soon as I had Paul safely forced into his car seat (because of course the architect of this office complex had dared to include doors), I texted Andrew the good news. I also texted Tara to let her know that we had finally gotten a doctor on board with us, and hopefully give her the hint that I might not be quite so unstable from now on.

"Which ENT is he seeing?" she texted back.

"Melba Lewis," I wrote.

"How funny! That's who Michael saw when he had his tonsils out way back when."

Funny, indeed. This doctor who had treated her husband had been right there on our periphery all along. I swore to myself that I would never again see a doctor without asking for recommendations from everyone I'd ever known.

By the third day of the "good stuff," a high-dose antibiotic called Augmentin, Paul's tantrums were completely gone again. It was just in time, too, because on the fifth day of the Augmentin Paul began his second year of PPCD. Halfway through the second week of school we returned to Dell Children's Hospital, where we'd been just three months earlier, and Paul had his tonsils taken out.

This time I didn't hesitate in the recovery room. I climbed right up in the hospital bed and lay gently across him before he had a chance to wake up. Caressing his sleeping face, I whispered, "Hopefully, this is the last time I'll ever have to do this, kid."

When he awoke there was wailing and thrashing and disorientation just as before, but this time I got to just relax and count by ones, twos, fives, and tens in his ear to help calm him until he finally passed out again from exhaustion.

"You deserve a medal," said the wide-eyed recovery nurse.

I shrugged flatly and said this was kind of a normal occurrence for us. I think my cold delivery made her uncomfortable, and I wish I could have told her not to worry, I was doing fine—in fact, I was great! Today was the happiest I had been in a very long time, my dead eyes notwithstanding. But before I could figure out how to be convincingly cheerful, they moved us away to a private room to spend the night.

A short while later Paul woke up and vomited, and this seemed to clear the anesthesia out of his system just as with his previous surgery. He calmly settled in to watch some DVDs we'd brought, and genuine emotion started to seep back into the edges of my own anesthetized brain.

The results were better than we ever could have hoped for. Within a week he was back on solid foods (we were off the elemental formula by this time—more on that later), and Paul's mind was clearer than it had ever been. On his second day back at school Mrs. Allison sent home a note about how he was participating in class in ways he had never done before, even in the first week of school before the surgery, when we had already been happy with his performance on the Augmentin. That day she had actually overheard him having real back-and-forth conversations with several classmates.

"It's like something just clicked," she wrote. "He's doing all these great new things!"

We could see it, too. He was talking more and starting to ask us legitimate questions about things. During one of our first few walks out to the mailbox again, he bent down, looked through a hole in a neighbor's fence, and asked, "Whose back yard is that?"

This was how I became convinced in the end that Paul did have PANDAS, or a related syndrome. After the tonsillectomy he wasn't just a happier, pain-free version of himself. There was notable neurological improvement. At our first school conference a few weeks later, Mrs. Allison gave me the news that we had been daring to hope for: with the changes he'd shown postsurgery, Paul was now on track to be fully mainstreamed for kindergarten.

Chapter 15

Code of Silence

IT WAS DURING this time, the fall of 2010, that a stunning but largely ignored change in the medical understanding of autism occurred.

Thanks to an abundance of medical bills, we received an even greater abundance of correspondence from our insurance company. In an ideal world they would have been in parity, one insurance statement to match each office visit, but I'm pretty sure medical insurance companies are outlawed in ideal worlds. Instead Andrew and I played the "what's in the envelope" lottery at least two or three times a week, taking bets on whether any given piece of mail from the insurance company would contain good news or bad news.

Good news meant a basic statement informing us of a payment made to a doctor who accepted insurance. This was relatively rare because we didn't see many doctors like that anymore. As we had recently learned the hard way with Dr. Shikari, bedside manner is everything when it comes to special needs, and the local message boards were rife with recommendation requests for a cardiologist, or a dermatologist, or even a urologist Who Is Good With Autistic Kids. It wasn't enough to find doctors who were merely talented in their fields. We needed the most compassionate, patient, and skilled specialist in town to deal with the added layer of difficulty we brought everywhere we went.

Earning someone's WIGWAK seal of approval on the boards was a big deal, and sometimes these doctors found themselves inundated with autistic patients after word got out that they were the ones to go see. I can think of at least six families that I have sent to Dr. Lewis, for example, and I wasn't even the first autism mom to stumble upon how great she was. Such popularity comes at a premium, and any doctor who is that good is also likely to have a long list of customers. Accepting insurance is a luxury they don't have to offer, a headache they can afford not to deal with. By now I had gotten so used to filing our own claims for reimbursement that I did a literal double-take whenever someone charged us only a co-pay.

Better news was when the insurance envelope contained a reimbursement check for one of these many self-filed claims. If it were actually made out for the correct amount, we hit the jackpot.

Too often, however, it was bad news.

Of course stories about unfairly denied medical claims are so common as to be cliché. Sometimes it is mere apathy and ignorance on the part of the insurance company, but, as more than one journalist has exposed, sometimes it is an outright attempt to defraud patients and providers. Setting aside the question of motive, my experience is that their poor reputation is well deserved, and perhaps even too kind. I estimate that at least 40 percent of our self-filed claims suffered major processing errors, each of which took anywhere from two to nine months of additional paperwork to resolve. This rate held steady across several different insurance companies over the years, so it seems endemic to the industry.

To be fair, they are not the only ones gaming the system. Many medical offices do it, too. Hanlon's razor posits that we should "never attribute to malice that which is adequately explained by stupidity," but I've received far too many incorrect bills from doctors to believe that they are all accidental. I've received bills for the full amount, when in fact insurance has already paid and I owe nothing, on more occasions than I can count. I've had hospitals insist on payment up front, even when we've confirmed that our annual deductible has been met, and then conveniently forget their promise to send us a check for any overpayment they receive. I've received bills for dollar amounts that can't be arrived at by adding or subtracting any combination of the numbers on the itemized list.

I would like to believe that most medical billing staff are innumerate dullards because the alternative is even less polite. Sometimes, though, the fraud is undeniable. My old general practitioner—the one who gave us two positive strep cultures for Paul but couldn't produce a third—never bothered us with extra bills, but close attention to the statements from the insurance company revealed that he always filed every claim twice: once immediately after the appointment and once exactly three months later. About a third of the time the insurance company would not notice that a claim had already been filed and pay him again. When it did get noticed, it simply got marked as a duplicate and dismissed, since it is assumed that errors are unavoidable in such a complicated, bureaucratic system. I stopped seeing him when it became obvious to me that this was not a series of accidents but office policy.

Unlike medical offices, who always apologized and corrected their errors the first time they got called out, insurance companies usually took several attempts. There were layers of bureaucracy that had to be drilled through, starting with customer service representatives who were not empowered to fix problems, only to write them down and then "send it back for review." I have never figured out where this mythical back area was and was certainly never allowed to speak to anyone in it, but any paperwork sent there took a two- to three-week vacation before emerging. I would then receive another statement in the mail, which might or might not contain the corrections I had discussed with the lowly customer service representative. If we were really unlucky, there would be new errors added.

Fortunately, I learned some tricks along the way for speeding up the process. To begin with, I always kept copies of the forms I sent in, because on more than one occasion I experienced a conversation like this:

"Yes, ma'am, I see here your claim was denied because the location code was missing."

"No, it wasn't."

"I'm sorry?"

"I'm the one who filled out the form. I'm looking at it right now. There is clearly a 3 written in box 37."

"Uh, hold a moment while I check the scan. . . . Huh. Don't know how that happened. Okay, I've sent your claim back for review."

"Great," I would drawl in a calm, legalistic manner. I always imagined myself as Bill Lumbergh, the boss from *Office Space*. "And what was your name again?"

It always made them so uncomfortable to repeat their name, even though they'd already told it to me once at the beginning of the call. The implication of personal liability is powerful. Combine that with a request for the official reference number for our call, and my average resolution time dropped dramatically.

On this particular day in November we were not winners in the envelope lottery. The statement declared that my most recently submitted claim had been denied due to an incorrect diagnosis code. An unlikely scenario, since I had been using the same codes for over two years now, but at least they kept it interesting by screwing up something new on occasion. I no longer felt the urge to fume over incompetence versus fraud anymore; it was all just part of the process. I shrugged and added it to my to-do pile.

When I called the next morning to walk the customer service representative through the transcription error, however, I received a shock. For once it actually had been my mistake, though there was no way I could have known it. Paul's diagnosis code was no longer valid.

On October 1, 2010, the American Medical Association had issued the latest version of its diagnostic code manual, a thick tome that assigns a three- to five-digit code to every single malady known to man. Insurance claim forms have space for at least four codes at a time, since if you have a broken arm (diagnosis code section 813), it is likely that you also have a laceration on the elbow or forearm (section 881) and perhaps a post-traumatic wound infection (section 958). Codes are given additional specificity with decimal points. If your broken arm is a closed fracture of the shaft of the radius, it would be coded as 813.21, whereas an open fracture of the distal end of the ulna is 813.53.

The code that we had been using since it had been handed down by the neurologist was 299.0, defined simply as "autistic disorder." In its latest update, however, the AMA had seen fit to distinguish this into two new code categories: 299.00, autistic disorder current or active state; and 299.01, autistic disorder residual or inactive state.

This was a subtle but ground-shattering change. Imagine having "residual" or "inactive" Down syndrome. It's not possible. Down syndrome is something you either have or you don't. There is a range of symptom severity, just as in autism, but ultimately it is code 758.0, no additional modifiers needed.

Now, however, they were saying autism was different. It was no longer something you had or didn't have. It could also be something you *used to have*, or, more specifically, something that was kept in symptom-free remission by some unspecified combination of treatments, just as Dr. Jepson and many others had been saying for decades.

"Residual or inactive state" was a fundamental acknowledgment that kids were recovering. There had been only a few widely publicized cases, but of course there were thousands upon thousands of recovered children nationwide. I knew many of their parents on my message boards. They weren't getting broad attention from the media, but nonetheless, these children had made enough of an impact somewhere that the AMA had changed its tune.

Of course they didn't send out a big press release about it, nor did they make any kind of effort to educate ignorant doctors about the meaning of this change, and they certainly didn't bother telling the hundreds of thousands of parents who were still not seeking effective medical treatments for their children. No; the only people immediately aware of this change were the insurance companies, because of course they were going to want to know if they shouldn't have to pay for a procedure, if the patient's condition were residual.

As instructed, I altered our diagnosis code to 299.00, current or active state, and addressed the envelope to the claims corrections department.

I was glad the medical community was coming around, but at the same time it raised an interesting new quandary.

In the biomedical community we often referred to "true" recovery versus "maintained" recovery. A child in maintained recovery would be symptom-free and appear outwardly neurotypical, but only if he remained on his diet and perhaps some combination of medications or supplements. A bite of the wrong food or a skipped med, and symptoms would start coming back, revealing the hidden disease still lurking underneath.

Though I personally knew many kids in maintained recovery, I heard only occasional rumors of kids who had been fully cured, who had gone off their diets and never regressed. Often parents claimed they'd gotten there, but then a year or two later they'd show back up on the boards, admitting that the regressions were slow at first but did eventually become obvious, and that they were putting their kids back on treatment.

I still wasn't convinced that true recovery was possible, to be honest. Maintained recovery was a lofty enough goal for any of us, and I certainly would be satisfied with it if we ever got there. Getting Paul off meds would be nice, but I felt no desire to ever go back to eating a junky American diet again.

But the other common way to describe maintained recovery was that a child had "lost his diagnosis." Until now autism had always been a diagnosis based on symptoms alone. No outward symptoms meant no diagnosis, regardless of what the parents had to do to keep it that way. This new change in the codes meant that a diagnosis could now follow a child, even when there were no longer outward symptoms. A good thing or a bad thing?

On the one hand, the right doctors would need this information in order to understand that a recovered child did still have special medical requirements, even though he might not appear any different than other children. On the other hand, the wrong doctors—or schools, or someday even employers—could view the diagnosis as a black mark, despite the lack of any actual impairment, and use it to discriminate against him.

I wanted to reach the endgame, where the medical nature of the diagnosis was openly accepted in society and my son's future needs could be considered no more hampering than a diabetic's. I wanted autism to be just a thing he happened to have, effectively treated and not otherwise noticeable. But the path to that endgame was going to be rough, as social change always is, and the pioneers were going to suffer, as they always do. "He never really had autism" was in fact the nicest thing said right now to people who stood up and declared recovery was possible. Usually the dismissals and accusations were far nastier. Yet if no one stood up and took the abuse, if we all tried to erase history and just slip quietly into the normal world as soon as we were able, then we'd never reach that endgame.

It was a question of social obligation, ironically enough. If we ran from the diagnosis, we would be abandoning everyone we knew who was still struggling for acceptance. If we embraced it, we risked a permanent label that might not lose its stigma in Paul's lifetime. Did we owe it to others to be among those who stood up and forced the issue?

The urgency of this dilemma was being highlighted by very real milestones. On Halloween, just a few days before my revelation with the insurance representative, Paul finally figured out how to hold still and smile for a photo. He was dressed up as a slice of pizza, which was funny because he couldn't even eat one, but he had seen the costume at the store and requested it appropriately, so a slice of pizza he was. He not only stood patiently by the front door, delaying his trick-or-treating adventures for the sole purpose of photography, he even held for a moment afterwards until I checked the shot on the screen and confirmed that it was a good one.

He was almost four and a half years old and still in diapers, but in that moment he had made a prosocial choice. He had participated in something he didn't care about simply because someone else cared about it, and demonstrated yet another sliver of new understanding. The list of things he couldn't do had just gotten one shorter, even as our insurance company threatened to commit the original list to permanent memory. It was hard to decide how I felt about that.

Did I want the world to tell me my son had never had autism to begin with? Or did I want everyone to admit that he used to have it and open ourselves to the lowered expectations that might come along with that? Did I want credit for all that we had accomplished together, or did I want blessed anonymity?

Realistically, I had already made my decision. Paul's videos were on the Internet and had thousands of views already. I had even been contacted a few times by college students looking for permission to use them as part of a class project. I could delete the originals, but nothing can ever really be deleted from the Internet. Once it's out there, it's out there. His story was committed, whether I'd really thought about the implications of that or not.

And if we were out there, we might as well be *out there*. I did have a social obligation, I decided, as well as a genuine desire to help others struggling behind us. I had continued running my GFCF Lady website even when Paul's diet had become far more restricted, and over the years I had responded to hundreds of e-mails and even a few phone calls from people around the world, asking for help not just with diet but with supplements and other biomedical treatments as well.

I wanted to do more than just share our story and run a recipe website. I wanted to treat autistic children directly, with the medical therapies that I knew worked.

It was time to get a job at Thoughtful House.

A full medical school degree was not something I was prepared to pursue, but a nurse practitioner license was well within reach. The University of Texas offers an accelerated two-year licensing program for students who already have an undergraduate degree in something other than nursing, and I was missing only nine prerequisites. As a nurse practitioner, I would be able to write prescriptions and manage treatment of patients independently, with minimal oversight from a supervising doctor. One biomedical doctor could oversee the patient load of several nurse practitioners, and this was one way the small number of informed doctors nationwide were successfully shortening their wait lists.

I laid out a plan to take those nine missing prerequisites over the next two years, starting in the spring of 2011 and finishing in time to begin the real nurse practitioner program in the fall of 2013, when Marie would be entering kindergarten and I would have full days to myself again. One of my courses that first semester was nutrition, an easy A for me if there ever were one. My final paper in that class was titled "Gluten Intolerance: A Hidden Epidemic," and the list of foot-noted references was half as long as the paper itself.

Chapter 16

The Specific Carbohydrate Diet

As I MENTIONED, we had weaned Paul off the elemental formula a couple of months before strep had really taken over our lives. This had been a stressful decision, since he was doing so well on it, but we had known the liquid diet could never be a permanent solution. He had to go back to eating real food at some point.

First, we ran the full IgG and IgE allergy panels again, and the results were encouraging. He was down to just five severe foods, plus a handful of lesser ones. Here was proof that the formula had accomplished at least one thing we'd desired, allowing his immune system to settle down and "forget" most of the foods it had labeled as aggressors. Still, Kirsten warned us to go very slowly and carefully with the reintroduction of foods and to start with only well-cooked, pureed vegetables, as one would with an infant.

We tried giving him a spoonful of pureed butternut squash, but after three months of tasting only one thing, the onslaught of flavor made him retch and gag. We had to go even more slowly than single bites, apparently.

The "frog in a boiling pot" technique has something to offer us metaphorically, even if it is not literally true. Often a routine-driven or overly sensory child will accept a change after all, as long as it is introduced so painfully slowly that he doesn't notice the evolution going on right in front of him. The level of patience this requires can be enough to drive one mad, but I am nothing if not stubborn. I took one teaspoon of pureed butternut squash and mixed it into an entire twelve-ounce sippy cup of formula. In mathematical terms, his drink was only 1.4 percent butternut squash. He didn't notice, so we continued this ratio for the rest of his cups that day. The next day it became two teaspoons in each cup. And so on. After a week and a half I'd worked him up to three tablespoons of squash per drink, and the formula was starting to take on a subtle orange hue, which I caught Paul examining suspiciously. Spooked that I might be moving too fast, I started phasing in teaspoons of pureed cauliflower because it was white, and then pureed zucchini because green balances orange. At the same time I was decreasing the amount of formula each day to make room in the sippy cup for the other foods.

Next I tried adding chicken broth, with the idea of eventually turning it into a proper vegetable soup, but I could never get past more than a few milliliters without hitting a line of rejection. For some reason the flavor of chicken broth stood out more strongly than any other to him. The only way to get in any measurable amount of chicken broth was to mask the flavor with equal amounts of fruit juice, which kind of killed the whole "vegetable soup" theme, but whatever. It all got mixed together in his stomach anyway.

Eventually, he was down to just a few tablespoons of formula blended into this weird vegetable, chicken broth, and fruit juice "smoothie." The ingredients were not logical, or complementary, or easy to assemble. Not even the most brazen nouvelle cuisine chef would be inspired to create it. But that's how evolution works: each small change is a reaction to a specific pressure here or there, independent of what may have come before. Each mismatched body part of the platypus developed to fill a need, and it thrives in its ecological niche despite the fact that the beaver tail and duck bill never compared notes to discover how ridiculous the whole thing would look when it was finished. If we lived in a world where butternut squash were white instead of orange, Paul's pureed concoction would have veered along a totally different path of ingredients, yet in the end, they would likely have been just as weird. I was responding to nutritional and preferential needs as they arose, but the social acceptability of a recipe was not a pressure we were concerned with, so I ignored it.

If I had presented Paul with this final product in the beginning, he would have retched at the smell alone. But the transition happened so slowly over a period of months that he not only accepted it, he demanded it. "Mix juice," as he called it, was *the thing* he drank now, and I couldn't have given him plain fruit juice even if I'd wanted to.

Eventually, the last of the formula was out, and we were ready to attempt soft solids like very ripe banana. We had towels strategically in place the first few times, but everything stayed down. Not long after that he was able to eat a real meal on a plate for the first time in four and a half months. I even took a picture of the momentous occasion.

Later, after the tonsil ordeal was over and I had a chance to reassess where things stood with his diet, I noticed a problem.

Paul had gained several pounds while on the formula, catching up on a deficit that had started when he was about fifteen months old. As an infant he had always been above the 75th percentile for height and the 95th percentile for weight, but then his growth had slowed dramatically, around the same time that his digestive and behavioral problems began to really tank. This is a common trend in the growth charts of autistic children, potentially due to malabsorption of nutrients in a damaged gut.

Putting him on the easily absorbed formula had provided a secondary benefit of rapid growth, but we now realized that he'd lost all that weight again since stopping the formula and was back down to just the 13th percentile. It didn't yet qualify as a medical emergency, but given his previous growth curve, it was a dangerous red flag. Small kids are normal and healthy as long as they grow steadily from wherever they started out, but big kids are not supposed to unexpectedly turn into small kids.

Scanning backwards through our growing stacks of medical paperwork, I realized that if you ignored the brief spike and drop from the formula, Paul had not grown at all in over a year.

It occurred to me that perhaps we could continue to supplement with elemental formula, adding as many extra nutrients throughout the day as we could while still keeping him on a full diet of real food. Several friends on my biomedical message boards had used a brand of elemental formula called Splash for their children. It was generally agreed to have a worse flavor than Elecare, but the big benefit was that it came as a premixed liquid in brightly colored juice boxes instead of cans of powder. It needed no refrigeration and could be sipped at the school lunch table without stigma.

This time, however, we were stuck buying it ourselves out-of-pocket because our insurance company would cover elemental formula only as an exclusive diet. Our policy specifically ruled out nutritional supplementation, even with a medically demonstrated need to gain weight. During one of several phone calls about this, I also learned that when the company had approved the formula the first time, someone had been under the mistaken impression that Paul would be consuming it through a G-tube, or a semipermanent catheter that is installed in the abdomen when a child's physiological problems impede swallowing. Had they known he was drinking the Elecare orally, they likely wouldn't have covered it. I decided it was time to stop arguing before they revoked their earlier coverage and demanded their money back.

Direct from the manufacturer, Splash was $140 per case, but you could get it on eBay for around half that. If I were forced to speculate, I might guess that the individuals selling it on eBay were those fortunate enough to have a full-coverage prescription for their child, and by selling or even giving away their extra boxes each month, they were technically committing insurance fraud. But it was a moral gray area, since otherwise the extra formula would just be going in the trash. I never asked any questions.

We made enough room in the budget—that is, went further into debt—for Paul to have three cases per month, which worked out to about 30 percent extra daily nutrition on top of everything he was eating normally. He drank the formula willingly enough, but I wasn't completely pleased with the results. His behavior seemed to me to be

negatively affected, potentially because the Splash included some artificial sweeteners that the Elecare hadn't. (Yet somehow it tasted worse:
you'd think the R&D department could have spent some time on that
conundrum.) But it was only a little hyperactivity, nothing unbearable,
and we thought the trade-off might be worth it for some weight gain.

It didn't work. Sometimes he would go up a couple of pounds
but then drop them again a few days later. Meanwhile, his stools were
still on the mushy side most of the time—not the most horrible they'd
ever been but definitely not perfect. We limped along, unable to afford
more boxes but too afraid of weight loss to stop them entirely.

The good news was that his cognition was holding steady at a
mainstreamable level. He might be the weird kid with minimal social
skills, moderate echolalia, and no fine-motor strength whatsoever—
despite his advanced reading ability, he still required a whole page
to crudely form one letter of the alphabet—but he would be able to
function in a regular kindergarten classroom without major behavioral or academic problems. Part of me felt I should be satisfied that
we'd reached that goal and that it was nothing short of ungrateful to
demand more. But I wasn't going to give up on full recovery, and I
wasn't going to ignore even slight GI symptoms like poor growth and
semisolid stools.

Until his digestion is perfect, we're not done.

But what was left to do? There were only two big things we hadn't
tried yet, digestively. First, there was a diet, more advanced than just
GFCF, called the Specific Carbohydrate Diet. It had been designed
in the 1960s by a woman named Elaine Gottschall, with the help of
a rather progressive gastroenterologist named Dr. Sidney V. Haas, in
order to cure her daughter's ulcerative colitis. SCD had in fact been
mentioned in Dr. Jepson's book as the most successful diet for children
with autism, but at the time I hadn't been mentally or emotionally
ready for anything more difficult than eliminating gluten and dairy.
SCD called for the removal of not just gluten but all grains, including
corn, rice, and all of the common gluten-free alternatives like chickpea, sorghum, and amaranth flour. Baked goods were not impossible,
but they were limited to nut flours, such as coconut or almond. As a

reference to this, the biggest informational website about implementing SCD for autistic children was called Pecan Bread.

SCD also eliminated all starches, gums, and thickeners, as well as all sugars and sweeteners except honey and the fructose found naturally in fruits. Strictly speaking, the original diet allowed a few forms of dairy, but it was generally agreed that autistic children should do a dairy-free version.

The chemical basis for which foods were allowed had to do with whether they could be broken down by the body into monosaccharides or polysaccharides, and this mechanism was explained in great detail in Gottschall's book, *Breaking the Vicious Cycle*. Polysaccharides, it was said, were consumed by pathological intestinal bacteria, and by eliminating them from the diet, the intention was to literally starve out a presumed chronic imbalance in the gut flora, thus clearing the way for only the beneficial species to colonize. There were a few exceptions for foods with surprising chemical properties—for example, bananas actually contain a starch that converts to fructose as they ripen, so bananas were allowable only if they were extremely ripe and covered with brown spots—but the general idea was that on SCD, one should eat only meats, eggs, fruits, vegetables, nuts, and seeds. It was a very ancestral sort of diet, the kind of thing humans evolved to eat for tens of thousands of years before the relatively recent development of agriculture. Indeed, it had a lot in common with another popular regimen along that theme called the Paleo diet, though there were several notable differences between the two.

In some ways the Specific Carbohydrate Diet was actually easier than a typical gluten-free diet. There was no need for rare ingredients, or replacement pastas, or special bakeries. Every grocery store has a produce section and a meat counter, and that was all that was needed. Meals were broken down to such basics that cooking dinner became as simple as grilling a seasoned piece of meat, steaming some vegetables, and slicing up a little fruit for dessert. Nothing more complicated was necessary because nothing more complicated was allowed.

The trick, of course, was getting a kid to actually eat it. We'd already done the hard work of taking away everything in order to put him on the formula and now had discretion over which foods we chose to bring back. Paul was eating a good amount of vegetables in his smoothies and was always happy to eat any fruit we put in front of him. We still had not reintroduced grains of any kind, so they could just continue to stay out of the picture.

The difficulty, oddly enough, was meat. Even as a baby he'd had a major aversion to it, and the only kind of meat he was willing to eat was processed lunch meat. Under the rules of SCD, this was illegal, since it invariably included starches, sugars, and preservatives. I tried a dozen preparations of every fresh meat I could think of, including exotic things like buffalo, elk, lamb, and rabbit, but he refused all of them. I even purchased a full-sized deli meat slicer so I could try to make my own lunch-meat equivalent, but the slices just crumbled. Real meat doesn't hold together in a smooth, magical loaf without the help of fillers.

It's true that I could have brought out my behavioral therapist persona and spent dozens of hours methodically training him to eat meat because I said so, but having just escaped the Summer from Hell, I wasn't ready to jump back into battle mode yet. I already lived in a permanent state of exhaustion.

The elemental Splash boxes weren't SCD-legal, either, and the theory went that the artificial sugars in them were actually holding him back, maintaining the intestinal damage even as they were absorbed as well as anything could be in his current state. It would be a leap of faith to stop them in the hope that with the formula, the lunch meat, and a few other incidental sugars like salad dressing all removed, a large amount of healing could take place, and this would then improve his absorption ability so he could begin gaining weight on his own again. There were many such anecdotes on the SCD message board I sometimes perused, stories of stick-thin, malnourished children suddenly gaining five, ten, even fifteen pounds after just a couple of months on SCD. But they all stressed the importance of eating plenty of protein early on in the diet so that these children didn't go so far as to lose weight while their digestion dealt with the upheaval of a major microbial die-off.

Paul was still allergic to eggs and sensitive to most nuts, so without meat I didn't see how the diet would be possible for him. Others might be able to manage it, I told myself, but they didn't have to work with our unique situation and constraints. This thinking was foolishly parallel, of course, to that of the parents whom I regularly exhorted to be brave enough to try a GFCF diet. The tasks behind us seem so easy, while the ones in front loom impossibly high. I just kept staring SCD in the face, knowing we had to go there but terrified to step forward into another major dietary undertaking.

The second thing we hadn't tried yet wasn't a thing but rather a person. On just about every message board I frequented, Dr. Arthur Krigsman was regularly mentioned as the top gastrointestinal doctor in the country for autistic children. I already knew through others' experiences that taking an autistic child to a standard pediatric gastroenterologist was an exercise in futility. In their eyes, the slope between treating autistic GI disease and being accused of antivaccine sentiments was short and slippery, and just by sharing a medical specialty with Dr. Wakefield they were already one step too close for comfort.

One friend of mine had attempted to get help from a local doctor without mentioning autism at all, but she'd still been rebuffed. The appointment was going well, and the pediatric gastroenterologist was nodding and discussing various testing and scopes that could be done to investigate her son's obvious GI symptoms. Suddenly he stopped and stared at her son, who was flapping his hands over a puzzle in the corner of the room.

"Tell me," he asked, "has your child ever received a diagnosis of autism?"

"Well, yes," my friend admitted. "But—"

"I'm sorry," he interrupted, holding up one hand. "But that's just not a rabbit hole I can go down with you. If you're concerned about diarrhea, I recommend trying some Imodium." And he had abruptly ended the appointment.

Dr. Krigsman maintained offices in both New York City and Austin, flying back and forth between them every month so that he could help as many patients as possible. Everyone had extremely positive things to say about him, both personally and professionally, and it seemed like taking Paul to see him should be an obvious choice, especially since we were lucky enough to have him right in our hometown. The fact that most of Dr. Krigsman's patients voluntarily got on an airplane with an autistic child to go see him was a testament to just how talented he was.

However, one of the requirements of his practice was that every child must have a complete intestinal scope before he could begin treatment, and like all of our doctors, he didn't take insurance. He had a staff member who would call your insurance company on your behalf, help you file your own forms, and generally do everything in her power to get you the most coverage possible, but he couldn't take that reimbursement gamble himself.

The full scope procedure had three parts. The first two, a colonoscopy and upper endoscopy, were routine operations for any GI doctor and almost certain to be covered by insurance, albeit at out-of-network rates. These traditional manual scopes only travel a few feet into the body from either end, however, leaving over a dozen feet of intestines unexamined in between. Dr. Krigsman had found in his research that most of the damage in autistic children was typically in the small intestine, which was inaccessible by standard scopes. So he also used a special "pill cam" to cover the area in between.

This technological innovation was a tiny camera the size and shape of a pill, which would be swallowed by the patient and travel through the entire digestive tract, taking a flash photo every half-second. These images were transmitted wirelessly to a small receiver box worn on a belt and could later be downloaded and viewed in sequence. It was a diagnostic marvel, when you considered it: no anesthesia, no nurses, no hospitals were required. The cost of the pill cam was less than the sum of the other two scopes, plus it covered more ground. Yet because the technology was still relatively new, the pill cam was frequently labeled as experimental or unnecessary by insurance companies, and coverage was denied.

The funny thing was, they were kind of right. It was unnecessary, because in almost all of the children he examined Dr. Krigsman found exactly the same type of damage: small white lesions that were unique to autistic children and unlike any other known bowel disease such as Crohn's, celiac, or inflammatory bowel disease. Sometimes there was evidence of these other diseases in addition to the lesions, but the lesions were the hallmark characteristic of autistic enterocolitis. It would have been so much easier to treat his patients empirically; that is, to simply begin treatment without a scope and look for a positive response in symptoms as evidence that the disease was in fact there. This "try it, and see it if helps" method is used by doctors every day across all disciplines. Some fields, such as psychiatry, use nothing but empirical treatment because there is no biological way to prove the presence or absence of any of the diseases they specialize in.

Unfortunately, because of the political nature of associating gastrointestinal disease with autism, Dr. Krigsman was under much greater scrutiny than a normal doctor was. In a general sense he needed the pill-cam images in order to publish more research proving that the majority of autistic children do indeed have a real and unique bowel disease. But in the short term he also needed the images to prove that *his patients* undeniably had a physical GI disease that he was treating, and the fact that all of his patients also happened to be autistic could be left as an interesting side note if the state medical boards started getting nervous. The results of the procedure might be depressingly predictable to everyone involved, but if patients with a well-established and understood disease like Crohn's still had to undergo scopes and biopsies for confirmation, then certainly autistic patients must be expected to as well, both to protect Dr. Krigsman in the present and to pave an easier way for children in the future.

Aside from the cost of a hospital visit, I had been putting off going to see Dr. Krigsman for another reason. To a certain degree, it felt like giving up on true healing for Paul. We had seen such great things with dietary management, and I was afraid that if we added traditional GI medications into the mix, we would simply be hiding symptoms rather than eliminating their cause. I did not want antidiarrhea medicine to artificially clog things up; I wanted his body to stop reacting with diarrhea in the first place. But several other mothers convinced me that

Dr. Krigsman's approach was different and that his goal was indeed to force the disease into full remission rather than putting Band-Aids on it. He considered his prescription pad to be just one piece of the puzzle alongside dietary interventions, probiotics, and more.

"He actually had a plan to get my son off daily MiraLAX," one wrote to me, "and he did it. No other doctor ever even acted like that was a possibility."

It was a lot of money to spend with no guarantee of getting any back from the insurance company, but every improvement we gained now meant less therapy needed down the line. Pay for it now, or pay for it later.

And maybe if he works his magic, we won't have to commit to SCD, I was secretly thinking. Those who do not learn from history are condemned to repeat it, and I was not done learning yet.

Before we could see Dr. Krigsman in person, we had to complete an intake packet that included about thirty different blood, stool, and urine tests. These covered everything from bacterial infections to viral titers, Crohn's markers to celiac antibodies, liver enzymes to thyroid hormones, Vitamin D levels to white-blood-cell counts. The paperwork explained that although the list of labs was admittedly onerous, it would provide Dr. Krigsman with a comprehensive picture of the child's problems from the very first appointment, allowing treatment to begin immediately and minimizing his waiting lists. Strangely enough, since we were expected to gather all of this information before the first appointment, he couldn't be the one to order the labs because we were not officially his patients yet. We were instructed to take the order forms to any cooperative doctor with whom we had a relationship.

I decided to take our packet to our old pediatrician, the one I had told off in a four-page letter almost two years earlier. We had seen her twice since then, not out of medical need but because I was a self-righteous brat who intended to make good on my promise to convince her that recovery was possible. Under our insurance, annual well checks were free, so once a year I would show up in her office to flaunt our progress, at no cost to me and considerable awkwardness to her. Whether she ever started to believe me or not, she certainly didn't want to see me but was apparently too polite to tell me not to come back. It was my guess that she'd have her nurse sign anything I wanted if it meant she could avoid seeing me face-to-face in the exam room.

I was right. We were in and out in ten minutes flat.

Of course, as the ordering physician, a copy of all the lab results were going to be sent to her, as well as to Dr. Krigsman, and I was pleased to have another way to passive-aggressively shove Paul's abnormal physiological markers in her face. Eventually, my imperiousness would taper and I'd leave the poor woman alone, but at this point my soapbox was still firmly wedged beneath my feet. I was mad at doctors in general, and I took it out on her more than she deserved.

Chapter 17

Shalom, Y'all

LIKE THOUGHTFUL HOUSE, Dr. Krigsman's clinic was well tailored to his clientele's needs. His personal office opened directly into the waiting room, and he held appointments at his desk with the door open so that the children could continue to play in the never-ending buckets of toys while their parents sat comfortably on a couch going over symptoms and treatments. He was happy to move to a table out in the waiting room if greater supervision was necessary. Another area of the office suite, away from public view, had been remodeled into a small bedroom and bath, where he stayed overnight during his monthly Texas trips. A calming background track of bird noises played in the waiting room, and there was a large mural of a rain forest on one wall.

Beside his office door hung a small plaque reading, "Shalom, Y'all." His dry wit and New York accent somehow blended seamlessly with a distinct sense of Southern charm, and I got the impression that he could have worn cowboy boots along with his ever-present yarmulke and no one would think it out of place. He made it seem as if every one of his patients was his favorite, and it was probably true.

"Where's the notebook?" he asked me at our first appointment.

I didn't understand.

"The notebook," he persisted with a sly twinkle in his eye. "The one four inches thick, with every lab he's ever had in his life, and all the food diaries—the one all you autism moms have. You *do* have a notebook, don't you?"

I blushed. "I didn't know I could bring it without looking like a kook."

"Nah! You moms are just incredible. None of my colleagues have patients as good as mine. You all know what's what, and I love it. So! Let's talk about these labs."

The results weren't too bad, at least not for an autistic kid. No major infections like *Clostridium difficile* or *Helicobacter pylori*, and his white blood cells and liver enzymes were at low but sustainable levels. Lots of inflammation markers, but that was to be expected. This meant we could move forward without any more preliminary steps. Dr. Krigsman took great care to explain the purpose and mechanism of the proposed scope procedures, but I waved away his reassurances.

"We're definitely on board with it," I said. "That's what you do, and that's why we're here."

He chuckled again to himself about autism moms. Towards the end of the appointment, after he'd taken an extensive account of Paul's development, sensitivities, diet, supplements, and family history—over an hour in all—he suddenly stopped and gave me a serious look.

"So, tell me exactly, what is it you want me to do for Paul?"

My stomach turned. Was he telling me he couldn't help us after all? "Um . . . I want you to make him stop having diarrhea?"

"Okay, good!" he said, relaxing again. "We can do that. I have to ask, you know, because people come in here with different agendas. I don't cure autism. I won't prove for you that this thing or that thing caused his illness—some people come here, and what they really want is for me to go to court and testify. I don't do that. And I don't make any promises about the cognitive situation."

He held out his hands. "Do most of my patients show impressive cognitive gains along with the digestive treatment? Yes, absolutely!

But some don't, or maybe it's very minimal. What I treat is the GI disease. The rest, we just hope we get lucky."

"I understand," I said. "But I do know we're going to get lucky in his case."

He grinned. "And I know better than to argue with you."

Our hospital date was scheduled for mid-May, which would be Dr. Krigsman's next trip to Texas and Paul's last month of PPCD before heading to kindergarten in the fall. But a week later, he called me with bad news.

While giving our family history I had made a quick note about a condition called malignant hyperthermia. I didn't actually know what it was, to be honest. The story was that back in the 1960s Andrew's aunt had once taken a very long time to wake up after an operation. A few decades after that Andrew's mother had casually mentioned this tale about her sister during one of her own medical procedures, and the nurse at that time had declared that her sister probably suffered from "mild malignant hyperthermia." She instructed my mother-in-law to always tell doctors that there was potentially MH in the family whenever she, or any of her descendants, had to undergo anesthesia.

My mother-in-law had shared all of this with us when I had begun my crusade to get Paul's tonsils and adenoids out, so I had been sure to mention it at both of those procedures. Each time the anesthesiologist on duty had just made a note of it and moved on, so we had always been under the impression that it was not a big deal, whatever it was.

Not so, said Dr. Krigsman. Or at least that was what his anesthesiologist was saying to him. Malignant hyperthermia is a severe muscular reaction to a certain class of anesthetics and can cause the heart and lungs to seize up suddenly while the patient is unconscious. It is frequently fatal, and there's no telling when the reaction may or may not happen, so the fact that Paul had already gone under anesthesia twice without incident was no guarantee that it wouldn't happen in the future. In short, Dr. Krigsman's anesthesiologist was uable to do the procedure until we could confirm that Paul did not, in fact, have malignant hyperthermia.

I told him I would research it and get back to him. Who cared if Paul had to have one more blood test? I could get that done within the hour, if I had to.

Unfortunately, it wasn't that easy. There is no simple blood test for MH, or even a genetic screening. The only way to rule it out, I learned, was a muscle biopsy. They would have to remove a piece of muscle tissue, subject it to an extremely high dose of anesthetic, and see if it seized. If it didn't, Paul was in the clear.

The more I researched it, the more ridiculous it got. For one thing, a patient had to go under anesthesia for this biopsy procedure to find out if it was safe to go under anesthesia. For another, it was only a specific, well-defined group of anesthetics that could trigger the reaction, and the general recommendation for people who did have the condition was simply to use one of the dozens of other anesthetics available. Furthermore, taking a long time to wake up from anesthesia was not, in fact, a symptom of malignant hyperthermia at all, as that random nurse had told my mother-in-law so long ago.

I spoke with Dr. Krigsman's anesthesiologist on the phone, but she was adamant. MH was an official part of our paperwork now, and she was unwilling to accept my assurance that we were pretty sure my husband's aunt had not had this condition after all. Nor was she swayed when I suggested she just use a nonreactive anesthetic. The primary risk, it seemed, lay in the fact that most endoscopies were done in small surgery centers, rather than the large hospital environment where Paul had had his previous procedures. With a reaction of this kind, an outpatient center's preparedness was roughly equivalent to attempting the procedure on our own at home.

"So you're telling me we have to get a muscle biopsy; that's the only way?"

"Well, I suppose actually your husband should be the one to get it done. The inheritance is autosomal-dominant, meaning if he doesn't have it, none of his kids could have it, either. And the test isn't very reliable on children anyway, so it's best if he's the one to get tested."

That was something, at least. I talked to Dr. Krigsman about what else could be done, but he didn't have privileges at any of the large hospitals in Austin. He did think his regular hospital in New York was equipped to handle it, so potentially we could fly there to have the scope done, but in that case we'd have to give up our procedure date and reschedule for another month or two down the line.

Meanwhile, Andrew had gone into overdrive after hearing the news that he could be the one to have the MH test. Here, finally, was something he could do. He had always felt guilty that the majority of Paul's care fell on my shoulders, and he attacked this task with all the undirected ferocity he had been saving up for years. They were not going to block us based on his genes; no way.

Yet the situation was even worse than we knew. First, Andrew found out there were only five labs in all of North America that could do an MH test at all. None of them were the kind of clinic you could just walk into; these were all large-scale hospital environments requiring appointments weeks in advance. And none of them were in Texas.

Andrew spent two days straight making phone calls, leaving messages, and sending e-mails until he had managed to contact the right person at each of the five hospitals.

The first was a veterans' hospital in Maryland, which wouldn't do anything for us because Andrew wasn't a service member.

The second had a policy that they would perform only one MH test a month, and their schedule was booked for over a year. When Andrew tried to get someone to explain the reasoning behind this policy, he was reminded that the hospital was in Canada, and things were just done differently there.

The third location was in California, and they said they could fit us in no sooner than late July, over two months away. It remained to be seen whether this would be on a faster timetable than taking Paul to New York, should it come to that.

The fourth possibility was at Wake Forest University in North Carolina, and it had potential, since Dr. Krigsman had colleagues there who were also working on the GI disease of autistic children. He thought perhaps he could pull some strings between departments, but the staff at Wake Forest were extremely reluctant in all of their communications with us, so if it were going to happen, Dr. Krigsman would have to coordinate it for us himself.

Finally, there was the hospital at the University of Minnesota. Unlike the others, who seemed to be coming up with excuses to turn us down as soon as they'd picked up the phone, the staff at UM were cheerfully ignorant about who would make the decision at all. Person A said they couldn't see why not, but best to talk to Person B. Person B said oh, yes, we could easily do that; just call Person C to get approval. Person C was happy to approve the procedure, but really we needed Person D on board. And so on, and so on. Eventually, Andrew was given the direct office number of a low-level lab technician, who was bewildered to learn that the decision apparently rested on her shoulders.

But if everyone else had already said it was okay . . . "Uh, then sure, I guess," she said. "Do you want to come in next week?"

Victory!

Dr. Krigsman was doubtful. "We're getting pretty close to the deadline," he said, referring to our hospital date for the scopes. "We're going to figure out a way to get this taken care of, I promise, but it may be time to make the call that we're going to delay until a later month. You know, maybe give that slot to another mom like yourself, who would be pretty grateful to get to move up a month."

"No, no, we're going to get it done in time," I insisted. "We already got Andrew on the schedule with the University of Minnesota for next Monday."

"Wonderful," he said, surprised. "When will they have the results?"

"They said it will be immediately. They'll fax them to the anesthesiologist before he leaves."

"Hey, with a whole week to spare," he joked. "So you're not shipping the sample, then; this whole thing is actually happening in Minnesota?"

"Yep, we already got him a plane ticket. It can't be shipped because the muscle tissue has to still be alive when they do the test. They won't actually sew up his leg and take him out of the operating room until they know they got a good sample."

"Interesting. I didn't realize the sample had to be so large."

Large, indeed. This wasn't going to be a little eraser-sized bite of flesh, like most biopsies. The MH test required a strip at least eight centimeters long, and it had to come from large, continuous deep-muscle tissue, preferably the upper thigh. That was why the anesthesiologist had said the test was no good on young children: their leg muscles often weren't even long enough to get a good sample. We had watched a video of the surgery on the Malignant Hyperthermia Association's national website, and it was gruesome to see how much they'd be removing.

"It's like leg fajitas," Andrew noted with grim amusement. The thought of backing out never crossed his mind, though. Friends and coworkers marveled at his dedication, but to us it was an obvious choice. What father wouldn't undergo surgery to save his kid? Others may have viewed this whole thing as elective, but we knew otherwise. And even if we were wrong, even if all we did was save Paul's gut and not his brain, it would still result in less pain for him throughout the course of his entire life. The idea that Andrew would refuse to take a little bit of pain on Paul's behalf was beyond absurd.

"But what if it turns out he's positive for the MH?" Dr. Krigsman asked.

I rolled my eyes. "He's not. Now that we've actually researched it and gone back and talked to his aunt again, there's no way. I'm a hundred percent sure. We think what she has is something called pseudocholinesterase deficiency, which is completely different from malignant hyperthermia. We're just doing the test because it's the only way to get the scope."

"I'm impressed," he said.

"Well, we haven't taken care of everything yet," I admitted. "We're still working on getting insurance to pay for it."

That was a bit of a problem, actually. We had put off thinking about it while we were frantically trying to schedule the procedure at all, but this test was a real operation, at least as expensive as the one it was a prerequisite for. Including those two little words in our family history had been a several-thousand-dollar mistake on my part.

So now Andrew spent another few days on the phone, moving up the chain of insurance supervisors. The hospital in Minnesota was out of network, but we could apply for an exception if we could prove that none of the labs that were in network could provide these same services. Of course we already knew how short the list of possible labs was, but, unsurprisingly, they wouldn't take our word for it. So Andrew dutifully called all of the local places on the insurance company's list, which were mostly just walk-in clinics with a few chairs for blood draws, and got the name of a contact person at each one who would officially agree that they could not perform an MH muscle-biopsy test—after he explained to them what that even was.

Then back to the insurance company, which approved the exception and agreed to pay for it at in-network rates. Then that paperwork was sent over to the Minnesota hospital, which wanted an assurance that it would get paid before anyone did anything. Finally, Andrew had to schedule a last-minute appointment with his regular doctor so that she could sign a prescription order for the MH lab work to be done. Again, he had to explain to her what the test was in the first place and tell her exactly what she needed to write on the prescription pad.

All of this was orchestrated from the small office area that he shared with four other people, so his coworkers were intimately aware of the situation. "Never seen anyone fight so hard to have his leg cut open," one chuckled.

Towards the end of the week, Andrew talked to his mom on the phone. He gave her the latest updates and let her know that she could quit trying to get a copy of her sister's hospital records from forty years ago, since it was all a moot point now.

"But what will Jennifer do with the children while you're in the hospital?" she asked.

"Same thing she usually does." He shrugged. "She'll just be at home with them like normal. She'll give me a ride to the airport Sunday afternoon, and then she'll pick me up Monday night when I get back."

"Oh, Andrew! No. I don't like that."

"What? I mean, sure, if the flight gets in late, I can take a cab home or whatever. But it's not a huge deal for her to put the kids in the car and drive to the airport."

He looked at me for confirmation, and I nodded. There was a passenger-pickup loop at the Austin airport, where you could just keep driving in circles until your traveler showed up on the sidewalk. The kids wouldn't even have to get out of their car seats. No big deal.

"No, I mean you can't fly there by yourself!" she cried. "You'll be in a hospital in another state. What if something goes wrong? How are you possibly going to drive yourself back to the airport when you've just woken up from anesthesia?"

"There's actually a train that goes straight from the airport to the university and back. I've talked to the lab tech at the hospital. She said it's a really simple procedure; I may be limping, but I'll be able to walk out of there."

"I don't think—"

"And I'll be able to sit down on the train," he added. "It'll be fine."

"I think I need to go there with you."

"Mom, really, that's totally unnecessary! It'll be a big waste of money, just so you can spend all day sitting in a hospital and then turn right back around."

"No. When one of my children needs me, I will be there. When Christine had her surgery, I was at the hospital with her, and when Joseph had his—"

"But they were in the same city, Mom! You didn't have to fly to Minnesota to be with them."

Beside him, I was nodding in agreement. She was making a big deal out of nothing.

"Look," he warned playfully, "I'm going to play my Nintendo DS on the flight and not talk to you at all. You will be so bored."

Nonetheless, she insisted on learning his flight details and a short while later called us back to let us know that she had booked matching tickets. "If you're not going to be with your wife on Mother's Day," she said firmly, "then you're going to be with your mother."

Andrew and I looked at each other in surprise. Oh, yeah. Sunday was Mother's Day, wasn't it? We'd both forgotten. Every day was Kids' Day; that was pretty much how it worked in our house.

Well, it was her money. If she felt she had to travel with her thirty-four-year-old son and hold his hand, we would just have to indulge her.

We were so lucky that she did. I don't know what we were thinking. He was going under full anesthesia, and if YouTube has taught us anything, it's that people are hysterically impaired when they wake up from a medical procedure. Whoever it was at the hospital who had told him he would "walk out of there" had lied to an extreme degree. Instead Andrew had to be rolled down to the train station in a wheelchair and lifted into a seat, giggling and speaking nonsense most of the way. My amused mother-in-law called me once he had been successfully transferred again into an airport wheelchair, and I got to talk to him briefly. I don't remember exactly what he said, but I know I was sorely disappointed that neither of them had a video camera.

Later he told me that the doctor had been shocked to learn that Andrew had originally planned to travel home alone. "We wouldn't have allowed it," he scoffed. "Legally, we can't let you leave without someone to escort you home after anesthesia. You would have had to stay here overnight." Why no one at the hospital had thought to mention this during one of his fifteen separate phone calls to their facility was a mystery. Thank goodness for my mother-in-law's overconcern.

Even after she got him safely home, recovery was worse than we had expected. The pain meds prevented his leg from hurting too much for the first few days, but it was also unusable. The upper leg muscle would not respond at all. He couldn't use crutches because he couldn't bend his bad leg enough to keep it off the ground. Instead he used a large wooden curtain rod to push himself around the house in his office chair, like a gondolier in Venice.

As mobility came back the pain got worse, but as soon as he could manage crutches Andrew went back to work. His boss would have let him continue to work from home as long as he needed, but Paul was making that impossible. Dr. Krigsman had instructed us to take him off all digestive supplements and medications for two weeks prior to the scope, and we were all feeling the effects.

"We need to see how bad his disease really is," Dr. Krigsman had said, "and we don't want anything masked by things he's already taking."

That meant no digestive enzymes, no anti-inflammatories, and no antimicrobials. We knew from experience that removing any one of these would cause an uptick in behaviors, and suddenly going cold turkey from all of them was serving as a very strong reminder of why we were doing all this in the first place. On Paul's second day off his supplements, Mrs. Allison e-mailed to let me know that something was very wrong. He was tantrumming, stimming, unfocused—a completely different kid.

I explained the situation to her and apologized. "Let me know if he gets too difficult," I said, "and I'll just keep him home from school until the scope is done."

She assured me she could handle it; she was just glad to know there was a reason for the sudden change.

By the time Andrew got back home from his surgery, Paul was already a week into his downward spiral, and I didn't blame him for wanting to run away to his office in spite of the leg pain. I had been wanting to run away myself for years.

He had just managed to switch to a cane by the time Scope Day arrived. I wanted him to bring the crutches to the endoscopy clinic instead, so the anesthesiologist might feel a little guilty about what we'd been through, but Andrew refused to "pose as a cripple." He did agree to wear shorts, however, so that his long line of stitches would be grotesquely visible.

It was effective. As we went through the preprocedure paperwork, the anesthesiologist tried not to stare. "Well, you must be relieved to know," she finally said, nodding at his leg. The MH test had come back negative, of course. "Now you never have to worry about it again."

"Yeah, we weren't really that worried," replied Andrew with a dry smirk. His tone wasn't resentful, though. Our attitude was one of triumph. The universe had tried to throw a roadblock in our way, and we had dodged it so thoroughly and efficiently, no one could believe it. We were beyond proud; we were downright smug.

"You're kind of a hero around the office," Dr. Krigsman said to me later. "We all thought there was no way you were going to pull it off in time."

I grinned. "Did I tell you, we got it covered in network, too?"

"In a week," he said, shaking his head. "Don't mess with you, right? Don't mess with you."

More like don't mess with Andrew, I thought. This victory was all his.

Chapter 18

Kindergarten

IT TOOK A while for Paul to get back to baseline behavior after the scope, and during this time we passed his fifth birthday and entered the summer before kindergarten. At his transition ARD at the end of the school year, the one major remaining concern was his fine-motor skills. If given a boxed outline, he could form shaky letters at a reasonable size, and if you strung together a series of boxes, he could write clear words as if he were filling out a crossword puzzle. But without the visual constraint of a box for every letter, he couldn't create even a rough mental boundary of where to start and stop, and his pencil wandered dramatically all over the page. Each letter would be eight inches tall and stacked on top of the others in a giant jumble. Other representational imagery—therapist lingo for "drawing pictures"— was still completely beyond him. Letters were the only thing he could or would reproduce, while his peers were busy drawing clear pictures of cats and spaceships and members of their families.

Otherwise, however, everyone agreed that Paul could be successfully mainstreamed. He would be given preferential seating near the front for greater supervision and be allowed to use a visual schedule if necessary, but his future teacher already used a written daily schedule on the board for all students, and since he could read we agreed this would probably be sufficient. He would continue to receive an hour a week of speech therapy to help him expand his sentence usage, but in general he was capable of making his needs understood. Over the winter he had finally, finally become potty-trained, and if he had to leave the classroom to go to the bathroom, his teacher promised she would always send him with a buddy to make sure he made it back.

As we had hoped, he might be the weird kid in the class, but he was going to be a real kindergartener, with no personal aide necessary. We had come so far already, and I knew Dr. Krigsman was going to take us even further.

A couple of weeks after school let out he called me to go over the results of the pill cam. I was in the middle of anatomy class at the time, and my guilt over slipping out the door with my vibrating phone was somewhat assuaged by the notion that I would at least still be discussing anatomy for the next half-hour.

We had already seen the photos of Paul's large intestine from the manual scopes, since those had been printed out on the spot in the hospital. There had been some areas where everything looked normal, but other areas were covered with swollen yellow lumps. These were labeled *lymphoid hyperplasia* on the scope printout. It had been pretty horrific to my eyes, but "not the worst I've ever seen," according to Dr. Krigsman.

The pill cam found similar results in the small intestine. The characteristic white lesions were there, as well as more patches of swelling and inflammation, but there were no surprises. The signs of the disease were as expected, he said, and very treatable.

We were to begin with a course of prednisone, tapering down over a period of six weeks, as well as an ongoing corticosteroid called Entocort and an anti-inflammatory called Sulfasalazine. In three months we would follow up on Paul's progress and adjust medications as necessary. Dr. Krigsman warned us that some kids became hyper, irrational, or aggressive on the prednisone, but we should do our best to be patient and fight through it because it would provide a tremendous amount of healing that would hopefully kick-start the long process towards remission.

Luckily, we saw almost no moodiness. In fact, Paul was noticeably better focused, better behaved, better speaking, better *everything* on the steroids. He had better stools, of course, too. It was like magic, and the gains just kept coming as the summer went on. He started coming up with startling new things to talk about almost every day.

Even so, we didn't realize quite how much he'd gained until the first week of kindergarten, when he brought home a picture he'd supposedly drawn in class. There was a figure with a tall rectangle body, including not just limbs but also hands and feet and an array of hair around a smiling face. What's more, there was a sun, grass, and a background object that was obviously a playground slide. Beneath the parallel S-shapes with the evenly drawn ladder leading to the top, his teacher had written the apparent inspiration for this picture: "I like recess." Paul's name was written along the top of the page in a ragged but completely age-appropriate handwriting. The tallest height of any letter was no more than an inch, and there were no guide boxes around any part of it.

"He didn't draw that," Andrew said as soon as I'd shown him. Then he frowned. "Did he?"

"I don't know," I said. "I can't imagine that he did. But I'm pretty sure kindergarten teachers don't sit there and draw things for their students, do they?"

I had the chance to ask Mrs. Miller a few days later, and she confirmed that Paul had indeed drawn the entire thing by himself. She gushed about how cute the picture was, but she wasn't operating from the same frame of reference we were. To her, it was just a normal kindergarten drawing. To us, it was . . . *a normal kindergarten drawing!*

Like many sentimental moms, I keep samples of my kids' artwork in binders. I dug through Paul's now, looking for some recent comparison to make sure I wasn't crazy. He had always hated coloring, so I had to go back a couple of months before I found something that involved an actual writing utensil instead of gluing.

It was a Father's Day card from June, just one week after he'd begun the steroids. There was some haphazard scribbling on the front and a rat's nest of marks on the inside, which, if you looked carefully enough, could be broken down into the constituent letters

H-A-P-P-Y-F-A-T-H-E-R-S-D-A-Y, all half a page tall and stacked on top of each other at random locations.

I photocopied the two works of art and brought them to Dr. Krigsman at our next appointment.

"I know you give a lot of presentations and publish papers and whatnot," I told him. "So, this is evidence. The first picture is his fine motor just as he was starting the steroids, and the second one is three months later. There was no therapy or writing practice of any kind over the summer, just the medicines. You have my permission to use it however you want."

"Amazing, isn't it?" He beamed at the papers I'd handed him. "I used to start with just the corticosteroids, but over the years I've found that prednisone is truly the most effective way to treat this disease."

He tucked the pages carefully away in a folder. "You look good!" he said to me. "Better. You've gained what, five, ten pounds?"

I laughed awkwardly. "Uh, I guess so. I don't know."

"I know, you're not supposed to say that to women. But for you, you needed it. Yeah, I think ten pounds. You look like you're doing better."

"When he's better, I'm better," I agreed. "I get to spend more time on things like eating and sleeping. But . . ."

"But what?"

"Well, we finished the prednisone a couple weeks ago, and he started regressing within just a few days. I mean not completely, still leagues better than he was before we started it, but the hyperactivity is coming back, the lack of focus. I don't know if we're allowed to do more, but he definitely still needs them."

Dr. Krigsman took some more details, checked Paul's latest lab results to make sure white blood cells and liver function were still holding steady, and agreed to do one more round of prednisone, but shorter this time.

"What if? . . ." I said, too afraid to finish.

"Don't worry," he said. "Some kids do seem to just keep needing more help. It's true you can't stay on steroids forever, but there are other options, other medicines that he can be on long-term, if it comes to that. Anything that modulates immune activity in the gut has the potential to help. We'll just see how he does. It may take a few years to really get everything into remission, to find the right balance that works for him. But you're on your way," he said with a grin.

In October of that year, I had a true awakening to how different Paul was now, as powerful as the moment when I first believed he really had autism. We had been invited to a birthday party for a boy named Jack, whom Paul could legitimately call his friend. They played Legos together every day during free centers, and Paul reported that at recess he and Jack played games like "outer-space cops" or "ninja fighters." These were no doubt invented and led by Jack or other boys, but it was still a miracle that Paul had managed to understand and participate in a pretend role-playing game and that the other boys seemed to want him around.

The celebration was being held at a popular bouncy-castle warehouse, where groups would progress through a series of smaller arenas in stages, thus giving the impression of having the entire facility reserved for your child when in fact there were up to four parties going on at once. As the first big event of the year, there hadn't been time yet for kids to start deciding which classmates they didn't like, or for parents to get burned out on buying presents, so the classwide invitation received nearly classwide attendance. Crammed into just a few inflatables at a time and hyped on the promise of cake, this fire hazard of children swarmed and ricocheted off vinyl and body parts in equal measure. The constant drone of air pumps played bass beneath the harsh treble of squealing youth, turning an already overwhelming experience into the worst dance club ever. It was more than enough to put a sensory kid over the edge.

Yet Paul was fine. He was chasing, and being chased, and laughing—not that tight, forced sound that actually was about to become a scream but a happy, casual laugh. His friends called out to him, and they pointed finger-guns at each other and shouted with glee as one side or another faked an explosion after a deftly aimed *pew-pew-pew.*

And me, I sat on a bench by the wall, chatting with the other moms.

I actually sat. Out of direct view. And we made small talk about normal, stupid Mom Stuff. Things like after-school programs, and the latest Pixar movie, and whether our husbands could be coerced into helping with chores.

Internally, I was dumbfounded, even as I performed outward pleasantries I had forgotten I knew how to do. I should have been slowly prowling the arena, keeping Paul in my sights at all times, ready to distract him the moment he started inappropriately grabbing at another child or speaking gibberish, making sure the total stress didn't accumulate into a meltdown . . . but for the first time in his entire life, I didn't have to. He was playing with friends, and they were playing with him. Fifteen, twenty minutes would go by during which I had no idea where he was, and it was okay because I actually knew and believed that he would come find me if there was a problem. He would not have done that even at the beginning of the summer, but he would now.

This was new territory for me. I hadn't gotten to be a normal mom since Paul had started walking at ten months and I'd had to start chasing. The conversation turned to how hard it was to keep kitchens clean, and it was downright inane. I reveled in it! No one was lamenting about cleaning poop smears off the walls every day, only about how tough it was to keep those darn fingerprints off stainless steel. Mothers fretted over how they were going to manage the vacation to Disney this year, what with the big beach trip, too, as if they'd never even heard the words "crushing medical debt."

It was so dumb, yet so wonderful.

The topic shifted to getting kids to eat healthy foods, and I felt a momentary twinge of outsiderness, a reminder that I still lived in a completely different universe than they did, with our vegetable smoothies and dozens of pills. But these mothers didn't know that. We were incognito, and nothing about Paul inherently revealed us as different anymore.

For the first time I was not the mom that everyone stared at and silently judged as a poor disciplinarian. I was not the one they wished would just go home, the one who should have had the good grace not to bother the general public with her loud, physical, irrational child in the first place. I was not one of these carefree moms surrounding me, either, and probably never would be. But here I was, passing for a native. They didn't know what we had been through, or what we continued to go through, and for once it was my choice whether to tell them.

This casual little birthday party with its meaningless conversations made my heart ache with joy. Three years ago I had been transported to a foreign, brutal place, with little hope of ever getting home. They had tried to convince me it was Holland, but most of the time it was Beirut. Can't fool me; Holland doesn't leave those kinds of scars. Like a soldier carrying a worn photograph of his family, I had been fighting relentlessly for an abstract child who I knew was out there somewhere but hadn't seen in years. Now, suddenly, I had been shipped home, the armistice signed and the crusade apparently over without warning.

I found with surprise that civilian life suited me fine. These scars could be carefully hidden *just so* under casual clothes, as long as I didn't accidentally stretch my arm out too far. I could pass in polite society as someone who had never known the horrors of combat.

Welcome to Italy.

Chapter 19

In Pursuit of Italy

MOST OF PAUL'S kindergarten year passed by in a blur. Life was no longer a steady drumbeat of horrific experiences by which to measure the days and months; it was just uneventful and mostly forgettable. This must be what normal parents felt, I realized, when they said it seems like they grow up so fast. Until now it had felt like Paul was growing up so, so slowly.

There were still some quirks to his personality, of course. It was never our goal to change who he was, only to remove the barriers and set that inner person free. For Christmas that year he begged for detailed medical anatomy posters, like the ones he saw in the school nurse's office each day when he took his lunchtime meds. We got him three—skeletal system, muscular system, and brain structures—and they hang in his room to this day. When he told his friends after the holiday break that he'd gotten something even better than their Transformers, he meant it.

There were some especially touching moments that I do remember, small paybacks on the emotional debt we'd accrued over the last three years. At more than one birthday party his friends pulled me aside and made sure I'd brought a cupcake he could eat because they didn't want him to feel left out. One of them even asked me gravely, "Do you know that Paul has to be on a special diet?"

Then there was the day that he graduated to the big kids' group in Sunday school, which meant he spent the first part of the service in the sanctuary with us. As he stood on the pews so he could read the hymn lyrics on the projector screen, Andrew and I both found ourselves getting choked up. The last time Paul had set foot in that sanctuary, he'd been kicking and screaming, "Guitars! Guitars!" Now he was singing.

He even started taking tae kwon do classes, and I finally got that gold-belt photo I had been so jealous of. No one at the tae kwon do facility knew he'd ever had a diagnosis.

Ironically, Paul's successful social integration created some social awkwardness for me. As I secretly walked among the normal folks, I felt my tight bonds with other autism moms begin to slip. I simply didn't struggle with the same things they did anymore, and though I certainly never brought up this fact, I sometimes felt like I had no right to be there.

Maybe that was just the way of the world. When I got married, I lost most of my single friends. And when I had a baby, most of my friends without kids drifted away. And when my kid got diagnosed with autism, I lost most of my friends with normal kids. Maybe there was nothing I could do to stop the quiet exodus of my autism friends now.

At the same time, though, I knew I didn't fully belong with the parents of neurotypical kids, even if none of them knew. I was unfairly trapped in the middle, with a past I could neither go back to nor ignore. My ideal social group would have been other parents with fully recovered children, but how many of those were there? I had been trying to make more with my grand "Go Back to School and Become a Nurse Practitioner" plan, but even that was rapidly tarnishing.

Time in recovery had allowed me a chance to get back to myself, to remember who I was before I became Autism Mom and nothing else. Our initial successes had given me a kind of altruistic high, a conviction that I could help others because *if I can do it, anyone can!* It was only as this rush faded over the course of several months that it slowly dawned on me: I don't really like people that much.

I mean, I like the people that I like, but I have only bare shreds of empathy naturally available to me, and the last thing in the world I would want—the real me, that is, not the force-molded Autism Mom I'd had to become—is a job where I have to care about whining strangers. I wanted to help others, no doubt, but I'm a problem-solver, not a problem-*listener*, and I absolutely couldn't deal with people who weren't willing to work for their own success.

The problem was, this was turning out to be most of the parents I came across.

When Paul was first diagnosed, I was obsessively driven. Nothing in the world could stop me from seeking more information, researching every angle, trying anything it was remotely possible for us to try. As the years passed and I became a knowledge source rather than a sponge, I had the chance to talk to many new parents and share our experiences. There were PPCD birthday parties, newcomers to the online message boards, coworkers from Andrew's office, neighbors of relatives, friends of friends, and loose acquaintances of loose acquaintances. Everyone who knew us passed my name along to anyone they knew who had received a diagnosis, and after countless lunch dates, phone conversations, and e-mail threads, I was finally coming to the realization that my intensity was not the norm.

Some were not ready to hear the diagnosis in the first place and felt no need to do anything because that would mean admitting there was a problem. They just stuck their heads in the sand and repeated the "wait and see" mantra. Often this type of parent could be found newly arrived on the message boards, making a lengthy introduction about their child's exact history of speech delays and behavioral problems, then asking for the "best" place to get an "accurate" (by which they meant nonautism) diagnosis.

The stock response from me and many others was always "If your child has such a severe speech delay, then they need speech therapy, regardless of why they have the speech delay. Don't get bogged down in labels. Get them the help they need as soon as possible." After several similar replies, all telling them the opposite of what they wanted to hear, these parents usually slunk away in silence and did not post again.

Others accepted the diagnosis readily enough but couldn't fathom that their doctor might be misinformed or ignorant about treatment options. Often they cited an abundance of caution in not trying anything that hadn't gained mainstream acceptance, morphing "wait and see" into "wait until all the evidence is in."

"Absence of evidence is not evidence of absence," I would quip. "We don't have time to wait around for the twenty-year population studies. Like it or not, our treatment window is now."

Often I would bring up the bee analogy. "You know, for decades scientists studying aeronautics said they couldn't figure out how bees fly. As far as they could tell, it was mathematically impossible; the wings just weren't big enough. But that doesn't mean bees can't fly! Of course they can fly. And eventually they did figure it out—something to do with how the wings actually move in circles and create a vortex in the air—but the honey farmers didn't just stop what they were doing because there were all these studies proving bees couldn't fly. What mattered is what they saw with their own eyes."

Nonetheless, I watched scores of parents face autism with staunch resignation, unwilling to gather their own personal evidence until society could agree on what was true. The doctors told them bees couldn't fly, so they chose to abstain from honey until someone proved its existence was possible.

These first two types of parent were disappointing to me, but not excessively. There are plenty of people in the world making parenting decisions that I don't agree with, or mired in denial about any number of issues. If they weren't asking for my advice in the first place, I had no right to feel betrayed if they didn't accept it. The worst, however—and what seemed, at least to my skewed perspective, to be the most common—were parents who were interested in biomedical treatment, who knew they needed to do something, but didn't have the strength to commit.

These were the parents who would reach out to me, marvel at Paul's progress, and intently ask dozens of questions . . . but before long it would become apparent that their line of questioning was shaped more like an asterisk than a straight line. They would ask about diet just long enough to understand that yes, I was really telling them they had to eliminate all bread products, then they would deftly switch to the topic of vitamin supplements instead. When they learned that vitamin B12, critical for rebuilding damaged neurons in the brain, was most effectively delivered via injection, they would again hop trains onto probiotics. When they heard that most retail probiotics contained dairy, and they would need to pay more for higher-quality probiotics that would actually get the job done, then the real grasping would begin.

"What about music therapy?" they would ask hopefully. Or "Have you ever tried horse therapy?"

I would shrug and tell them the truth: their child might enjoy these activities, and it was indeed important to find enjoyable activities for any child, but those "therapies" were augmentative at best. If listening to special music or riding a horse for thirty minutes a week were sufficient to treat autism, we wouldn't be having this conversation. They might be a nice way to round out a comprehensive treatment plan, but assuming the parents were working under the typical constraints of time, money, and energy, I told them in no uncertain terms that their efforts would be best directed elsewhere. Somehow, though, these parents usually ended up trying the fun therapies before any others, because they were interested in the easiest solution, not the most effective one.

At one point a friend booked me on a blind lunch date with her neighbor, whose daughter had just been diagnosed. I stayed long after the waiter had brought the check, answering all her questions and corroborating everything our mutual friend had told her about Paul's dramatically altered path. I even offered to go shopping with her at her grocery store, to help her locate all the GFCF products without having to do the research.

She shook her head. "I'm just so scared, you know?"

At first I thought she meant scared of autism, scared of having an eight-year-old still in diapers, scared of having her disabled child live with her for the rest of her life. These were the things I was afraid of, the things that had motivated me so highly to find effective treatments. But it turned out that no, she meant she was scared of having to learn a new way to cook. Scared enough, in fact, that she would just have to cross her fingers on the rest of it.

"I believe it would work," she admitted. "I just don't think I have it in me."

"It really gets easier; I promise it does," I said.

But she shook her head sadly again. "I mean, we go to Applebee's like once a week. I don't see how we could give that up."

Her eyes begged me for forgiveness I couldn't spare. *You don't have it in you to stop brain-damaging your child?* It was disgusting.

Refusing her compassion wouldn't change her mind, though; I could tell. She was already deep in self-loathing, and if that couldn't motivate her to make a better choice, my added condemnation wouldn't matter. So I tried to fake it, because the world has enough cruelty in it already. I nodded and murmured some meaningless comforting syllables, as if there really were no clear answer to her predicament. Then I changed the subject to how she might at least fit a couple of hours of therapy into her family's busy restaurant schedule. What else could I do?

I reached out to her a few more times after that, just in case I'd been wrong about her ability to rise to the occasion after all. But she never responded to my e-mails.

This pattern repeated itself again and again. Occasionally I would come across another truly dedicated mom, who would leap in with both feet and soon be providing as much information to me as I was to her, but the vast majority were interested only up to the point where they had to change their own lifestyle. They couldn't seem to understand that caring for an adult on the spectrum was going to have its own lifestyle requirements, far harder than the ones they were shying away from now.

It was one thing to sternly stick to conventional therapies or to deny the autism diagnosis completely. But seeing the answer in front of you, and believing it, yet refusing to do what you knew was right for your child? It was too painful to deal with parents like that at all. At least as a nurse practitioner, I thought, I could mostly avoid them through self-selection. Instead of running triage on every parent thrown at me, I could remain farther back and spend time helping only parents who knew for sure they wanted my help. The Applebee's connoisseur I'd wasted my afternoon with would never make an appointment with a biomedical doctor because she'd already heard enough to know that wasn't a path she was going to bother exploring. Once I was tucked safely away behind the professional battle lines, I would never have to face the charnel house of children whose parents "didn't have it in them." They would still be out there, of course, but I could insulate myself from feeling personally responsible for the ones whose parents I had failed to convince. I told myself that once I was a nurse practitioner, I would no longer have to lie awake at night, sick over the possibility that if I'd said something differently, explained something more thoroughly, I could have made a difference for those kids after all. Once I was a nurse practitioner, I would only have to lie awake at night worrying about whether I'd given my patients the right advice, and that would be an improvement.

However, during one of our own appointments at Thoughtful House—which had recently expanded its services and renamed itself the Johnson Center for Child Development—Lucas inadvertently revealed how false this assumption of mine was.

"I am so, so sorry about that," he said, taking the chocolate wrapper Paul had found on the floor and tucking it deep inside the trash can by his desk. He sighed. "We had a family in here earlier who said they were 'almost' GFCF, 'just the occasional candy treat.' I had to really get on them, not just about how important the diet was, of course, but how it was completely inappropriate for them to bring that sort of thing into this office, of all places. A kid could find something on the floor—well, like what just happened! Lucky for us Paul's not going to do anything, but a lot of kids would put it right in their mouths."

He took off his glasses and rubbed the bridge of his nose. "Anyway, I know I'm preaching to the choir here. It's just pretty hard to believe sometimes."

"Wow," I said. "You would think, being patients here, they would get it, you know?"

"You would think," he agreed. "Sadly, it's pretty common. If I'd known when I started this how many of my patients were going to just completely ignore my advice—advice they were paying for, you know, so why would they keep showing up? But they do; they keep coming here and telling me, 'Well, he's only getting a little gluten,' or 'It's too hard to give him medicine that tastes bad; I just hate seeing him cry.' And then they demand to know why their children aren't getting better."

I'd had this experience myself. Many of the same parents who told me they couldn't commit to radical dietary changes nonetheless kept asking me questions. The same questions over and over, as if somehow this time I would give them a different answer, something easy that would solve everything. One Weird Trick to Cure Autism! One acquaintance had a habit of e-mailing me every couple of weeks with endlessly detailed monologues about how her son had been behaving well, saying certain words, accomplishing a whole list of age-appropriate activities—and then he had binged on cheese and lost everything for the rest of the day.

"Do you think it could be the dairy?" she would ask, *every single time*, apparently hoping that I had changed my mind and could give her absolution for choosing not to act.

I tried being as explanatory and polite as I could for who knows how many of these e-mails. I matched her paragraph for paragraph, covering all the biological functions involved, citing medical studies, and urging her to please, please just give it a try. Then, a few weeks later, our little Groundhog Day routine would begin again, as if she'd never spoken to me on the subject before. Finally, one day I could be gentle no longer.

"YES, IT'S THE FOOD," I wrote back. "Yes, yes, yes! That's how I feel; that's how I'm always going to feel." End of discussion, click send.

Yet still she sat on the fence and continued to share every doubt and wonder in her mind with me while never actually trying anything.

Eventually I had to just start deleting her e-mails as they came in, for my own sanity.

But what if she were the norm after all? What a nightmare that would be. What was I getting myself into, entering a career where all I would do, every day, was face this type of parent? I would gladly bend over backwards to help those who were willing to engage in acrobatics themselves, but I could not subject myself to the daily nullification of my efforts by parents who would ignore everything I said yet demand that I repeat it anyway.

Lucas shook his head a fraction to get himself back on track. "Anyway, nothing you can do except keep telling them what they need to hear and hope they start listening someday."

I don't know whether that conversation was the last straw for me, but it was certainly one of the penultimate few. If our own nurse practitioner, who had gone back to school for the sole purpose of treating autistic children, just as I intended to do, was miserably warning me away from it, that was advice I needed to consider seriously. My impression of him was one of extreme patience, and knowing that I couldn't lay much claim to that trait myself made my chances even slimmer.

So I quit school after just three semesters. Officially, I put things on hold, reserving the right to start back up again whenever I pleased, but in truth I knew I was done.

Many years later this decision would be proven right for me in a poignantly sad way. I was cornered at a birthday party by an autism mom who grilled me for over two hours on everything I knew. I shared willingly, as I always did, and she showed great excitement, as they always did. With the party drawing to a close, she pulled out her cell phone.

"Would it be okay if I took down your number? Just in case I have any other questions? I just feel like there's so much to learn, and I really want to do what's right for him, you know?"

"Sure," I said, spelling my last name.

"Oh. Huh," she muttered. I looked at the screen and saw her dilemma.

I was already in her contact list. Name and number. I didn't remember ever meeting her before, but then again I'd had this exact conversation with a hundred mothers over the years, and they tended to blur. Clearly, she and I had been through this scene already. She must have been just as enthusiastic the first time, asked for my number in just this same way . . . and then forgotten all about it.

She never called me the second time, either.

Chapter 20

The SCD Lady

As THE SCHOOL year drew to a close, we began to acknowledge that my fears about poststeroid regression had been justified. Again and again Paul lost skills, speech, and behavioral control within days when we tried to wean him off the steroids, and we'd hurriedly start him on another round. On the steroids, he was a completely normal kid. Off them, it wasn't working, and the urgency to find a permanent solution grew even as the cold realization was sinking in that our visa to Italy might be temporary.

We tried transitioning him to one of the long-term options Dr. Krigsman had mentioned in the beginning, namely, an immune suppressor called Methotrexate, but it simply did not keep him at the same level as the steroids. He did get to the point where he could maintain his level of recovery on a relatively low dose of Entocort alone, without boosts from the harsher prednisone, but still the day came when Dr. Krigsman said Paul had reached the limit and absolutely must come off the Entocort for good.

"We'll keep playing with other immune suppressors," he told me, "and we will find the right combination that works best for him eventually. But the steroids are done. No more. I know how great he is on them, I know it's hard to deny him that, but there are real side effects.

You will not thank me if he starts coming home with broken leg bones, a broken pelvis, a failing liver . . . ”

In fact, we had already started to see some unusual leg pain in Paul. Some nights he would wake up crying that his legs or his feet hurt, even though we could feel with our hands that the muscle was loose, not cramped. Several people tried to tell us it was growing pains, but it came with no increase in height whatsoever. He ran somewhat gingerly now as well, gave only halfhearted kicks at tae kwon do, and completely avoided bouncing on the trampoline or jumping off even low platforms on the playground. On his worst days he used his seat belt as a kind of rappelling rope to carefully lower himself out of the minivan.

Andrew and I agreed that the risk of side effects was too close to becoming a reality, but still we didn’t regret his treatment thus far for even a moment. Of course we didn’t want to have to make the decision in the first place—no parent would—but if we had to choose between his brain or his legs, we would choose his brain every time. Without his brain those strong legs wouldn’t be good for anything except running into traffic. Paul might never make it to the Olympics now, true, but he wouldn’t be going to the Special Olympics, either. We accepted the trade-off.

But if steroids were off the table and immune suppressors weren’t enough to keep the disease at bay, then what else? How much could we stand to lose? What if this were a full-fledged *Flowers for Algernon* situation, where Paul was destined to fall all the way back to square one, with all our hard work only causing more suffering for him as he would now be aware of what he was being robbed of on the way down?

Losing him the first time had been bad enough. Losing him a second time would kill me.

Of course I couldn’t really say that nothing other than Entocort was working when I hadn’t actually tried everything yet. The Specific Carbohydrate Diet still lurked in the corner, waiting for me to own up. Could I do it after all? Paul still had not gained any real weight with the elemental Splash boxes, so getting rid of those would not be a hardship. But the question remained, how to get him to eat real meat instead of lunch meat?

Really? I chided myself. *After everything you've been through, you're gonna wuss out over some stupid lunch meat? You're better than this! Quit being a coward.*

So I did.

Goodbye Splash boxes, goodbye deli slices, and hello to pounds and pounds of wasted meat as I once again ran through every preparation of every known animal, trying to find something he would reject slightly less than the others. I finally found minimal success with an SCD recipe for "chicken pancakes," which meant blending up raw poultry with cooked pears, then spooning the resulting batter onto baking pans and broiling it in the oven. The texture was actually very similar to the industrial meat puree nicknamed "pink slime," except of course mine was made with whole meat instead of mechanically separated scraps and ligaments and didn't have to be rinsed with ammonia to kill off rampant bacterial contamination. The final product was surprisingly close to fast-food chicken nuggets, minus the breading. But even this, drizzled liberally with honey, was a battle over every bite.

I asked for help on the SCD message board, and it was suggested that we try a betaine HCl supplement. HCl is the chemical symbol for hydrochloric acid, just like the stomach produces, and there is evidence that chronically low stomach acid can result in not just poor digestion but even reflux and heartburn, the supposed hallmarks of too much stomach acid.

There are some who cynically believe that pharmaceutical companies are already aware that their prescription acid blockers will actually make the problem worse for half their customers, and that they are deliberately maintaining the cycle of illness and pill purchasing for these patients. Personally, I think the average heartburn sufferer's diet is a far larger contributor than any counterproductive medications they may take, but I do agree that there's no money in selling a cheap, unpatentable substance like plain old hydrochloric acid, so at the very least no pharmaceutical company is going to research and promote it.

Other than general digestive problems, which could be caused by many things, the one notable symptom associated with low stomach acid was a strong distaste for meat. This was enough to convince me to try it for Paul, and miraculously, it worked. Within two days he was happy to eat his chicken pancakes without any prodding. Just to be sure, I took the supplement away, and soon he was again telling me that they tasted bad and he didn't want to eat them anymore. The betaine HCl returned to his daily pile of pills, and his appetite for meat came right back, as it had the first time.

Another hurdle down. The GFCF Lady was now the SCD Lady, though it would be years before I mentioned any of this on my website.

The Specific Carbohydrate Diet may be simplistic, but it is also incredibly labor-intensive, as every single meal must be prepared from scratch. Food preparation becomes a full-time job, just as it was before the conveniences of modern society. The best thing since sliced bread once was, in fact, bread that someone else had sliced for you, and even today you can find old cookbooks calling for "prepared mustard," which any budding cook at the time would have understood as an instruction to mix the powdered spice with vinegar in order to create that well-loved condiment. If blending one's own mustard seems bourgeois to our refined plastic-bottle sensibilities, well, at least it didn't have to be boiled down for hours like tomato ketchup did. Whoever ran the household on a turn-of-the-century farm would scarcely finish cooking breakfast before lunch preparation had to begin, and this schedule was not designed to prevent one gender from rising up but to prevent both genders from starving.

Compounding the kitchen labor problem is the fact that, for the first few weeks or months, the patient on SCD is usually ravenously hungry, and will eat two to three times the expected amount of food. Partially this is because it takes an entire plate full of broccoli to equal the calories in just two slices of white bread, and we are simply not used to bestowing such generous real estate to vegetables. On the other hand, an infinite amount of white bread could not provide the abundance of nutrients available in broccoli, which leads to the second reason for this insatiable appetite.

The human metabolism is surprisingly adept at recognizing long-term trends. Doctors always advise against starvation diets because refusing to eat merely teaches one's metabolism that there will be extreme lean periods within the historical pattern of prosperity, such that when food is reintroduced, the body will pack away an even greater amount of fat in preparation for the next lean period. In the same way, the typical Western diet can be seen as a historical leanness of nutrients rather than calories. When the body is suddenly exposed to so many readily absorbable vitamins and minerals, it acts like a greedy child, demanding as much and as often as it can. Not only are lifelong deficiencies made up for, but more beyond that is craved for storage because the metabolism expects another nutritional lean period to begin at any moment.

Eventually, the hunger subsides to a more normal level, but in the beginning it can be almost impossible to keep up with the demands for food. When we first began SCD, Paul's daily consumption was five pounds of vegetables, a pound and a half of chicken, and perhaps another half-pound or so of fruits. He ate the equivalent of a second full lunch during snack time at school and a third upon arriving home. Each night he would frantically chug down one last smoothie in the bathroom before committing to brushing his teeth for bed.

If not for the modern advent of the freezer, which later expanded into a second stand-alone freezer in our garage, I truly would have had to turn in my jeans for a farmhouse smock. As it was, cooking in bulk still didn't last me very long. My standing special order with the meat counter at our grocery store—twenty-four pounds of ground chicken thighs, split into eight packages for easier handling—had to be repeated every two weeks, while the staples of his vegetable smoothies, butternut squash and zucchini, had to be purchased, peeled, chopped, and frozen fifteen to twenty pounds at a time every few days.

At first the tiresome response from every cashier was "Whoa, are you baking a bunch of zucchini bread or something?" There is nothing quite so American as assuming that the only possible use for a vegetable is to be baked into a confectionery treat.

"No, it's actually all for my son," I would reply, never able to decide whether I was embarrassed or proud of this fact. "I puree it and hide it in smoothies for him. He has no idea it's there, drinks them all day long."

"Wow, what a great idea!" they would all say. "I'm going to try that with my kids."

I'm sure they never actually did, but at least no one ever told me that I was a mean mother, only a crafty one. Eventually, all the cashiers came to recognize me as the lady who buys all that butternut squash and zucchini, and the comments stopped. One time Andrew made a grocery trip for me, and as he loaded bags and bags of zucchini onto the conveyor belt, the cashier announced, "Hey, I know your wife!"

Yet despite eating seven pounds of food every single day, Paul still gained no weight. We did a nutritional evaluation with Kirsten, and she confirmed that his new diet was well balanced and very healthy. Most importantly, it contained enough plant-based carbohydrates to sustain him. This is not always easy on a diet with no grains or sugars, and the temptation to consume too much meat instead of produce is a dangerous one. Without some form of carbohydrates, the body is forced to break down protein for energy instead, a process known as ketosis, and many well-meaning parents have made their children extremely ill by attempting SCD without really understanding the nutritional principles behind it. It's not enough to take away the bad stuff; you still have to do the hard work to make them eat the good stuff, too.

"Actually," Kirsten told me with a chuckle, "the only thing he could use more of is sodium. I've never had to tell anyone this before, but you should add a little more salt to his diet. Only about half a teaspoon per day should do it. Everything else is perfect."

Generally speaking, Paul was better on SCD, but it was not the complete shock we had seen when starting either GFCF or elemental. On the one hand, his hyperactivity was completely eliminated, to the point that I stopped even measuring it in my daily notebook. However, he had been slowly ramping up new symptoms of stuttering and generalized anxiety for at least six months, and SCD didn't halt their progression. His behavioral symptoms were moderately improved, but still not as good as they had been when he was on Entocort. Nothing was as good as when he had been on Entocort.

We had been told to expect a long progression, though. SCD is a process of live cultivation, and you can't grow a garden overnight, whether it's in your back yard or your belly. In fact, there is evidence that many species of pathogenic gut bacteria can go dormant for up to three months. When they can't hold out any longer, some finally starve to death, but then the remaining bacteria feed off their dead compatriots and hunker down for another three months. Many people on SCD report going through successive rounds of die-off in very predictable three-month intervals, and though later rounds are usually easier than the initial transition onto the diet, we were told that these quarterly cycles could be expected to continue for up to two or three years, depending on how rampant and hardy the original gut flora had been.

Paul's first three-month mark was in May, right at the end of kindergarten. We hadn't been watching the calendar, despite the warnings we'd been given, because his initial entry onto the diet had been relatively gradual, with grains being taken out of the picture several months before finally phasing out the last of the sugars. Nonetheless, a stunningly out-of-character occurrence did give us pause.

He was in gym class, which our school system called Wellness to account for the dual curriculum of both exercise and diet. (This was something I approved of only begrudgingly because it mostly meant teaching the kids how to read processed-food labels and keep saturated fats and sugars under certain thresholds. It wasn't at all relevant for a truly healthy diet, but I suppose it was a step in the right direction.) The Wellness teacher was demonstrating to the class how to make a "power smoothie," which to her credit contained several vegetables along with the fruits, but also included a Crystal Light packet for flavoring. Paul was by now perfectly aware that he was not to eat food that came from outside our home, and he had on many occasions turned down things like cookies, candy, and birthday cake when an adult who didn't know better tried to give them to him. On this day, however, he walked right up to the Wellness teacher's table, grabbed a paper cup, and tossed it back before anyone could stop him. She was stunned, and they raced him to the nurse's office and called me.

I wasn't too freaked out. Mistakes happen, and I never would have expected Paul to do what he had done, either. The amount of sweetener he'd consumed was small, and the reaction wasn't much, just a day or two of looser stools before everything was back to where it had been before. The bigger question was why in the world he had decided to drink the smoothie in the first place. When I asked him, he said he didn't know. In fact, he could hardly remember doing it at all. Was it because he was overwhelmed with a sugar craving stronger than any he'd ever felt before? Was a colony of pathogenic bacteria in his gut sending fierce signals to his brain in a desperate last attempt to survive? We'll never know for sure, but the experience certainly seemed to line up with that of hundreds of other parents who have put their children on this diet.

Two months after the infraction with the smoothie, Paul unexpectedly vomited all over himself, in the absence of any other symptoms of illness. At that time it wasn't connected in my mind to die-off, but this would in fact become a cycle for him over the next year, spontaneously vomiting for no reason once every three months almost to the day. Just one more interesting piece of data that I never could have kept track of without my daily notebooks.

But while SCD may have been slowly working its multiyear transformation in the background, we were busy dealing with the present. By the summer after kindergarten, Paul was stuttering badly, verbally stimming again, and having anxiety-related emotional breakdowns. These weren't like the irrational tantrums of his preschool years, but they could escalate to that if handled badly. Once he announced that he was going to marry his sister when he grew up. I began pleasantly explaining to him why that wasn't possible, and the next thing I knew he was weeping uncontrollably.

"But *why*, Mommy?" he wailed, face in his hands. "*Why won't they let me?*"

I assured him that it was no big deal, and by the time he was a grown-up he would have met lots of different girls to fall in love with, but he only cried harder.

"I just, just don't know-oh-oh-oh-oh-oh how I'm ever going-ing-ing—how I'm going-ing-ing to choose!"

During the days and weeks that followed this, he would at times randomly cry out, "I just don't know who I'm going to marry!" (I'll let you imagine the stuttering for yourself.) This also began extending to what college he was going to attend, where he was going to live, what he would name his children, and any other unknown variable in the future. One night he woke up sobbing and gasping from a nightmare, and when I asked him what the dream had been about, all he could get out was "I was trying, and trying, and trying, but I just kept failing!" An understandable nightmare for a thirty-something mother, perhaps, but not so normal for a six-year-old.

More traditional behavior problems were starting to creep back in as well. He began resisting tasks that weren't his favorite, arguing about any change in his routine, and even yelling and throwing himself on the floor if we offended him in some small way, such as by suggesting that he try to use the restroom before we left even if he didn't think he had to go. Conversations were becoming less frequent and less meaningful, and obsessions with video games and YouTube were taking their place. Once again he lost interest in drawing discernible pictures, instead choosing to create obsessive geometric patterns that sometimes started out as spaceships but always ended up filling the page with layers of overlapping triangles and bisected lines.

The longer Paul stayed off the steroids, the further things were slipping away from us. The Methotrexate wasn't working, and if SCD was working, it was doing so very slowly. We were losing him.

Chapter 21

Tulips in the Rubble

As THE NEW school year approached, Paul began to fret more and more about who his first grade teacher was going to be. At his annual ARD before the end of kindergarten, we had fought for a concession allowing us to choose his teacher every year. Mrs. Miller had been handpicked for Paul by Mrs. Allison, and he had even spent the last few months of PPCD visiting her classroom on a regular basis, to let each one get a feel for the other. This process had worked out well for us, and I wanted to have that kind of insightful selection every year.

The school officials had refused. They argued that since the IEP was a legally binding document, they could find themselves in an impossible situation if the district needed to lay off a teacher whom we had been promised. In the worst-case scenario, they claimed, there was even the possibility that our chosen teacher could blackmail the school for higher pay, or else she would quit and leave the door open for us to sue the district for not upholding his IEP. They readily agreed, however, that it was to everyone's benefit for Paul to be placed in a classroom with a teacher who could understand his differences because a bad placement would only lead to disruptions for everyone. So they included a generic "preferential teacher choice" as one of his accommodations, and we were allowed to pick three names. Barring any unforeseen staffing changes, the principal promised us that there was no reason we wouldn't get our first choice.

Over the summer, however, a new elementary school opened in the neighborhood, and many staff members from our school left to fill positions there. This included the school principal, Paul's speech therapist, and Mrs. Miller. In addition, Mrs. Allison left teaching entirely to stay home with her new baby, and even the ARD coordinator moved on to destinations unknown. Suddenly, every single person who had been in the room when it was agreed that Paul's teacher needed to be chosen carefully was gone.

Would the new principal even think to read our IEP before making the class rosters? We had no personal advocates left in the building, but I didn't want to call and be That Parent before she'd even finished unpacking her office. If I tried to tell her how to do her job, she might assign us to a different teacher out of spite. Yet the uncertainty was killing Paul. Several times a day he would declare in a wavering voice, "I just don't know who my first grade teacher is going to be!"

"I'm excited to find out, too," I would cheerfully reply, deflecting his real emotion on the subject. "But it's not Tuesday yet, so we can't talk about it."

It may sound cold, but we had been told by several books and professionals that reassuring a clinically anxious child only makes the problem worse. Unlike the average fears of a neurotypical child, for whom a quick hug or explanation will soothe their worries and give them confidence, clinical anxiety is a completely different psychological state. It is a positive feedback loop, such that more attention to the issue only encourages more fear, and a parent's natural instinct to comfort their child will in fact heighten the obsession. When dealing with clinical anxiety the only beneficial action is to extinguish the cycle outright. We were told to set a concrete time and place when Paul could be certain that we would talk about a particular fear, then kindly but firmly refuse to discuss it at any other time.

Our deadline, Tuesday, was the "Welcome Walk," a unique event at our school where teachers drove around the neighborhood and visited the houses of all their new students the week before school started.

The idea of having a first meeting on home turf had its appeal, but at the same time, listening for a stranger's knock at the door, which could happen anytime during a two-hour window, would be a nerve-wracking experience for him in itself.

When Tuesday finally came I opened the door with Paul hopping beside me, and a friendly woman in an official school T-shirt introduced herself as Mrs. McGregor.

She had been our third choice.

Admittedly, I didn't actually know any of the three teachers we'd chosen. I had only had private conversations with those at the school who knew Paul well—everyone who was now gone—and taken their unofficial recommendations about who they thought would work especially well with him. The names were ranked based on who was recommended by the most people, nothing more. I had no reason to think that Mrs. McGregor would be anything but an excellent teacher.

Still, I had to wonder. By what logic should we have our last choice when I knew for sure that our first two choices were still teaching at the school? It had to be deliberate; there was no other explanation. The new principal might as well have said to me, "I'm too afraid to go off-list for legal reasons, but I'll damn sure do what I want within those boundaries."

I would later be quietly told by other staff members that yes, the new principal had a habit of micromanaging, much to the chagrin of the longtime staffers, and had a particular chip on her shoulder against parents who had the gall to request teachers by name. I can certainly understand that it's not something you can allow for every student, but ours was a unique case. It wasn't about playing favorites; it was about finding the person who had the best chance of coping with him at all. Perhaps it is arrogant, but yes, my child was special. That's why they call it *special ed*.

Our third choice was still preferable to teachers we hadn't named at all, though, and Mrs. McGregor certainly seemed like a patient and kind woman as we chatted in our entryway. We would just have to hope for the best.

Now that he knew his teacher, Paul switched to "just not knowing where his classroom would be," but at least that was something new for me to hear about all day long. Then, after we did get to visit his classroom in order to drop off his school supplies, he dutifully updated to "just not knowing what first grade will be like." As the books said, his anxiety was a self-perpetuating thing, not based in any real outcome that could be disproved.

Saturday morning, two days before school started, we got a phone call from the principal. Her news was startling. The district had reviewed our school's final rosters and determined that the second grade had too many students per classroom, violating the student-teacher ratios mandated by state law. Perhaps this was something the principal had overlooked when creating the rosters, or perhaps some new children had transferred in at the last moment. Whatever the reason, it had to be fixed, and there was neither time nor money to hire a new second grade teacher. So the school had made the painful decision to turn our first grade teacher, Mrs. McGregor, into a second grade teacher at this last possible minute and evenly disperse all her students among the other first grade classrooms, which still had just enough headroom not to bump up against their own maximum number of students.

Our new teacher, she told us, would be Ms. Pallick.

She was number two on our list.

Even now she was screwing with us! Andrew was the one who took the phone call, otherwise I likely would have argued the point despite my nonconfrontational nature. But fuming over the principal's repeated power plays was not something I could waste time on now. This switch had the potential to be a major disaster for Paul.

He'd met his teacher. He'd seen his classroom. He had a plan for the first day of school. You couldn't just tell this child *never mind*, at least not without giving him steroids first.

I tried to explain the change to him, and he began creating fantasy scenarios in which both Ms. Pallick and Mrs. McGregor would be taking turns teaching him in the classroom he'd visited, or that he would be taught by some mutant blend of the two named "Mrs. McPallick." I told him in several different ways that his classroom would be different now, and he agreed that yes, the number over the room with the monkey decorations would change.

This was bad. I could easily imagine him marching into the wrong classroom on the first day of school and refusing to leave because he just knew this was the room he was supposed to be in. A meltdown on the first day was not the way to start the school year.

So we drove to the school. It was a Saturday, but with only two days to go I figured there must be at least a few teachers on campus finalizing their classrooms. Surely Mrs. McGregor herself would be there, frantically changing the name tags on everything and advancing her whole curriculum by a year. Even if all I could do was get inside the building and put Paul in front of his new classroom door, locked and dark, that would be better than nothing.

We walked in slow circles around the building for half an hour, knocking on doors and peering in windows, until we finally caught someone on their way back from a lunch break. I explained the situation, and she was more than happy to let us in.

"Mrs. McGregor actually isn't on campus right now," she said. "A bunch of other teachers stayed up all night with her, moving furniture and helping her get ready. She didn't even get to keep the same room."

"That's crazy," I said. "I had no idea the district could order something like this, not without at least providing money for a new hire."

"You'd be surprised how often it happens," she confided. "I was at a school once where they did this exact same thing, only they did it a week after school had already started!"

I shook my head and silently counted my blessings.

She escorted us down the first grade hallway. "But anyway, I'm actually pretty sure that I saw Ms. Pallick here earlier," she said, "so that would be even better for you."

Sure enough, Ms. Pallick was in her classroom, and we had the opportunity not just to introduce ourselves but to talk about Paul's idiosyncrasies in much greater depth than had been possible in our entryway with Mrs. McGregor. And now that he had replacement visuals in his mind for both his new teacher's face and the new classroom layout, Paul had no trouble understanding that this was where he'd be instead.

Just in case, we walked by Mrs. McGregor's old classroom on the way out so he could see that it was completely empty—no more monkey decorations. By the time we left I was feeling more confident about school than I had been before we'd unexpectedly changed teachers.

I was wrong, of course, but it was nice to feel confident for a little while.

For the first two weeks of school, things did seem to be going okay. I had explained to Ms. Pallick that Paul responded very badly to the idea of failure and that positive reinforcement was more effective than threats of punishment. He would be especially crushed, I said, by receiving a "red day" in his daily folder. Time-outs might be forgotten from day-to-day, but that crimson stain would continue to sit on his calendar for the rest of the month, stressing him out every time he opened his folder, convincing him that he couldn't be calm even if he tried.

This was all true, but the unfortunate result was that I didn't get a complete picture at first about what was going on in the classroom. I saw green days and received no other e-mails or phone calls, so I thought all was well.

At our first conference Ms. Pallick was encouraging, which I've come to realize is a steadfast requirement of all parent-teacher conferences. I imagine even Jeffrey Dahmer's teacher would find some way to put a positive spin on his first two weeks of school.

Paul was doing really well, she enthused, only melting down maybe once a day.

"Wait, like really melting down?" I asked. "Tears and shouting and everything?"

Ms. Pallick had special ed certification, and she hadn't considered it unusual for a child with autism to have regular meltdowns. I assured her that it was definitely not normal for Paul, and she was relieved.

"You know, that makes a lot of sense," she said, "because early on I asked the resource teachers what sort of strategies worked best for him when he was having a meltdown, and they just told me, 'He doesn't.'"

"Resource" was code for "special ed." As the number of special education students had skyrocketed over the past two decades, school districts statewide had been able to (well, forced to) expand from one special education classroom per school into a variety of different types of classes serving different subsets of children. In our district there was FAC for more severely impaired children, FCC for those who might show normal intelligence but were low- or nonverbal, SCORES for high-functioning autistic children who spoke well enough but had too many behavioral problems to be mainstreamed, ACHIEVE for the emotionally disturbed . . . and the sea of acronyms changed not just from district to district but also year to year within a given district.

Not all schools had all specialties, and students would be bused to the nearest school offering the most appropriate environment, but every school had a "resource room" for those special needs students who were able to be mainstreamed for most or all of the day. These were informal come-and-go classrooms that provided occasional help with anything from social skills to dyslexia. Sometimes they served simply as a place to stay during the one part of the day that a child couldn't handle, such as lunch in a crowded cafeteria or recess when there was minimal supervision.

There were at least two teachers covering the resource room, and as a student with an IEP, Paul was assigned to one each year, though either could help him in a pinch. During kindergarten, his resource teacher had only come periodically to observe him in the classroom and make sure everything was going well, which it always had been. I had met her only once at an ARD, and I'm not sure Paul ever had. This year, however, Paul had already referred several times to "visiting Ms. Bryan's classroom," and I only now realized that he hadn't been talking about the whole class doing some activity with another class; he had been talking about going to the resource room.

"No, he shouldn't be having meltdowns," I said. "I mean, his anxiety is a lot worse right now than it used to be, but not that level. That's not normal."

I told her about our medication roller coaster and how Paul's symptoms were very strongly tied to his overall health. Throughout kindergarten we had been slowly reducing some of his supplements as we determined they weren't needed anymore, but I committed to bringing several of them back, even though it pained me to do so. We were still going downhill, and I would do Paul no favors by being in denial about it.

Ms. Pallick reported a few days later that the supplement changes had indeed made a big difference in the classroom, and the meltdowns had been brought mostly under control for now. I warned her that things might still get worse the longer we were off the steroids, and she promised to tell me as soon as there were issues so I could try to stay on top of it.

Even without major behavioral problems, though, he was definitely back to being the weird kid. He talked compulsively, and the topics came out of left field, assuming they made any sense at all. He might sometimes greet his classmates normally, but he was just as likely to run up and shout the punch line to a joke without any context. Kids who had been his good friends in kindergarten began to shun him, and they couldn't really be blamed. These days he only wanted to play his games, his way, and he never, ever wanted to lose. He also wouldn't allow himself to be labeled the "bad guy" even for pretend purposes, and the other kids were understandably getting tired of his demands.

I had to continually remind myself that there had been a time when I had only dared to dream that he might be the weird kid in a mainstream classroom. But being back in Holland now was so much harder than it would have been if we'd never left at all.

That was another problem: it *was* looking suspiciously more like Holland this time around, not Beirut. I was tired. I hadn't given up fighting, but there were days when I allowed myself to consider the possibility of defeat. I hated myself for it, yet in some ways giving up had its own allure. A small part of me felt comforted to really belong somewhere again, rather than feeling like an interloper in all social groups.

I had known that losing him again would kill me, but it turned out to be a euthanization rather than a mauling.

While Paul's functioning level was inching lower by the day, the expectations at school were rising, making the gap between them ever more apparent. There were spelling tests and math tests every week, and these were guaranteed to ruin his morning if not his whole day. The very idea of testing meant the possibility of failure, which was something he couldn't cope with.

On the spelling tests he was terrified to write a word unless he was absolutely certain he was spelling it correctly. Having learned to read fluently by four, he was a better speller than most already, and of course there would have been no public humiliation or dire punishments in store had he misspelled something. Here again, however, clinical anxiety is not based in reality. He could not commit to anything that might be imperfect. Each time Ms. Pallick read a word out to the class, he would protest loudly that he didn't know how to spell it, and her encouragements to "just do his best" like the rest of the students did not satisfy him. He would rather turn in a blank page than one that might contain errors, and for the first couple of tests, he did.

Ms. Pallick finally made some progress when she told him he could write only the first letter of a word and stop there for now, but in order for him to keep up the internal lie that the goal posts had been moved, he would also put just the first letter for words he did know how to spell. He couldn't allow himself to be proved an occasional failure even by his own successes.

The math tests were timed, which was even worse. They were deliberately unfinishable, intended to measure improvement over the course of the year. In September the student might reasonably expect to complete the first five arithmetic problems in one minute, and the test would be repeated every two weeks until by May they would hopefully be able to do all twenty on the page. The entire design was to fail less over time rather than to succeed more. It didn't matter if Paul finished more math problems than any other child in the class, which he usually did. All he knew was that he'd failed to complete the test yet again.

This sort of thing usually led to moderate outbursts. Not a complete loss of control, but perhaps breaking down in tears or becoming so frustrated that he would yell, make angry faces, and stick his tongue out at Ms. Pallick. Before long I learned that Paul was spending more than his allotted time with Ms. Bryan each week, working on emotional stability and appropriate ways to interact with others when he was upset.

My standby description of his educational setting to others had always been "mainstreamed without an aide," but given the one-on-one attention he was receiving now, could I even really say that anymore? I tried not to think about it.

A speech therapist friend of mine once told me that in her experience, first grade and third grade are the two big benchmarks when high-functioning kids fall apart. "First grade for the sudden academic demands," she said, nodding at me, "and third grade is when the kids get mean and the bullying starts."

Her timeline was outdated, however. We had more than one bully situation even among these six-year-olds, and as the year wore on Paul became more entrenched as an outcast. He played by himself most days, but one boy would regularly organize several others to approach him one at a time and ask if he wanted to play. When Paul excitedly replied yes, they would sneer, "Just kidding!" and run away. Some of these were boys who had been his good friends in kindergarten, so he was taken in by the ruse every single time and hurt even more when the rejection was delivered.

There was another boy who understood that Paul got in trouble when he had an outburst and would deliberately goad him past the point of no return. Whether it was snatching Paul's glasses off his face, singing annoying songs at him on endless repeat, or putting a modern twist on the "I'm not touching you" routine by inching his peanut butter sandwich across the line to the nut-free end of the table, he was constantly looking for ways to push Paul over the edge and then delight in his punishment. Ms. Pallick understood what was happening and did her best to keep the two of them separated, but in the end, if Paul had an outburst it had to be addressed, regardless of whether he had started it or not. Things were only going to get harder for him in the coming years if he couldn't learn to control himself.

One afternoon on the way home from school, Paul casually informed me that he'd spent all of recess lying on a bench crying until

Ms. Bryan had come outside to get him. I was dismayed to hear this, but he just shrugged and said, "It's okay. I have tears at recess a lot."

This horrible statement, and the calmness with which he delivered it, struck me like a fist. Paul was giving up. His was a different kind of fight than mine, to be sure, but he was wearing thin just as I was.

I knew what would come next, because this was the story of my own childhood. Soon he would begin to view his isolation as not just inevitable but a definitive part of who he was. I had defiantly embraced misery in my adolescence, fulfilled the role above and beyond expectations just to spite them—this nebulous "them" that began as a few childhood bullies but soon came to encompass the whole world—and only finally discovered in my teens that I could just as easily choose to be defiantly happy instead. But Paul didn't have that same spark of independence. His sister surely did, we could already tell, but Paul was a sweeter, kinder soul than I'd ever been. He needed other people. Even when he'd lost control on the outside, in his heart he was hating himself for it, desperate to earn forgiveness from the very ones who had pushed him too far.

A meltdown was never a calculated choice to get what he wanted, nor was it an attempt to inflict equal hurt upon those who had hurt him. It was a sudden, panicked slip in the tight throttle he fought to keep around himself at all times. The maelstrom didn't start from nothing; it was always there, contained only by force of will out of love for everyone around him. His body may have grown, but on the inside Paul was still that same toddler, running around the room making sure no one ever stopped cheering. He would not be forged stronger by the fire of rejection, as I had been. He would simply allow himself to be consumed.

I had been feeling so sorry for myself, waking up outside the borders of Italy again and questioning whether I had the strength left to attempt another invasion. Finally, with that one wretched sentence, Paul got me moving again. Life had started to look like Holland to me, and I might have had it in me to put up with Holland after all if he had been happy. But he clearly wasn't, and that was the motivation I needed.

My war was back on.

And it's still ongoing. Because the truth is, Paul was not the child that I rescued from autism, at least not yet.

It was my daughter, Marie.

Chapter 22

Marie

MARIE HAD BEEN born just before Paul's second birthday, when things were rapidly shifting from difficult to impossible with him. She was a scheduled C-section because my obstetrician had convinced me that the risks of attempting a natural delivery after my first C-section were not worth it in our case. Aside from my natural genetic tendency to develop large and unpredictable keloid scars, sonograms had revealed that Marie was a giant baby, estimated at over nine pounds. The added strain of trying to deliver such a large baby might cause my old scar to rupture, which could put both of our lives at risk.

The benefit of this decision was that we knew exactly when I would be delivering her, so there would be no chance of us running to the hospital in the middle of the night and having Paul wake up unexpectedly to someone who was Not Mommy. But on the downside, it meant I would be gone for twice as long, a minimum of three to four days in the hospital. At this point in our lives Paul still suffered from extreme separation anxiety and routinely screamed for as many hours as it took for me to come back. His sister's birth would be the ultimate test of how long nonstop screaming could truly last. I honestly believed he might go for the whole three days.

When the time came we called in both my mother and Andrew's mother to stay with him at our house together. We told them this was so neither grandmother felt slighted, but actually it was so they could provide relief for each other when he inevitably became too much to deal with. Better to imply that they were jealous of each other's time than to admit that I didn't think either one of them could handle him alone for three days without dumping his body in the woods.

I wrote up a long translation dictionary of all the strange words he used for his favorite foods and videos so they would have a chance of understanding his consistent but backwards language. I also transcribed many of his common echolalia scripts so they wouldn't waste energy trying to figure out what he wanted when in fact he was just reveling in his own voice.

We were still almost a year away from Paul's diagnosis and had never heard of a social story, but we did read him lots of books about new babies and big brothers, trying to prepare him as best we could. We already had one perpetually needy, awake-at-all-hours, Mommy-centric creature under our roof, and we had no idea how he would react when a second one arrived. We joked that it would be just like having twins, except with one big enough to break things.

About three hours after the delivery, they brought Paul up to the hospital to see the baby. My mother reported that the morning at home had gone poorly, as expected, but at least he'd stopped screaming once they'd put him in the car and he'd understood that he was being taken to see me.

He was surprisingly enthralled with his new sister, so much so that he didn't even try to take the room apart, which was a relief. We managed to snap a couple of happy family photos in which Andrew is obviously struggling to keep Paul facing in the general direction of the camera, but that was a pretty accurate representation of our family, after all. Shortly after that, though, things got problematic, as Paul became desperate to climb up into the bed with me. We could not risk his squirmy legs kicking open my stitches. He began fussing, then fighting and yelling, and after a few minutes we all agreed it was time for him to go home again.

I could hear him screaming down the hall even after the elevator doors closed, only eventually fading as they slid downward below the concrete floor. Later phone reports indicated that seeing me for just that brief time had upset him even more than he'd been in the morning, and by early evening I insisted that Andrew go home to help take care of him.

"Are you sure?" he asked.

"Absolutely. I'm fine," I said. This time I hadn't gone through twenty exhausting hours of labor before the surgery, I pointed out, and we'd been rightly told that it gets easier every time. My friend Tara had had four C-sections herself, and after the last one she'd voluntarily checked out of the hospital and gone home after just twenty-four hours. At the time I'd thought she was insane, but considering it now, it didn't seem impossible at all. I felt energized and happy. Abdominal surgery was way easier than taking care of Paul all day.

"Marie's sleeping, and I can reach her just fine if she wakes up," I assured him. "You're the one who needs to sleep. Are you really going to try and tell me you want to sleep on that awful thing?" I gestured at the vinyl futon, which strained the definition of the word "bed" so badly it probably gave it stretch marks.

"No," he admitted sheepishly. "But I could at least wait until later, if you want."

"If you're going to go, you might as well get there before they attempt to put Paul to bed without you. It's still not going to be good enough for him, obviously—"

"Yeah, thanks," he said.

"—but better you than neither of us. And if he sees you come home from the hospital, maybe that can sort of help with the idea that the hospital is a place people can leave, that I'm not stuck here forever."

"Yeah, not really buying that argument," he said wryly. "But I gotta admit, sleeping in my own bed sounds really nice. Are you really, really sure you don't need me here?"

"One hundred percent positive. Bring me chips and queso in the morning; that's your job."

"What if they aren't letting you eat yet?"

"Screw them. I'm starving; that means my body is ready to eat. I'm about to call the nurse back in and demand like ten more Jell-Os."

He kissed me and left. I lay back and stared at my beautiful baby girl, sleeping peacefully in her clear plastic bin beside my bed. Not squalling for the first twenty-four hours of her life, like her brother had. Just dozing, and nursing, and dozing again, completely satisfied and making no demands of the world. Marie the sweet angel, polar opposite of her tempestuous brother.

"There are two rules about having children," my Grandma Ethel had once said. "Number one, your first child will completely change your life. And number two, your second child will be nothing like your first."

God, I hoped she was right.

We waited two days before attempting to bring Paul back to the hospital again, after I was healed enough for him to safely crawl into the bed with me. Andrew had spent only a few sporadic hours at the hospital himself since leaving the first night, because frankly there was nothing for him to do there and plenty for him to do at home. Paul's stalwart grandmothers were wearing thin.

Even knowing this, I was shocked to see how awful Paul looked when they arrived. His face was blotched and puffy, and he had deep circles under his eyes. Andrew had told me he did eventually stop screaming in his crib after several hours each night, but he was pretty sure it was an involuntary collapse from exhaustion, and Paul had been waking early each morning still in a panic. Nevertheless, Paul gave a huge grin as he burst through the door and immediately dove at me.

"No, no," my mother-in-law began tiredly, but I waved her off and gently shifted my body to the side so he wouldn't be lying directly over my stomach. Paul scrabbled up the inclined bed and took my face in both hands, pressing his forehead urgently to mine.

"Ay-yuh-yuh Mommy, ay-yuh-yuh Mommy," he said again and again.

"Yeah, honey, Mommy's right here," I said.

"Ay-yuh-yuh Mommy," he repeated, pure joy shining from his exhausted, emotionally battered little face.

He eventually let go of my cheeks, but we stayed tightly twisted together on the bed for at least twenty or thirty minutes, he endlessly reiterating what he'd been wanting for two days and I confirming that he had it. It was the closest thing to snuggling he had ever done with me, despite the fact that his body was rigid and unable to stay still.

Finally, he sat up and peered over at Marie.

"Do you see your sister?" I asked.

"Do you see your sister," he repeated, a statement rather than a question. Then, gravely, "Ay-yuh-yuh-yuh-yuh *baby*."

And I saw with great relief that he was looking at her with the same loving desperation that he'd had fixated on me moments before. I knew then that he would not be jealous of his sister. She was an extension of me, as far as he was concerned, and that was all that needed to be said.

When we finally brought her home the next day, he leaned into her baby carrier and gently placed his forehead on hers, just as he so often did with mine. He adored Marie and wanted her to be with him at all times, just like me.

Marie was nine months old when Paul was eventually diagnosed, and she was still his favorite person and my peaceful cherub. She was patient, happy, alert, and talkative. She was content to be held and even laid her head on my shoulder, something Paul had literally never done since becoming strong enough to hold up his own head. She used a handful of meaningful words, including "Mama" and "Dada" and "bath," reached her arms out to be picked up, and pointed at things with one finger. She crawled normally, if a couple of months later than her peers, and had no sensory aversions except an extreme dislike of the noisy blender, which wasn't unusual for a baby. Everything about her development was the opposite of Paul's.

I had one autistic child and one neurotypical child. No doubt about it.

While Marie cruised happily along from nine months to twelve months, the rest of our world turned upside down. During that time we started seeing Melanie, weighted all of Paul's toys, attempted and abandoned the skin-brushing protocol, removed dairy from his diet, began services with ECI, got evaluated by the school district, and eliminated gluten. Marie had to hop on her brother's dietary band-wagon, just as I did, so by eleven months old she was completely GFCF.

The day after we took gluten away from her, I remember thinking that she was in a particularly chipper mood and wondering if we'd somehow dodged a bullet by getting her started on it so early. That curious musing was quickly pushed aside for more urgent concerns, like dealing with her brother's violent withdrawal, but it continued to nag at the back of my mind as we approached her twelve-month appointment with the pediatrician.

I had one autistic child and one neurotypical child . . . so far. Children with autism commonly regress at twelve months, eighteen months, sometimes as late as three years. What was our risk? More im-portantly, could we do anything about it? Was there even the slightest chance that we could prevent—or inadvertently cause—such a regres-sion in our thus far unaffected daughter?

Of course we'd read about the vaccine controversies, both before and after Paul's diagnosis, and until now I had never once questioned the medical establishment's insistence that there was no link between vaccines and autism. I am a regimentally scientific person, and I be-lieved in the system. (I still do believe in the system, in fact, but I've come to realize that sometimes the bad data takes longer to be rooted out than we would like to think. And there is always bad data, or else why would we need a system of peer review in the first place?)

Still, scrutiny of one's own beliefs is always a good thing, so we looked back carefully at Paul's development, just to be sure: Had we ever seen a major regression of any kind, after a shot or otherwise? The answer was clearly no. There were some children who regressed suddenly and without warning, but Paul was not one of them. He had been on this skewed path since the beginning, and there had been no-table sensory and developmental oddities as early as three months old.

Then again, he'd also received a shot the day he was born, and a few more at two months, so symptoms at three months old didn't necessarily rule out vaccine complications for him altogether. Frankly, though, what may or may not have happened in Paul's past didn't matter to us. Andrew and I are both very good at compartmentaliz-ing our experiences, and for us, the phrase "what's done is done" is not just a guilt-smoothing platitude but a sincere worldview. For now, our only concern was the shots that Marie was about to receive at her twelve-month checkup: the MMR and the varicella shot, more com-monly known as chicken pox.

Neither of those specific shots had caused Paul's autism, that much was certain.

Nevertheless, I was deep into my obsessive researching by now, and I'd come across some studies indicating that a percentage of autis-tic children were found to be harboring live measles virus in their in-testines without showing the typical outward symptoms of the disease. In all cases it was genetically confirmed to be the modified live strain used in the MMR vaccine. The shot had effectively given them a per-manent case of "silent" measles. The researchers in those studies had suggested two possible explanations: first, that the virus had evolved, presenting in some cases with neurological symptoms rather than the classic skin rash; and second, possibly in conjunction with the first, the inherently broken immune system of an autistic child might not rec-ognize the virus as a pathogen and would thus allow it to unnaturally flourish inside its host.

The measles itself was still not the sole cause of the autism in those cases, because though the number of children with a live measles infec-tion was significant—especially considering that it should have been zero—the majority of autistic children studied did not harbor the vi-rus. In addition, treating the infected children with antiviral therapies did improve their autistic symptoms to some degree in all cases, but it did not eliminate the autism entirely, just as eliminating Paul's strep infection a few years later would help him tremendously but did not magically solve everything.

As the decision inched steadily closer, we pondered every risk and every reward. As best we could tell at that time, it seemed that autistic children began with immune systems that were faulty in some unknown way, for some unknown reason, and each additional challenge—be it vaccine or natural infection—risked starting the ava-lanche of neurological symptoms.

Did Marie have a flawed immune system like her brother? There was no way to know. She had no allergies, no chronic ear infections, no obvious signs that anything yet had begun to go wrong. She didn't even suffer from a lot of digestive gas, as Paul had as a baby. Yet there was, maybe, that improvement we thought we saw after taking her off gluten. And beyond that, simply being related to us put her at a huge disadvantage. A child with an autistic sibling is somewhere between eight and seventeen times more likely to also be on the spectrum.

The knee-jerk reaction would be that if there's even the slightest possibility of the shot hurting her, then don't give it. But viewed from a different perspective, this theory we were trying to piece together between ourselves also implied that it would be just as dangerous for Marie to actually get measles—perhaps even more so. Outbreaks had been on the rise in recent years, so it was not inconceivable that she would be exposed to it someday. In fact, over the course of her whole lifetime, it might even be likely. Such an exposure might prove even more devastating to her, assuming she had this secret time bomb lurk-ing inside her.

"To be honest," I told a friend, "I kind of feel like my children were the ones who would have died from stuff like measles, back in the day."

The comedian Louis CK does a brilliant bit known as "Of Course . . . But Maybe," and although he didn't actually perform it until 2013 (first broadcast on April 13, in fact, exactly four years to the day after the upcoming well-check appointment we were so torn over), he managed to put into words something that I was pondering a lot back then.

"Of course," he begins, "*of course* children who have nut allergies should be protected. Of course! We have to segregate their food from nuts, have their medication available at all times, and anybody who manufactures or serves food needs to be aware of deadly nut allergies. Of course!"

Then the sideways grin appears. "But maybe," he simpers, the audience already laughing in anticipation of the punch line, *"maybe . . . if* touching a nut kills you, you're supposed to die."

Callous though it may seem, there is value in thinning the herd, and that fact is not lost on me just because I have a personal stake in the herd. (As does Louis, who quickly admits he has a nephew with a severe nut allergy.) Saving every child from every mortal disease is good for the individual, but it is decidedly bad for the population as a whole. From an objective, biological standpoint, those with weak immune systems should be removed from the genetic pool or else their bad genes will only be passed on and amplified over the generations.

Perhaps it was the case that I, or my parents, or even my grandparents, should have died from measles, or polio, or diphtheria, but modern medicine had allowed us to pass on our weaker immune systems when nature would have wisely weeded us out. Perhaps the same was true of one or more of Andrew's relatives, and as we combined weak with weak, generation over generation, we were fast approaching the breaking point of our brittle evolutionary branch. Nature always wins in the end, and maybe our earlier attempts to thwart it meant only that our descendants would now be prevented from procreating by developmental impairment instead of death.

However, evolution is a complex thing. A trait that is valuable today might be a liability tomorrow, and a trait that seems universally unhelpful might nonetheless be naturally paired with another trait that is superior. The classic example is sickle-cell anemia. Although this disease confers many unpleasant symptoms, often leading to an early death, it also happens to protect against malaria and thus surprisingly leads to greater survival in Africa, where malaria kills hundreds of thousands each year.

As a child I was nearsighted enough to qualify as legally blind; that is, I was unable to identify even the large E at the top of the vision chart. In ancient days I would have been useless to the tribe and probably would have walked off a cliff or stepped on a venomous snake long before escaping adolescence. Yet I'd like to believe that my other contributions to society as a glasses-wearing adult have made my survival today worthwhile and atoned for my parents' evolutionary sin of passing on such bad genes.

That same collection of genes also gave me supernaturally healthy teeth, for example. I know for a fact that I did not brush my teeth once between the ages of six through nine because, like Paul, I found the sensation to be extremely unpleasant. I simply wet the toothbrush in the sink and claimed I'd done it, every single night. Even after getting caught and earning myself closer supervision, I still didn't brush consistently until I was in my teens. I don't recall ever seeing a dentist until I started orthodontic treatment in middle school, and even now I only bother to go once every few years. Yet by some genetic miracle, I have never had even a hint of a cavity. Dental hygienists, when I actually go visit them, always rave about what a "great flosser" I must be, and I try not to smirk.

In the tribe, some companion with weaker teeth might have died from malnutrition while I chomped happily away on that tough mammoth meat. Maybe blurry food wasn't as bad as food you couldn't eat at all. So who was I to say that a weak immune system was a bigger negative than some of the other positive traits our genetics had to offer? In fact, what if humans' ability to compensate for each other—my friend spotting the mammoth with her keen eyes and I pulverizing the meat for her to gnaw on with toothless gums—was what made us collectively superior to other species? Maybe my faulty genes deserved preservation simply because protecting the weak was a superior behavioral trait for other humans to cultivate in themselves.

Like all philosophical musings, however, none of this bore any real relevance. Eugenicists might argue that I and my descendants had a moral imperative not to procreate, and they might even be right. But that didn't sanction the suffering of living children. Our only moral imperative here and now was to prevent triggering Marie's disease as best we could, even if it meant she might pass that time bomb on to her own children someday. That would be her choice to make, not ours.

The question of whether vaccinating her was "best for society" was similarly irrelevant to us, because such big-picture arguments can always be expanded even further until they are logically moot. On one level, giving her a shot regardless of the personal risk might be viewed as better for herd immunity, but zoom even further out, and one could argue that our socially irresponsible instincts needed to be weeded out of the herd in the long run anyway—assuming they actually were a bad thing to begin with—and thus, we should be encouraged to follow our conscience, whichever way it might point. Those of us with individualist tendencies ought to embrace that path and let nature judge which attitude was fittest. The final, unassailable response to both herd-protecting and herd-thinning arguments was that the system already accounted for us, no matter what we did. If we made a bad choice, the consequences would ensure that those behaviors stopped with us. Conversely, if we did manage to keep Marie's hypothetical disease under wraps—or if we recovered Paul to the point that he could marry and have children after all—then our very ability to do that deserved, by definition, to be passed on. Our sickle-cell individualism could be outweighed by our antimalarial determination, intelligence, and self-discipline—and if it *could* be, then it *should* be.

The choices were complicated yet surprisingly simple: give the shots now, later, or not at all. All three had risks, and we were guessing blindly about which risk might be larger than the next for our daughter's particular genetic situation. The more we studied it, though, the more we began to believe that the most dangerous option might actually be "later."

Babies are born with a clean slate, having no targeted antibodies since they've never had any diseases. They ingest antibodies through their mothers' breast milk, thus borrowing her immune system until their own has had time to build up its library of disease-fighting blueprints. As long as the baby contracts something that the mother has already survived, her breast milk will wage the bulk of the war against it in most cases.

However, the mother's antibodies are good only for the time they're passing through. The immunity they give is not permanent, and ultimately, the baby will still need to be exposed to the actual disease in order to create her own regenerating antibodies. I was breast-feeding Marie still, but I wouldn't be forever. If she got the shot now, we reasoned, perhaps my antibodies would diminish the risk, help prevent any live measles from taking up residence in her intestines, and she would walk away with immunity, safe from later exposure. If we gave it later, the shot would still carry the same risk—whatever un-definable quantity that was—but without the benefit of my protection.

Ultimately, we decided that we would give the MMR now, while she was still heavily breast-feeding, and delay the varicella until a later time, if at all. There was less data on the risks of chicken pox in autistic children, and at that time no studies had confirmed the presence or ab-sence of a live varicella strain taking up residence in any of them. That would be a question for another day.

Our moderate, considered, risk-balanced decision failed to take into account one critical fact, however. I, Marie's surrogate immune system for the purposes of this decision, had not actually contracted and survived measles. I'd gotten the shot as a child, just like everyone else my age, and now, a quarter of a century later, it was questionable whether I still possessed any antibodies to measles at all.

Chapter 23

To Be Served Concurrently

So on April 13, 2009, two days after Marie's first birthday, we went to Dr. Felix's office for the appointment. We had last been there in January, a couple of days before Paul had been diagnosed by Melanie.

As she ran through her basic examination of Marie's vitals, Dr. Felix kept her eyes mostly on Paul, who was happily, if somewhat loudly, entertaining himself.

"So how are things going with the sensory integration therapy?" she asked.

"It's okay," I said.

"Who is the therapist you're seeing again?"

"Melanie."

"Ah, yes, Melanie. She's wonderful." (I can hear the speech therapists now: "Let's work on increasing the number of adjectives she can use to describe us. . . . ") Dr. Felix smiled encouragingly. "I'm so glad to hear it's helping."

"Well, actually," I began, a little irritated at her assumption, "what really made a difference was when we put him on the GFCF diet."

"The what?"

"We took him off all gluten and dairy."

"I see," she said. "And who ordered that?"

"I'm sorry?"

"What physician told you to do that?"

"No one. I just read about it online. We figured it couldn't hurt him, so why not try it?"

"Okay." She nodded. "So you just did this on your own, then."

"Yes," I said.

There was a long pause, and she seemed to be done with the subject, but I was not. "It made a huge difference," I reiterated. "He started saying all these new things. . . . "

"Mm-hmm." She nodded, continuing with Marie's paperwork. "But he was verbal before, wasn't he?"

"Yeah, but not like this," I said.

"Well, you know, we do worry about calcium intake, so I would make sure he's on a really good calcium supplement if he's not drinking any milk."

I told her we would look into it, although I was not really convinced that calcium was any more important than all the other vitamins and minerals that were seriously lacking from most toddlers' diets. He got his calcium from green vegetables, just like the cows got it in the first place. Did she grill all the other mothers about where their milk-drinking children got their vitamin A, or vitamin C, or vitamin B12? As a former member of that group, I knew she did not.

"So what shots are we doing today?" she asked.

I explained our plan to delay the varicella shot, which she seemed content with as long as we were still getting at least one immunization that day. She wrapped up the appointment, and a few minutes later the nurse came in with the injection kit.

I was nervous, feeling that we'd made the best choice we could under the circumstances but still tempted to opt for a later risk, regardless of the relative magnitude. My arm twitched, and I almost reached out and stopped the nurse, but instead I brought my hand to my face to steady it.

I have to know, came the thought to my mind. Now, just what the hell did that mean? I wasn't running an experiment; I was doing what we'd agreed was the safest choice. Wasn't I?

More thoughts were racing unbidden to the surface now, and I saw in my mind an image of Marie banging her head against the wall, lost in a self-injurious haze. The fingers I'd brought to my lips formed a fist and pressed hard against my mouth to keep me from yelling out at the nurse to stop what she was doing. I couldn't explain why, but I was suddenly terrified.

The moment the needle slipped into my daughter's thigh, I heard a booming in my ears like a burst of blood against the eardrum from a single, explosive heartbeat.

It's done—now everything changes was the last intrusive thought to echo through my brain before I shook free of it all. I took a deep breath and gathered up my crying daughter with the little cartoon Band-Aid on her leg.

That afternoon she developed a moderate but persistent fever and slept most of the day.

Two days later, just as the fever was finally starting to go down, a rash of red spots appeared on her neck.

Before the neck spots disappeared, she developed general cold symptoms with lots of thick, opaque mucus.

On the fourth day of snot bombing, April 22, I opened her diaper to reveal emerald-green diarrhea.

This was what Paul's poop had looked like since he was an infant.

In retrospect, that was when I really knew, staring at that first horrific diaper. I had broken my baby girl. Yet still, a part of me resisted. She was babbling much less over the past week, admittedly, but she was also markedly ill. Perhaps when the cold cleared up, she'd be fine.

I added some hefty probiotics to her daily multivitamin, but it made no difference. After another week the cold symptoms finally cleared, but the diarrhea remained. A few days after that she broke out in hives all over, from her scalp to her toes.

Marie's first notebook, laid out in vertical columns like her brother's and filled with the same scrawled yet obsessively detailed data, officially began on May 2, the day the hives first appeared, with additional notes about her symptoms going all the way back to the MMR on the 13th. It was time for me to accept that I was now treating two children with autism.

Marie continued to ride a roller coaster of multiple symptoms over the next five months. Sometimes the stools would seem to be improving a little, but at the same time she'd develop another case of hives, or her face would turn into a red faucet of snot and watering eyes for another week and a half. One day she'd have half a dozen explosive green diapers, then the next she'd be constipated with tiny pellets of rabbit poop.

Her cognition had a summer pass to the same unpredictable theme park. On May 26 I wrote in her notebook that she was distinctly avoiding eye contact with me, but on June 3 there is a note that she suddenly used the word "Mama" to encourage me to move a toy car and even looked at my face expectantly until I did it.

Just four days after that, however, I described an almost identical account of the terrifying vision I'd had in the pediatrician's office. "Banging head into wall?! Dragging head during multiple tantrums."

On June 11 she was "very talkative after nap"; then, on the 12th, she was "avoiding eye contact, not responding to name." One month later saw her "frozen with hands over her ears for two-plus minutes, avoided Andrew's eyes when he tried to snap her out of it," but then on July 16 she was "pointing at items in book" and making grunts as if naming them.

It was not a straight fall off a cliff, but the upticks were smaller than the drops, and the general trend was always down. Even now I can't say for sure what multiple causative factors may have been at play over those entire five months. What I can say with absolute, documented certainty is that the last time she was healthy, the last time she'd spent a single day without a rash, or a fever, or diarrhea, or thick mucus—and most commonly, a combination of those and more—was the morning before she had received the MMR.

When Marie was a baby I used to whisper all sorts of things as I rocked her at night, knowing she couldn't understand but hoping that some of it might seep through as my voice soothed her to sleep. During

225

the three-month window after Paul's diagnosis but before Marie's regression, I would secretly confess to her the difficulty of the job ahead.

"You're going to have to be patient," I whispered. "You're going to have to help him. Sometimes you'll have to be the big sister even though he's older. It won't be fun, and it won't be fair, but I know you can do it. We'll all get there together."

As her condition worsened, however, I was reduced to whispering just one thing, night after night.

"I'm sorry, baby girl. I'm so sorry."

By September her stools were dark green mush all the time, and she began regularly waking up crying in the middle of the night. Meaningful language and interaction were gone, and a thickly slurred "ma" was now the only babbling syllable she had left. We'd hear it once a day if we were lucky, but I clung stubbornly to it, setting my teeth against my maternal comforting instincts and instead putting up the therapist wall.

The one and only thing Marie expressed any desire for anymore was to be held, just held for hours on end, which meant it was my only negotiating chip. When she came to me, dully burying her face in my legs now instead of reaching out to be picked up, I refused to comply until she uttered that noise.

"This little baby wants her mommy," I recited from her old favorite book.

Her line, the one she used to happily deliver along with all the other words revealed under the flaps on each page, was "Mama!" Now she no longer wanted to read the book at all; she would just stay fixated on that one page, opening and closing the flap again and again.

She would stay silent at first, hiding her face from me, but by now I had plenty of experience at outstubborning her brother.

"This little baby wants her mommy," I would say again, with the exact same inflection. It wouldn't do any good to emphasize particular words or to raise the pitch at the end in the classic "I'm *waiting*" sound that all mothers instinctively know how to make, because changing the tone might as well change the entire meaning for a child on the spectrum. To drive home the cause and effect, it had to be the exact same every time.

"This little baby wants her mommy," I'd repeat; then I would form my lips into the M-shape and give the barest hint of her next line. Not a prompting "muh" but an "m—" cut off abruptly as if my vocal cords had stopped working. The actual first part of the word, not the way you would imagine the first part of the word if you already understood that words were made up of separate sounds, and that if two human beings were interacting, one human might try to help the other with a clue. For the purposes of therapy, I was not a human; I was a machine that gave one input, expected one output, and could not perform any other way.

I knew she knew the line. The memories were in there, even if she was no longer sharing them. "This little baby wants her mommy. M—"

Interminable pause. Longer than you thought it should be, because you never knew what speed the gears might be turning in there.

"This little baby wants her mommy. M—"

If ABA had a motto, it would be *We can do this all day*.

"This little baby wants her mommy. M—"

"Ma," Marie would finally sigh softly into my shins, and I would gasp with overacted joy and swing her into my arms.

"Mama! This little baby wants her mommy. Mama!"

She would smile, and sometimes even laugh, before burying her face in my neck. Then, a few hours later, we'd do the whole scene over again, her refusal to speak butting up against my refusal to pick her up until she caved. It took months, but persistence paid off, and finally, she began saying it without prompting when she first arrived at my legs. Saying "ma" or sometimes even the full "mama" to be picked up is the one and only word Marie never lost. She never became truly, completely nonverbal, thanks to that dopey board book with the flaps.

We lost pretty much everything else, though.

"God, I can't even imagine dealing with two," said a friend from one of my message boards who was *blessed* with only one gift of this nature.

"It's not so bad," I lied. "One of them's always making progress."

"Doesn't that mean one of them is always doing worse, too?" she asked doubtfully.

I shrugged and changed the subject.

I tell my children's stories separately here because it always felt like I was living two lives simultaneously. When one child had a big breakthrough, the other would inevitably be in the middle of a regression. If I'd allowed the fear and frustration of one story to stain the joy of the other, I'd never feel any hope at all. You can mix ice cream with your spinach, but it won't really make the spinach taste better; it just ruins the ice cream. So I mentally walled them off from each other. I was two mothers, with one child each. In this way I could think about whichever one was making progress and be happy, and only later unpack those worrisome thoughts about the second child and release the depression as needed.

Because of this dual life I often have to stop and compare dates in order to know exactly what the two parts of my brain were doing at any given time. The memories are separate. While Marie was slowly but surely falling apart, for example, Paul was improving by leaps and bounds on his new GFCF diet. It was exciting to see, and hard to reconcile the fact that the diet was doing little to nothing for his sister. Her stools were still as bad as his had been before starting the diet. There were a few occasions when she, too, was exposed to gluten by accident, yet the only reaction we saw was a weeklong skin rash on top of all her other symptoms, no change in speech or cognition whatsoever. Certainly nothing like the obvious, immediate behavioral reactions that Paul had.

Paul's mother was confident, defiant, taking on the status quo and succeeding. Marie's mother was guilty, frustrated, impotent, and completely terrified about the future. Marie's mother was achingly jealous of her doppelgänger, while Paul's mother in turn couldn't stomach the implication that recovery might be all down to luck after all. It's no wonder I had to keep the two of them apart. They resented the hell out of each other.

Of course it felt a lot better to be Paul's mother, at least right now, so I spent more and more time in that headspace as the months wore on and often found myself considering Marie as if she were someone else's child. It wasn't Paul's mother's fault for giving her that shot; that had been someone else. She could examine the symptoms dispassionately and research things objectively without having to really care if she succeeded because it wasn't her kid. Marie's mother was deeply depressed and producing no results; only Paul's mother was shielded from despair. If there were a way to turn Marie's story into Paul's story, only Paul's mother would know how to do it.

Generally speaking, the later the regression, the more severe a case of autism is likely to be. The worst cases are often those who were neurotypical all the way up to eighteen months. Having begun her regression at twelve months, Marie was clearly more severe than her brother, who'd had his disease triggered very early and always had plenty of language and good eye contact. Yet I still believed that, at the core, they suffered from the same disease. He was slipping and scrabbling for a foothold just below the edge of the pit, while she was so far down in the darkness that we couldn't even see her, but the nature of the rope was sufficient. We only needed to modify its length.

In fact, it's fair to say that Paul saved his sister in this regard. Our experiences with him so deeply convinced me that autism was an immunological, metabolic disease that we pursued biomedical treatments with Marie long past the point where a rational person, having only Marie as evidence, would have dismissed them as a failure. If dietary restrictions weren't doing anything for her, I thought, it must only be because we hadn't pushed it hard enough yet. Her gut was part of this; Paul had proved that. She just needed something more drastic.

And so it was that, as the autumn of 2009 approached and we considered putting Paul on the elemental diet for his ever-increasing food allergies, we took it as a given that Marie would do the formula, too. Her allergy tests didn't show even a fifth of his, but for all we knew she was still heading downward and would get there before long if we didn't step in now. If there was a chance we were ever going to have to do this for her, we might as well get it over with. She was practically still a baby anyway, and giving an eighteen-month-old formula wasn't unheard of in the real world. We knew she wouldn't fight it because she almost never bothered to fight anything. As long as I held her and let her bury her face in my neck for hours on end, she'd drink it.

And if we didn't need to plan out a long holiday weekend battle to get her started, well, there was no reason not to jump in as soon as we had insurance approval. So in late October, a whole month before Paul's transition, she stopped all food and began drinking Elecare.

Again, nothing changed. There was maybe a small increase in babbling for the first couple of weeks, but then she lost it again and continued sliding downward, even as Paul joined her on the formula and shocked us all with his newfound calmness and cognitive control. We started to see more ear covering from her, and more stereotyped behaviors. She began compulsively lining up her toys, except her muscle tone was so low that she would place them only as far as she could reach from a slumped sitting position, so they always ended up in an arc around her, following the radius of her arm. Then she would just sit and stare at them for as long as we would let her, a tamed giant on display for an amphitheater of plastic villagers.

"Why is she not in speech therapy?" my mother asked me just after Christmas.

I shrugged sullenly. "I dunno. I mean, we know it's medical, right? We've just been focusing everything we have on that, because that's clearly the way out of this."

Marie had officially become a patient at Thoughtful House just a couple of weeks after Paul's first appointment with Lucas, when he had noticed her wandering aimlessly around his office and asked outright if she'd ever been evaluated. I admitted that we'd seen some regressions since April, and he asked how old she was now. We had a silent moment of acknowledgment over the implied start date of her health problems.

"Well, let's get her in here," Lucas said. "No point in waiting for her to hit rock bottom. When you do the intake, tell them I said she's a sibling and to fast-track her. You can skip all the preliminary stuff."

Marie's initial lab work showed a lot of the same general metabolic issues that Paul's had, and we'd started her on a handful of supplements, some overlapping with Paul's recommendations and some unique to her situation. So far they might as well have been placebos. With Paul, the slightest change in his regimen was obvious, whether positive or negative. One dose of the wrong thing, and he went crazy within the hour; one dose of the right thing, and he was doing shocking mental gymnastics. Yet Marie just hung in limbo, unaffected by, and uninterested in, anything we did.

We just hadn't found her *thing* yet, I kept telling myself, the key that would give her that first big jump down the right path.

"She could do both," my mother said pointedly. "Trying everything means trying everything, doesn't it?"

She was right, of course. Yet somehow I couldn't bring myself to invest in therapy, either financially or emotionally, because I honestly didn't believe it would matter in the long run. My experience with therapy so far placed its effectiveness somewhere between a crude Band-Aid and an assertion that Mommy's kiss could make it all better. When we'd unlocked Paul's first major medical problem, he'd instantly begun wearing long sleeves without complaint, something that three months of sensory integration therapy hadn't come close to achieving. True, he was benefiting from some of the behavioral techniques used first by Melanie and then in PPCD, but Marie didn't need that kind of authoritarian wrangling. She'd listlessly go wherever you put her and never tried to run anywhere, let alone "away." Even our speech therapist from ECI had done nothing but encourage us to try dietary changes. If we couldn't get her back with research and empirical evidence, then I knew we wouldn't be getting her back at all. Therapy meant giving up.

In fact, starting Marie in therapy might turn out to be a detriment to my larger purpose, even worse than a meaningless gesture. I dreamed of a future where I could say, "I recovered my daughter without any therapy at all." Not many parents started treatment as early and as aggressively as we had with her, and we had a rare opportunity to present her to the world as an undeniable bulwark of biomedical effectiveness. Paul's story was already tainted to some degree with a commingling of interventions, and part of me believed I should try to keep Marie's tale pristine, for the greater good.

Nonetheless, my mother's accusation that we weren't doing everything we could stung badly. It was around this time that my father first suggested that, if we did recover Paul, the world would claim he'd never had autism to begin with.

"Good," I'd said, surprised by my own candor. "As long as they get the chance to say that, I don't care."

Was that really true? If so, then I needed to let go of my ego and recover my daughter in whatever way worked, using every tool available to me. The only thing that mattered was her recovery, not how people thought she'd gotten there. She was more important than my crusade.

Unfortunately, my continued ambivalence on the usefulness of speech therapy would become a self-fulfilling prophecy. I hadn't yet learned the importance of personal recommendations and didn't truly believe there was any point to this exercise anyway, so when I finally broke down and began looking for a speech therapist, I ended up signing on with the first person who accepted our insurance. I never even considered whether an exceptional talent might be worth hunting down and paying more for, because my battle was about science, not art.

Giselle was sketchy from the start. I didn't realize it until we arrived at the given address for our first appointment, but this therapist worked out of her home while her children were at school. Her "therapy room" looked no different than any home office, with disheveled stacks of paperwork spread across the desk and various bookshelves, and she made it clear that parents were not invited to sit in on sessions. Instead I was to wait on her living room couch, often watching the Disney channel in the company of whichever child was home sick that day.

In addition, Giselle told me that she never scheduled a session for more than thirty minutes because she felt that kids wore out and anything longer would be ineffective. I could see how this might be true for high-energy, distractible children like Paul, but Marie took at least ten minutes to even warm up and consider paying attention to an activity. I asked several times if we could pay for longer sessions but was politely turned down. As I sat surrounded by clutter, dust bunnies, and a house telephone that rang almost constantly—usually left unanswered while she was in session, but a distraction nonetheless—I got the distinct impression that it was Giselle herself who couldn't manage a longer attention span.

It was Marie's mother who trudged through those weekly appointments, seeing zero progress but not knowing what else to do. Paul's mother would have abandoned any doctor like Giselle immediately, but she somehow never made an appearance at Giselle's house. Therapy was not her game, and she was too busy thinking about other things.

Finally, that brazen half of me did find our opening on the medical front, with the discovery that several pathogenic bacterial infections had set up shop in Marie's intestines over the winter. They had not been there during her first round of lab work at Thoughtful House, but she had regressed quite a bit since then, and it wasn't surprising to learn that her immune system had been unable to handle the typical array of winter exposures.

With her first dose of antibiotics, Marie finally had that "aha" moment we'd been desperately seeking. No real speech came out of it, but the instant abundance of babbling, eye contact, and general awareness was more than we'd seen in almost a year.

And just as quickly, it went away when the antibiotics stopped. We were now in the spring of 2010, when Paul was already a couple of months into his roller coaster of antibiotics for tonsillitis. This was unlucky for Marie because I was already lobbying Lucas with all my credibility to obtain increasing rounds of medicine for Paul, and he was understandably skeptical of my belief that my daughter suddenly needed more antibiotics as well.

It didn't help that at their respective nadirs, she was a meandering shadow while he was a violent psychopath. As so often happened, the unbearable nature of Paul's behaviors earned him the most attention and the most aggressive treatment. Lucas felt it would be a good idea to rerun Marie's stool tests before agreeing to more antibiotics for her, and I didn't argue. I was just relieved he'd agreed to refill her brother's pill bottle one more time.

The test showed that her infection was still ongoing, and another round of antibiotics showed the same burst of improvement, but again we lost ground after the medicine stopped. Lucas repeatedly increased the dose and strength of the antibiotics over the next six months, but because she was so young, and we were already pushing the limits of what was FDA-approved, he insisted on labs before each refill.

In retrospect, I think he did believe we were on the proper course but was protecting himself with documentation, just as Dr. Krigsman did. The continued retesting and prescribing without refills was a very slow cycle, and I didn't demand better for her. That was the Summer from Hell, and it belonged to Paul. I pinned him screaming to the bed every day, Marie watched in eerie calm, and that was all there was until the end of August.

Chapter 24

From the Ground Up

I EMERGED FROM the strep imprisonment weary but wiser. I began taking note every time a doctor or clinic received the prestigious WIGWAK approval on the message boards, because you never knew when I might need someone of their specialty someday. One glowing recommendation from an especially trusted friend was for a new therapy clinic that had opened over the summer, an announcement that I had apparently missed while we had been housebound. It was surprisingly close to our neighborhood, and my friend effused about how wonderful the therapists had been and how she had seen notable progress in just those few months.

I could practically feel Paul's mother smacking Marie's mother across the face and jabbing her finger accusingly at the laptop screen. And, against all her hopeless instincts, Marie's mother listened for once.

Building BLOCS (which stood for Behavior and Language Opportunities Through Communication and Social Skills) was run by a two-woman team. Brandy was a speech language pathologist, and Christie was a board-certified behavioral analyst. Together they ran both individual and group therapy, with each borrowing from the other's specialty—Brandy used behavioral techniques to teach speech, and Christie always tied a child's speech needs into her ABA programs.

The clinic had a comfortable waiting room, including a proper reception desk behind a sliding glass window. No dust bunnies. Beyond that was a large main room, outfitted similarly to Paul's PPCD classroom: lots of colorful room dividers, picture schedules, and therapy items that could pass as plain toys if you weren't familiar with the particular needs they served.

A handful of doors led off the main room into small office spaces, which had what I now understood to be the classic layout of a focused therapy room. Each contained two chairs, with the small one set in the corner so a fidgeting child could be casually blocked in by the therapist's legs, limiting both focus and movement. The toys were all placed on a high shelf so that the child had to ask, point, or otherwise engage help in order to receive them.

All of these rooms were empty when we arrived for an evaluation. Even administrative tasks at the reception desk were being shared by the two therapists between sessions. Everything was sparkling and new, just waiting to be used.

Christie and Brandy took turns guiding Marie around the room through several activities, testing her abilities and deficits in a number of ways and talking to me as they did so, just as Melanie had done during her first evaluation with Paul. Back then, however, only one of the adults in the room had really known what was going on. This time I was either seasoned or jaded, depending on how you wanted to look at it, and there would be no bombshells dropped. They did not have to pretend to be evaluating the possibility of autism or couch obvious symptoms in terms of "red flags." It was only a question of what kind of therapy, and how much, she might need.

The two women explained that they had just finished a successful run of social-skills camps for older children over the summer, which was the program my friend's son had attended, and now they were looking to kick off an early intervention program for preschool-aged children during their first operating school year. It would be somewhat like PPCD, but smaller, with only three to five kids rotating between shared social activities, and extensive one-on-one time for individual goals. They would hold the three-hour class every day in the mornings and reserve afternoon slots for private therapy and older children.

The idea was certainly tempting, but we couldn't come close to affording the special introductory price of $1,500 a month, even though it was less than one would normally pay for that amount of therapy. Besides, it would be impossible for me to pick her up at noon each day when the PPCD bus was dropping Paul off in our driveway at that same time. Andrew could be enlisted for lunchtime chauffeuring duties if necessary, but it would require him to take a larger chunk out of his day than he was supposed to, which would mean working later, leaving me with even more hours in the evening to take care of the kids alone when I was already exhausted . . . no, I told them, the program sounded fantastic, but there was no way we could pull it off.

We did, however, sign Marie up for an hour a week of speech therapy with Brandy and fired Giselle posthaste. Within just a few sessions Brandy had Marie making activity choices by touching her hand to one of two picture cues, and soon she was dragging echolalia out of her as well. One trick she used often in the beginning was to turn off all the lights in their windowless side room and use only a small flashlight to point at an object. When all other visual information was removed, Marie was more likely to repeat the name of the item being illuminated. This was the kind of creative insight that had been completely lacking before, and I fiercely berated myself for not finding a better therapist sooner. Marie made more progress in two months with Brandy than she'd made in almost a year with Giselle —infinitely more, in fact, since her progress with Giselle had been precisely none. It was still hard for me to accept that medical treatment seemed to be doing very little for Marie, but as long as she was making progress somehow, I could force myself to live with the conundrum.

One day in November Brandy and Christie came to me with news. They had just become in-network with our insurance, which was something they'd been working on since we'd started with them, and it turned out that we did have some coverage for behavioral therapy available to us as long as it was filed with specific codes. In addition, the calendar year was about to roll over, at which point we would be granted a whole new batch of speech therapy visits. We were only covered for something like forty total visits per year, and we'd used all of those up with Giselle, but starting in January we could start filing again, as often as twice a week.

I nodded in slow consideration. "So you're thinking, bump it up to two hours a week with Brandy and add an hour a week with Christie?" I nervously began adding up the co-pays in my head and comparing them to what we were currently paying out-of-pocket for the noncovered speech appointments.

"Actually," Brandy said, glancing over at Christie, "we were thinking about the early intervention program again. You know, we've had a surprisingly tough time getting it going, and mostly it seems to be because no one wants to be the very first one to sign up."

"We've had lots of families who are interested," agreed Christie, "but it's like Brandy said, they all want to join an existing class. No one wants to be the only kid in here for a couple of days."

"We actually have two families right now, ready to join, but they both really want a third child to be in the class. And we were thinking, you know, Marie would just be the perfect choice."

"Oh," I said.

Christie continued quickly, "Because there's going to be so much one-on-one time within the program, we can just make sure on our end that she does that time with Brandy in particular, and bill it as a speech appointment just like we're doing now. Then the one-on-one time with me can be billed under that behavioral coverage we were talking about, and . . . " She looked at Brandy, then took a breath. "Basically, we'll get everything we can from insurance, and we're prepared to discount the rest to a level that you guys can pay."

I was silent.

"You'll probably want some time to think about it," Brandy said.

"No, no," I said, shaking free of my stupor. "I'm just . . . processing."

"So you think you're maybe on board with it?"

"Oh, my God, yes—we are totally, totally on board with it," I said. "I'm just kind of blown away. Thank you. Thank you so much."

They grinned.

"No, thank you," Brandy said. "We've been trying so hard, for so long, to get this class off the ground. We really need a third kid. And it was always part of our plan when we started this business—we never wanted to treat just the kids who had lots of money."

Of course the irony was that if we hadn't already had one child with autism, we probably could have afforded the full tuition, with the help of insurance. It would have been tight, as it is for any autism family, but we could have managed our debt in the same ways we were already doing, with all the benefits going towards Marie. With two, though, we were in the hole before she even got started and now found ourselves in the horrible position of trying to decide not just which treatment was the better investment, but which child was. It was battlefield triage, where wounds that might be treatable under other circumstances were written off because too many others would die in the meantime. The nasty but necessary question was: Who was going to get the most out of our limited funds? What if Paul were gaining five steps from a moderately expensive supplement, but Marie would gain only one, or less, from an equally expensive amount of therapy? Paul's two surgeries had cost us thousands of dollars each, but if he hadn't gotten them, Marie would have continued to suffer collateral emotional damage that might have canceled out any benefit she would have received from those funds anyway. There was simply no way to make it fair, for them or for us, but we couldn't pretend that the decisions didn't have to be made.

At this point, however, our budget for antibiotics and ENT appointments had just dropped dramatically, and Paul's teacher had just delivered the news that he was on a path to make it to kindergarten. Clearly, it was time. Marie had languished long enough, and she deserved our full attention.

We talked numbers, and I was surprised to see just how much insurance was going to take care of, now that we knew about the behavioral coverage. We'd be burning through our speech appointments twice as fast as before, but Marie would be eligible for PPCD when she turned three in April, so the whole situation would change then anyway. For the kind of opportunity she was being offered, it was worth it. Between credit cards, some help from my mom, and pruning back a few of Paul's supplements now that he was doing so much better, we could make it work.

My driving problem was solved by moving the class thirty minutes earlier, which was good for them anyway because it meant they could now start trying to fill a second class in the afternoon.

"So, when does it start?" I asked, still trying to fully grasp all the ways this was going to affect our daily schedule.

"Tomorrow morning," Brandy told me. "The other families are just waiting on the call that we have a third child lined up. We're ready to go."

So Marie became one of the inaugural members of the early intervention class at Building BLOCS. Brandy and Christie's hopes proved accurate as a fourth and fifth child quickly joined after that; then some split off to form the afternoon program, and soon it was full as well. Today the clinic has remodeled to add more classrooms, hired several additional therapists, and serves around two dozen active clients, not counting the many who have graduated from the program.

Marie's progress in individual therapy had been steady but slow. In the group, however, she began rapidly learning skills that had eluded her for over a year, simply by having the opportunity to watch a therapist teach another child how to do it. Here again was the lesson that my children were complete opposites. Paul both wanted and needed undivided attention and praise in order to learn a task, but for Marie, it seemed that the pressure of simple interaction had been too overwhelming in itself. If you focused attention on her, she would stay in a nearly permanent state of shutdown, but once she was given the chance to sit at a distance and watch something that wasn't directed at her, she could follow behind and complete the same task.

Armed with this knowledge, I began making an effort to conspicuously teach Paul things in front of her, even if they were things he already knew how to do. I also began to put every command in terms of her brother.

"Paul, put your shoes on."

"But—"

"Marie, copy Paul," I continued smoothly, pointing at Paul's already-covered feet and not looking at her. It was critical that I resist the urge to turn and check, because even a glance could shut her down, let alone forced eye contact. But after only a few tries Marie began responding, not only with shoes but with other tasks as well. Christie was only lukewarm on my method because it wasn't sustainable in the long run, but I was convinced it was a baby step on the right path.

One of the biggest rewards was that Marie effectively potty-trained herself at the same time that we finally won that battle with Paul, even though she was only two and a half compared to his four and a half. Though she was still mostly nonverbal and prone to shutting down at the slightest pressure, I clung to this one achievement as evidence that she wasn't necessarily so much worse off than Paul had been at her age. Her deficits were just different, I tried telling myself, not worse.

I didn't really believe it.

Others did, however. One friend in my group of biomedical moms had a pair of children who were shockingly similar to mine. Her son had been diagnosed first, with the daughter's diagnosis coming just six months later once they'd learned what to look for. Her son was echolalic and highly emotional, while her daughter had been nonverbal and passive. And though it had appeared for a long time that she was farther behind and not responding as well to biomedical therapies as her brother was, she had suddenly begun blossoming within the right therapy environment and eventually surpassed him, to the point of full recovery. In fact, my friend admitted, her daughter, now seven, did not actually know that she'd ever had a diagnosis. All she knew was that her older brother had mild autism, and she had GI disease.

"I think it'll be the same with yours," she said, crossing her arms as if the matter were already settled. "Lilah was just like Marie. We were so sure she was the severe one, but she came through. I really think it's because we started so early, you know, because of Patrick. We didn't see the progress at first, but it was there. Like she had to do all her developing internally before she could show it to us, you know? It's a girl thing. I'm telling you right now, Marie's going to be the one to recover."

"We'll see," I said. I was unwilling to say "I hope so," because living out her scenario meant that Paul wouldn't recover, and I wasn't interested in the smaller lump-sum payout. It didn't matter anyway, since a common sense comparison of my kids told me she was dead wrong. At Marie's age Paul had been making eye contact and parroting words constantly, and he hadn't even been diagnosed yet.

Yet Marie's glacial pace was remarkably consistent. They would introduce a goal in therapy, she'd take a week or two to learn it, and then they'd move on to the next one. Unlike her classmates, she never fought any particular goal very hard, and she rarely lost an old skill while learning a new one. Every fraction of a concept had to be taught, and she would never generalize a skill or make a creative leap on her own, but piece by piece they built, and no part of the tower ever crumbled. Then one day I realized she was outperforming children who had entered the class more advanced than she was—first by just one tiny increment, then two, but the distance widened each day.

I began to reform my thinking on the question of therapy versus medicine. It didn't have to be an either/or proposition, I concluded, but in fact ought to be a combination of both. It was like being in a horrible car accident that shattered your legs. Yes, you would unquestionably need physical therapy to learn to walk again—but if you didn't first get a doctor to set the bone, and sew up the gashes, and give you antibiotics for the infection that had made its way inside, then all the physical therapy in the world would not make you whole.

Without medical treatment for the underlying disease, behavioral therapists were trying to teach autistic children to walk on broken legs. A noble but flawed endeavor. Meanwhile, I had set Marie's legs in sturdy braces and expected her to get up and start running. Foolish and unreasonable. Now I finally understood that neither philosophy could overcome the problem on its own. You had to treat medically for the disease while using therapy to make up for the deficits the disease had caused. Marie was the only child in her class aggressively receiving both, so it didn't matter that she had started out so much lower than some of the other children. She was the one whose body was ready to make progress, whose bones weren't forever snapping again along misaligned ridges.

Chapter 25

District Policy

So when the time came to go see Dr. Krigsman, it was actually two children I scheduled, in back-to-back appointments, and I had to complete sixty preappointment lab tests rather than thirty. Then, after more than an hour of medical history, symptom documentation, and lab reviews for Paul, Dr. Krigsman and I spent another hour doing it all again for Marie.

"Excellent, excellent," he said when I explained that because of her brother, Marie had been gluten- and dairy-free even before her big regression. "That probably helped protect her to some degree. We'll see when we get in there," he said, referring to the pill-cam procedure, "but I'm thinking it won't be as bad as it could be."

"Really," I said flatly.

"Oh, yes," he said. "Look, outwardly these kids can be very different, even though inside it's the same lesions, the same fundamental disease. But I've been doing this a long time, and I can tell you, Marie's case is classic. Normal development, severe regression, loss of speech—all very standard stuff. She'll be easy. Paul is the one who is, I guess you could say, more diagnostically interesting."

He shuffled his papers sheepishly. "I mean, obviously, of course, interesting for me isn't necessarily great for you, but this is the thing that I do, so, you know, the more fascinating cases stick out. . . . "

"It's okay," I said with a grin. "I gotcha."

"I think he's going to be more complicated," he concluded with a nod, then gave a sly wag of his finger. "And Marie may surprise you. Like I said, we'll see when we get in there."

Meanwhile, Marie was nearly at her third birthday in April, which meant she could join Paul in Mrs. Allison's PPCD classroom. There would only be a six-week overlap before the school year ended, and then Paul would be headed off to kindergarten in the fall, but he was nonetheless very excited to have his favorite person in the world join him at school. As the date approached, however, Mrs. Allison informed me that her class was at maximum capacity.

"There will definitely be spots open in August," she said.

"I know; one of them is Paul's," I reminded her.

"Oh, that's true! So, yeah, she'll have priority then, but for the rest of this year they would have to bus her to the next-closest school with space, which I think would be Elm Park, or maybe Gibson. They were both close to full, last I heard, so I'm not sure."

When Paul had started, there had been plenty of space, and some of the classes Mrs. Allison was referring to hadn't even existed, but the number of children enrolled in special education programs had climbed at a monumental rate even in those two years. In fact, our school district later released an official report that between 2005 and 2009, the number of children in special education classrooms increased a staggering 400 percent. That's five times as many children in a span of just four years. What's more, this count did not include mildly affected children receiving weekly speech therapy or dyslexia services but only those being taught a modified curriculum in a self-contained classroom. Many have argued that these children were merely a result of better and more frequent evaluations and that most of them would have been forced to survive in the regular classroom in decades past, but my experience was in fact the opposite. If anything, school districts were working harder and harder to disqualify students from special education classrooms, even when the placement was clearly warranted, because they simply couldn't bear the costs.

One friend of mine had an eight-year-old son who was nonverbal and slapped himself in the head virtually nonstop. Yet he had been placed in a mainstream classroom with no additional help because he was rarely disruptive, and if you put a worksheet in front of him, he would usually fill it out with one hand while continuing to hit himself with the other. The school officials told my friend that as long as he could pass the written material, he was "on grade level," and thus they had fulfilled their duty to him.

This child was *not* counted in the 400 percent increase, so just imagine the children who were. And ask yourself if you, or anyone you knew in your entire school career, had a nonverbal, self-injuring child in any classroom you were ever in. Decades ago, that is a child who most certainly would have been in a special education classroom, but now he had been pushed out because of funding concerns. The increase is real, both in my neighborhood and nationwide, and it is not, in fact, smaller than it appears. It is larger.

"I'm not even going to worry about it, then," I told Mrs. Allison. "I want her in your class, not some random person I've never met. We'll just leave everything the way it is for the rest of this year and start her fresh on the first day of school."

I was happy with all the goals that Mrs. Allison had created for Marie's IEP, so when I strolled into the ARD meeting a few days after Marie's birthday, I was expecting no more than a pleasant chat with the staff members I'd already been working with for years and a quick rubber-stamping of forms. As quickly as such a convoluted and bureaucratic mess of forms can be stamped, anyway.

"Okay, um, I see you've put a different destination for her bus for next year," the ARD facilitator stammered. "That's, ah, that's . . . not a daycare."

"It's her therapy clinic," I explained. This was the semester that I had decided to go back to school and become a nurse practitioner, and the classes I needed to take in the fall would work only if Marie could travel from school to Building BLOCS without me. Most special education students rode the bus home after school, despite the fact that it was a neighborhood elementary with only a few transfers. State funding for transportation is based not on the number of vehicles or the distance traveled but on the number of students physically in the seats each day, so if there is even one child who requires a bus—and in special education, there always is—then it is in the school's financial interest to fill the rest of it with as many eligible students as they can. They don't care if you live across the street from the school; they practically beg you to let your special needs child ride the bus. Across the street is ideal, in fact, in order to minimize the fuel burned per tax dollar received. No doubt if the principal could play Sims with the neighborhood, she would line up all the special needs houses in one straight shot out from the parking lot.

"That's so wonderful that you have her in that program," the facilitator said, and everyone else nodded adoringly. Staff in ARD meetings are always fawning over what a joy it is to teach your child and how impressive their progress is even when they haven't made any. "Unfortunately," she said with a grimace, "it's the district's policy that we can only deliver a child to the home address, or to a day care to finish out the afternoon. We can't take them anywhere else."

"Why not?"

"It's the district's policy," she repeated, holding up her hands in a sitcom what-are-you-gonna-do kind of shrug.

"But it's closer than a lot of day cares," I pointed out, still confused. I had thought this would be an argument about the price of gas, if anything, and wasn't expecting to be denied on a technicality.

The facilitator just kept scrunching her face apologetically.

"Look," I said, "there's actually a day care, literally next door to the therapy clinic. You're saying you could take her there?"

"Sure!" she said, her pen poised to make the change on the form. "Will she be enrolled there over the summer?"

"No, she's not going there—I'm saying, it's the same distance; the therapists have the same liability insurance that a day care has to have. I don't understand the problem."

Mrs. Allison piped up diplomatically. "I think we just don't have the right people in this meeting. Katarina would be the one to make this sort of decision, don't you think?" She looked around the room for approval. "Why don't we just get everything else in place, sign off on everything except transportation, and we can have another ARD to deal with this when Katarina can come. She'll be the one who can answer your questions and make decisions at a district level."

I shrugged and agreed.

Later that day I got in touch with a friend who worked for the school district and asked her what was going on.

"It's about money," she told me. "Look at any decision a school makes, and it always comes back to the money."

That was true, I knew, but it didn't seem to be what was at play here. Was it?

"IDEA says that they have to provide everything the child needs," my friend continued. The Individuals with Disabilities Education Act was the sweeping special education reform law that had been passed in 2004, and all of a child's current educational rights could be traced back to that document. "If they take her to a therapy clinic, that could be seen in court as an admission that she 'needs' that therapy. Which means you as the parent could then demand they pay for it. There's been more than one case where families have sued their school districts for $100,000 in past therapy bills, and won. So they will not carry any child to any therapy, for any reason. It's pretty much the same everywhere in the state."

The uniformity of this sad policy was no consolation to me, but at least I now understood the angle I needed to pursue. At the next ARD meeting I would tell this Katarina person, point-blank and off the record, that I understood what they were really afraid of and that I would sign any document they wanted stating that the therapy wasn't necessary and waiving all rights to sue them for it. We'd had such a good relationship with everyone at the school so far, I felt sure that we could work something out.

Timing, in addition to naïveté, conspired against me. Instead of contacting a legal advocate and drawing up sample documents I'd be willing to sign, I spent the intervening month dealing with Dr. Krigsman's anesthesiologist, organizing a surprise plane trip to Minnesota, helping my crippled husband roll around the house, containing a child who was increasingly nutty the longer he was off his meds, and generally wishing I'd never spoken the poison words "malignant hyperthermia."

On top of everything, the school scheduled Marie's transportation ARD on the day immediately before the kids' simultaneous colonoscopies. As any experienced GI patient can tell you, this is not a pleasant day. For twenty-four hours before a scope procedure, you may not eat or drink anything except clear liquids. Once you're well and truly irritable, you then must consume a quart of laxatives and spend the rest of the afternoon and evening on the toilet until your insides are as empty and barren as your dignity.

Doing a full colonoscopy prep on two autistic children at the same time would be a punishment fit for criminals. And now they were telling me that halfway through this wretched day I would need to hop over to the elementary school for a significant legal discussion. I wasn't just unprepared; I had taken my game face and put it in an unmarked grave somewhere out in the desert.

Katarina, on the other hand—a name I can't help but spit with disgust, even to this day—was made of 100 percent pure extract of game face. Her job title was innocuously administrative, but in practice it consisted almost entirely of attending difficult ARD meetings. I learned, too late to do anything about it, that they brought her in only when it was time to brutally deny a parent who had gotten too uppity. She was a professional stonewaller, more like a lawyer than the therapist she had once started out as. When I mentioned her name among friends a few days beforehand, a swarm of groans and curses erupted down the length of the table.

"You won't win," one told me. "You might as well just cancel the ARD."

"Seriously, you don't even want to be in the room with this woman," another warned. "She's not just going to tell you no; she's going to infuriate you. She does this thing, where she goes into a speech about how 'as a mom' she understands. . . . "

"Oh, my God, she did that to me, too!" someone else cried.

"She does it to everyone. I completely went off at her, you know, because *she* certainly doesn't have any special needs kids. But you lose your cool, and she's won. She absolutely knows it will piss you off; that's why she does it."

I brushed off this unfair emotional judgement. *It's nothing personal*, I thought, *just business*. I was going to be appealing to her on a different level, offering to sign away my right to sue before she could pretend this was about something else. Surely this would engender a truce between us—not necessarily a friendly one, but a mutually beneficial arrangement.

Not so much.

I entered the ARD already exhausted, soaked with guilt for first starving my children all morning, then ignoring their desperate cries as Andrew held them back so I could slip out the door. Paul was angry, which I could handle, but Marie just wept endlessly, unable to understand my promises of when she would be allowed to eat again. For all she knew, it was never, and she had been refusing all comfort from me, the perpetrator of her torture. At the best of times she only needed me, never cared about me. Now I imagined I could see hatred in her eyes.

Katarina was already seated, a statue of smug alabaster dressed in a perfectly-tailored business suit that somehow made our cramped little conference room seem like an executive board meeting by her presence alone. She extended a limp hand as introductions were made, fingers forward as if I might kiss her rings.

As I had been warned, there was no discussion. This was simply a ceremony for the decision to be handed down, and the rest of the attendees were no more than legally necessary witnesses. After the initial greetings, no one except Katarina and I spoke during the entire meeting.

When I offered to sign away my right to sue, she shook her head in amusement as if I were a child negotiating a later bedtime.

When I suggested that Marie's disability prevented her from attending a regular day care, and thus their behavior looked an awful lot like discrimination to me, she requested documents showing that at least three daycare facilities had officially enrolled her and then kicked her out due to behaviors.

She gave only a pitying nod when I explained why I needed this, unmoved even by my tearful assertion that I had to get this degree so I could go back to work in order to afford these ridiculously expensive children. That was admittedly disingenuous, though it was true that we could always use the money. The tears were quite real, but I was crying only from the sum total of the day's frustrations, not because we were destined to be homeless. She didn't care, regardless.

"You know what I think would be a great option for you?" she said, placing her hand on the table for emphasis. "You and another parent could work out a carpool arrangement."

I narrowed my eyes. "That would be *two* fewer children on the PPCD bus. That costs you money. You're so afraid of me that you'd give up even more easy money from butts in the seats?"

She smiled wanly. "You know, as a mom, I get it. I know that you are the best advocate for your child. I, too, have had to advocate for my own daughter on her volleyball team. . . . "

Yes, as God is my witness, she actually compared autism to volleyball-team drama.

I didn't lose my temper, as my friends had told me I would. I was just too tired. As she began her speech, I put my head down in my hands and checked out. She kept right on talking, but I don't remember anything else she said until "Well! I think that we'll go ahead and wrap this up. Mrs. Noonan, I encourage you to pursue your legal options, if that's something you still wish to do."

School officials were supposed to be afraid of getting sued, and this one had just dared me to do it. I was foolish to think I'd ever had a chance.

"With the summer almost upon us," she noted pleasantly, "we won't be able to hold another ARD this year, but we can reconvene sometime in September."

Of course if the bus weren't taking Marie to Building BLOCS on the very first day of school, then the fight was over. Even if I had been willing to hire a disability rights lawyer, I was on a timeline, and Katarina wasn't. It would be nice if I'd had the money or energy to waste on setting a legal precedent for other children, but we'd been bereft of both for years now.

Instead of responding, I just stared at her with dead, unblinking eyes, still red-rimmed with tears. In my mind I was already back home, listening to my children wail and forcing them to sip electrolyte drinks. She took my silence as agreement and passed me the paper to sign.

"I hope you have a great rest of your afternoon," she said. "I am sorry we had to meet under these circumstances."

"Katarina," I said, "I'm sure you're a very nice person in all the areas of your life that don't require you to take a moral stand. But in this room your only job is to take away services from disabled children. The argument that 'someone has to do it' doesn't absolve you from the fact that you've allowed it to be you. So forgive me if I'm not impressed with your general character."

Just kidding—I didn't say any of that. You should know me better by now. That's the speech I came up with later that afternoon, the one that played through my head on a daily basis for months after this doomed confrontation, but right there in the moment, I caved as usual. Marie's mother silently ignored Katarina's proffered hand, out of broken indifference rather than spite, and gathered her things.

Suddenly Paul's mother muttered, softly but clearly, "It's okay. I'll recover my daughter without your help."

And in that moment, for the first time, I believed it. As awful as she was, Katarina had helped us after all. She had finally forced the yin and yang of Marie's mother and Paul's mother to merge into one proud creature. Contentedly defiant but neither afraid nor angry anymore. Well, maybe still angry at Katarina for a little while, but mostly just angry at myself for wasting my time. The unified me would simply do what needed to be done, and no condescending school official, or nervous anesthesiologist, or ignorant pediatrician would stand in my way. Not because I would knock them over but because I had finally come to the understanding that going around is always more efficient.

Over the next several months I stopped arguing with unconvinced parents about treatments for autism. I quit showing up at Dr. Felix's office for our annual in-your-face appointment because her opinion genuinely didn't matter to me anymore. I forgot about filming videos of Paul progress and posting them online. And shortly after that I tossed out my plans to get a nurse practitioner's license. I was no longer a warrior for anyone except my own children.

This overdue delineation of what *was* and *was not* my personal responsibility felt surprisingly similar to the beatific acceptance that many autism parents eventually reach, but rather than accepting my own lot, I was instead accepting the outside world for what it would choose to be. Other children might stay sick, doctors might stay ignorant, and that was not my problem. I would close my shell around my pearlescent core of impertinence and create a singular treasure, alone. Seeded by a lifelong belief that the rules didn't apply to me, it would now be polished to a shine by the lesson that the righteous don't have to convince anyone. If righteousness is truly there, it can speak for itself.

Chapter 26

The Nature of Love and Acceptance

THERE WAS AN added layer of complexity to our Scope Day, even beyond the pediatric and autistic natures of the patients. Each pill cam's wireless images were to be broadcast in a wide burst at a single frequency, without data encryption or multiple channels to choose from. All the receiver boxes made by the manufacturer were programmed to pick up that frequency, like radios that could tune to only one station. Thus, two patients with activated pill cams inside them had to stay at least eighty feet apart from each other, or else each one's receiver box might start picking up images from the other's intestines.

"That's ridiculous," Andrew complained. "Even Paul's walkie-talkies have multiple channels! We're not talking about cutting-edge technology here. Full duplex has been the norm since what, the '80s? They easily could have built multiple channels into the pill cams if they'd wanted to."

"I guess they couldn't imagine a scenario where two people in the same household would both be getting it done on the same day," I said with a shrug.

"Well, what about different patients in a hospital, with rooms close together? It's just bad product design, is what it is. Or what about interference? You have to work around a thousand other digital devices these days, and you never know what bands are going to be overcrowded. Our baby monitors have like fifteen channels! It is not unreasonable to expect a high-tech medical device to have two or three."

I heard several versions of this rant in the weeks leading up to the procedure, but reality stubbornly refused to alter at my husband's insistence. For eight hours after waking up from anesthesia, one of the children would not be able to come home.

The easy choice was Paul. During his two previous experiences with anesthesia he had been angry and disoriented at first, but after vomiting he'd been alert and relatively calm within an hour or two. Marie, on the other hand, had undergone anesthesia once for a dental procedure—with six cavities by the age of three, she'd clearly missed out on my glorious bicuspid genes—and she had been extremely groggy and irritable for the rest of the day. Her attitude would no doubt be worsened by this cumbersome receiver belt around her midsection. By now Paul could be made to understand the purpose and short-term nature of something unpleasant, such as the colonoscopy cleanout, or brushing his teeth, for that matter. He wouldn't enjoy the belt, but he'd wear it because we told him to. Marie still understood nothing, and every moment after waking would be spent crying and trying to remove this strange apparatus. In theory the belt could have remained somewhere within eighty feet of her and probably been fine, but I wasn't going to risk missing a single picture after all we'd gone through to get this done. She was going to wear it right up against her body like she was supposed to.

The unanimous advice from parents who had done this before was to cover the belt inside a one-piece pajama outfit and put it on backwards so she couldn't reach the zipper. I had a hard time finding one in her size, though. Three-year-old girls were supposed to be wearing Disney princess nightgowns, not baby onesies, and it had to be even a size larger than that if it were going to comfortably accommodate the box inside. There were plenty of ironic footie pajamas for large adolescents but nothing for the sincerely immature preschooler.

The largest one I could find on short notice still didn't fit her until I took a pair of scissors to the arms and legs. Add a buttoned flap in the back and give her a corncob pipe, and she could have passed for an Appalachian hillbilly. It felt strange to be mutilating a brand-new piece of clothing like that, but I told myself to think of it like a bridesmaid's dress. Sometimes you just have to buy something that you'll never wear again.

Marie had the first scope appointment of the day, so she and I awoke at 5:00 a.m. while Andrew and Paul got to sleep for another leisurely hour. Her already floppy muscle tone was even weaker than normal, being deprived of both food and sleep, and she rode listlessly in a stroller through the parking garage and up to the appropriate floor. We were just heading back to our prep room when the boys arrived to sign in, and Paul informed me that he'd "throwed up without any throw-up" in the car on the way there.

"He was retching," Andrew clarified.

"I'm sorry, sweetie."

"It's okay," Paul said. "But I'd really like a drink of water."

Andrew and I exchanged a look over this sentence, which was surprisingly conversational for him at the time. Once again I wistfully fantasized about using IV nutrition to eliminate eating entirely, and wondered if we'd taken him off the Elecare too soon.

Once Marie was asleep and her scope was under way, I went to join Paul in his prep room and got to witness the anesthesiologist's stifled reaction to Andrew's Frankenstein leg. Finally Dr. Krigsman returned to trade children with us.

"Everything looked good," he said.

"Good? Like . . . "

"Healthy and normal." He showed me the printed images and smiled. "This is exactly why we do the pill cam. If she had been given only the regular scope, they would have seen nothing, and some other doctor would have sent you home telling you it was all in your head. But it's not in your head; it's just up high in her small intestine. And we will see it."

Sure enough, the images downloaded a few days later proved that her white lesions and inflammation were there, although they were not as severe as Paul's, just as Dr. Krigsman had predicted. Her initial treatment plan was the same, and her outward reaction to the steroids was positive, although not nearly as impressive as Paul's. The tortoise and the hare, as always. While he made his last giant leap into Italy during this summer before kindergarten, then fell off the cliff again nine months later, Marie continued to plod relentlessly forward in only slightly larger increments.

It was during this time that Marie finally entered her terrible not-really-twos. Developmental specialists will tell you that even delayed children must go through this stage, regardless of when it actually happens or how long it lasts. Learning to identify one's own desires, fight to achieve them, and recognize which boundaries in life are immovable is a critical process of maturation that can't be avoided. As with everything else, she took longer getting there, but once she arrived she did it with unswerving diligence. When Marie threw a tantrum, she was not losing control of her emotions like her brother did. She was willfully punishing us for daring to countermand her. Tantrums were one of the few times she would look right at me, with her chubby expression as coldly threatening as she could make it. She would narrow her eyes and cock her head to one side as if to say, "See what you've made me do?"

Because of this, there is a photo in our family's digital collection that is charmingly titled *Second Day of School*.

Paul's first day as a real, mainstreamed kindergartener was supposed to be a huge celebration, the crowning achievement of everything we'd been fighting for. It was the flag on top of Everest, the flag on the damn moon! However, it was also Marie's first day of PPCD, and in an ironic turnabout, it went far worse for her than it had for him two years earlier.

My first unforgivable slight to her came at breakfast that morning, when Marie discovered that her sippy cups now had name stickers on them, as required by the PPCD classroom. She screamed and clawed at the hefty dishwasher-proof label instead of eating. That tantrum fed into a general refusal to get dressed, followed by an obsessive drawer-opening-and-closing routine, which was still in progress when the school bus arrived at our house. I barely managed to rush my one clothed child onto it, no camera at hand.

After another twenty minutes I finally had Marie calmed and ready to go, just in time to walk her to the front doors of the school myself like some kind of normal parent. The weather in Texas is still blisteringly hot in late August, but with overcast clouds and the sun barely risen, it was balmy that morning. A slight breeze urged the throng of excited children forward, all shrugging gleefully under oversized backpacks and calling out to friends not seen since before the eternity of summer. We casually strolled with the flow of the crowd, Marie's hand in mine.

Look at us, I thought, *just enjoying a run-of-the-mill life milestone like the rest of them. Or rather, look at how no one is actually looking at us!*

Even though Paul was a mainstreamed kindergartener, the special ed bus had robbed me of this particular experience with him, and I found my spirits lifting. Perhaps it was for the best that I'd ended up out on this sidewalk after all instead of back in bed the moment the bus had pulled away. The happiness of the crowd was impossible to resist.

Right as I began toying with the idea of getting a first-day-of-school photo of Marie after all, she came to the sudden realization that this wasn't an aimless neighborhood walk but a purposeful trip to a place she had neither vetted nor approved. She angrily dropped straight to her knees on the hard sidewalk, as she often did in those days to indicate refusal, and unexpectedly landed in a rain puddle from the night before.

With that my ten-minute respite was over and the screaming began anew. The stream of children and parents split awkwardly around us as she writhed on the sidewalk, furiously trying to strip off her wet clothes. I picked her up and continued towards the main doors, my face red with embarrassment if not exertion. These muscular arms had trained on a far more determined child, after all. By comparison Marie's kicks were barely more than wiggles.

The crossing guard chuckled at me. "Maybe leave baby sister at home next time, huh?"

"Special ed starts at three," I muttered back. Yet I knew the truth was that Marie didn't even look three. The comment we got most often from strangers was that she was "so big" because they looked at her soft, uncoordinated limbs and vaguely dazed expression and assumed she was a giant one-year-old, not a delayed three-year-old who was actually somewhat small for her age.

By the time I got her dropped off at her classroom, it had begun raining again. I made no attempt to stay dry as I trudged home, trying very hard to believe that this ruined day, this sudden role reversal of my children, was nonetheless a step in the right direction. Crying in the rain would be too cliché to bear, so I refused. Instead I resolutely pushed the wet strands of hair off my forehead and dove into my mental stew of research, mulling over the dichotomy between my children for the thousandth time.

Paul loved people, loved attention, loved the world. He opened himself to it, became completely overwhelmed and collapsed in shock, then imprudently opened himself to it once again. Yet as often as Marie threw herself on the floor screaming these days, she was just as likely to glare and retreat from any interaction, no matter how friendly. Somehow she had already mastered a teenager's disdain, not just ignoring but pointedly displaying her fundamental dislike for all of us, especially me. Andrew would sometimes threaten to let Mommy help her with a task if she didn't start cooperating, and that would always get her moving.

That last thought tickled a memory of a research study I'd read who knows when.

Much as we would like to believe that love is in the exclusive jurisdiction of the soul, the fact is that there are brain chemicals involved, which can be not only measured but synthesized. The hormone most responsible for what we experience as love is called oxytocin, sometimes nicknamed the "bonding" or "trust" hormone (not to be confused with the brand-name pain medication Oxycontin). Although its most dramatic effects can be seen in pregnant women, in whom oxytocin is responsible for triggering both labor and lactation, it is present at varying levels in all humans and has been shown to have a number of remarkable secondary effects.

When given a dose of oxytocin versus placebo, adult males in a committed relationship distance themselves from an attractive woman by an additional ten to fifteen centimeters and even approach photos of attractive women more slowly. Single males, on the other hand, are either unaffected or slightly more likely to approach the attractive stranger. Oxytocin encourages us to get into relationships and then stay in them.

In another study, adults of both genders recalled and shared more emotional details of past events when given oxytocin and were less able to recall the details of unpleasant events. This of course explains why, days or even hours after childbirth, many women think, "Sure, I'd do that again."

But most relevantly, adults diagnosed with autism had shown increased retention of speech, lower anxiety, improved mood, and an increased ability to recognize emotions in others after just one dose of an oxytocin nasal spray.

Paul needed no help in loving anyone, even strangers. But maybe Marie did? I asked Lucas about it, and he agreed it was certainly worth a try.

Within minutes of the first nasal spritz, Marie was laughing and bouncing joyfully in a way I hadn't seen since she was a baby. An hour after that she was screaming and flailing angrily on the floor, an about-face that continued unabated for the rest of the day.

I tried giving it more frequently, but short of dosing her every single hour, the ugly crash seemed inevitable. I shared all of this with Lucas and asked if there were a more sustained-release option available. He told me that pure oxytocin was destroyed in the gastrointestinal tract, which is why it was traditionally taken via nose spray or IV. However, a compounding pharmacy in Colorado had recently patented what it called a lipid-matrix method of delivery, which supposedly allowed the medication to pass safely into the lymphatic system, and from there into the blood stream, without exposing it to the destructive acids of the digestive system.

He sent them the prescription, and they shipped us the pills.

And finally, finally, came the second big "aha" moment my daughter ever achieved. The specially compounded oxytocin pills gave instant benefits and no crash. For the first time in two years Marie was happy, and everyone noticed it. Suddenly, she was cheerfully interacting with friends and teachers, at school and therapy alike. We had managed to arrange a carpool to Building BLOCS that autumn after all, and Marie began running up and earnestly hugging her classmate's father when he arrived. I didn't share that particular development with Andrew, however, because even with the medicine she still hugged the two of us only halfheartedly, and I saw no need to twist his knife to match mine. This was when I began to worry that my relationship with Marie had been permanently marred by what she'd seen during the Summer from Hell. But there was nothing to do except keep loving her and hope she came around.

At least she was talking to me more. Lots more, in fact. She went from indifferent to fully conversational in the span of just a few months. Paul's puzzle was a thousand tiny pieces that kept falling out of place, while Marie's was a handful of slabs that wanted only for the strength to heft them. Before long, in fact, she began to take the lessons she was learning in therapy and apply them to me as if she were the authority figure. One day, after I told her we didn't have time to go to the park, she raised her eyebrows firmly and held out two hands as if miming a choice.

"I want to go to the park," she repeated coolly. "You can say, 'Yes!' or 'Okay, let's go!' Which do you choose?"

Were it not for the sparkly headband and cartoon T-shirt, she could have passed for a behavioral therapist. I laughed uproariously at her gambit, and the professionally unperturbed look on her face melted into confusion. "What?" she asked, highly offended. My three-year-old teenager.

"What did I tell you?" Dr. Krigsman asked as I detailed her improvement during an appointment the following spring. "She surprised you, yeah?"

"Yeah," I admitted with a grin. It was hard to figure out when exactly it had happened, but in less than a year of GI medications and oxytocin, Marie had miraculously achieved the elusive designation of "better than Paul was at her age." Even with another year and a half to go, her new PPCD teacher was taking it as a given that she would be mainstreamed into a regular kindergarten classroom.

I did eventually come to appreciate our Second Day of School photo, and what it represented about our journey up to that point—a meaningful scar to add interest to the landscape. There is another photo, however, that I have never stopped hating, even though I displayed it on the mantel for years.

In this photo Marie is about two years old, and she is staring listlessly up at the sky as I hold her on my lap, smiling down at her. The smile appears completely genuine, and only I knew that it was not. As we played in the back yard that afternoon, Paul at the height of hopefulness and rapid improvement and Marie impassively stuck in the mud, I remember thinking as the camera pointed towards us that this would be an idealist depiction of maternal love. I would beam with an adoration that was in no way reciprocated and be a monument to grateful acceptance for the gift I'd been given. This was a photo of Marie's mother trying desperately to make Paul's mother shut the hell up, and by all outward appearances she had succeeded.

Only after I had unified my internal resolve, thanks to Katarina, could I admit to myself the falseness of that photo. Not only was it not whom I wanted to be, it was not the example I wanted to set for Marie.

Acceptance is almost always a philosophy of hindsight. Acceptance instructs us to look upon our misfortunes, whatever they may be, and believe that the path was destined. We are told to backfill our inadequacies with this false benediction and pretend that we are exactly where we have always wanted to be. Yet if we were truly grateful for the tough lessons life teaches us, we would eagerly seek out more such limitations and difficulties. We don't, of course, because we all know that acceptance is a rationalization, not a prize. This is not to say that the struggle isn't a necessary or even good thing in the long run— without it we are nothing. Who am I, if not the person who experienced this setback or overcame that pain? But to pretend that it is a good thing in the short term is to lose oneself just as thoroughly as if we'd never faced adversity in the first place.

I am not grateful for the tragedy itself; I am grateful for the opportunity to rise above it. I am grateful to have been given the free will and the strength to fight. No parent who is lucky enough to see improvement can claim that they preferred things the old way, and there is nothing wrong in admitting that. I believe that all of us can fully love our children, disabled or not, while nonetheless refusing to give up hope for something greater for them, just as we can love ourselves without dismissing all our goals and dreams.

I wanted to raise Marie to be the kind of person who never gives up, and this photo was hard evidence that I had once tried to convince myself to give up, even if only I knew what was going on behind that loving visage. I can hate that photo—hate Marie's mother in that photo—because I believe that it's fundamentally okay to be disappointed with the hand you've been dealt in life. Disappointment is what pushes us to try harder, and acceptance should only ever mean the opposite of denial, not the opposite of hard work. As I once told a graduate student who was studying the happiness levels of biomedical versus nonbiomedical autism parents, "I *accept* that this disease is real. I do not accept that it is permanent. There is a difference."

Even so, when I finally worked up the courage to replace the photo on the mantel, I didn't throw it away. I didn't even let myself reuse the frame. Today it sits in a box in the back of the closet, no longer a proud display of past weakness but still a cautionary reminder of it.

....

Chapter 27

An Alternative Vision

AFTER MRS. ALLISON left the PPCD class to stay home with her baby, she was replaced by Ms. Katelyn, which was actually her first name, as opposed to Mrs. Allison's first-name-sounding last name. (The therapists at Building BLOCS, meanwhile, used first names without any prefix, so that by the time Marie entered kindergarten, she was so confused about what to call authority figures that she often referred to her schoolteachers by their last name only, as if they were soldiers in her platoon.)

One day Ms. Katelyn stopped me in the school hallway and asked if Marie had ever had her vision checked.

"Oh, yes," I said. "Several times, actually. They keep swearing she can see."

"That's what the nurse said," Ms. Katelyn lamented, referring to the recent schoolwide vision tests. "But she squints!"

"I know!" I cried. "She stands a foot away from the TV and loses all interest if we make her move back. You can't show her anything at a distance."

"Exactly. Ms. Debbie and I both noticed that when we point at the high shelves, she really obviously squints and tries to make it out. We thought surely she'd fail the vision test."

"Well, and it would make sense genetically, too," I said. "Everyone in our family wears glasses. But I've taken her to the eye doctor twice, and they do that thing where they can take a picture of the shape of your eye, so they don't actually need her to read the eye chart?"

Ms. Katelyn, a glasses wearer herself, nodded.

"And both times the doctor said she can see just fine. But it's been about a year; who knows, maybe it would come up different now."

"I'd definitely take her again," Ms. Katelyn agreed. "That child can't see."

So I made a third appointment with the eye doctor we had first taken Marie to when she was just eighteen months old. Dr. Denise Smith was a developmental optometrist who had experience with autistic kids—another doctor who didn't take insurance, naturally—but she hadn't yet been able to run her full battery of tests on Marie. During the first attempt Marie had been totally nonresponsive, and the second time we tried, she had been openly defiant and royally pissed off to have been dragged out of the house at all.

This time she was swimming in oxytocin, and things were very different.

"Marie, do you see a letter A?"

"Yes."

Dr. Smith moved her stick a few inches closer. "Okay, how about now? Is there still one A? Or are there two As?"

Marie didn't answer.

"Marie, do you see two As?"

"Yes."

Dr. Smith moved it closer, about eight inches from Marie's face, and Marie immediately turned her head away.

"Marie, can you look at the A for me?"

Marie swung her head around, glanced at the A briefly as she passed, and looked away to the other side.

"Is it hard to look at the A?"

"Yes."

"How about now?"

She moved it back a few inches. Marie again turned to face the A and did her characteristic squint.

"Do you see one A or two As?"

"Two letter As."

"You see two?"

"Yes."

Each time Dr. Smith performed a test on Marie, she gave me a brief demonstration as well. During one task involving a red laser and special red-lensed glasses, Marie was asked to point on a number line where she saw the vertical line of light crossing. She pointed confidently to negative 12.

Dr. Smith took the glasses off Marie and handed them to me. "Do you see how it's on the zero, or somewhere close to it?" she asked.

"Actually, it's on negative two," I said.

Dr. Smith chuckled. "Well, not quite bad enough to recommend vision therapy, anyway."

She put a pair of 3D glasses on Marie and opened a book full of small gray stereogram images, the kind that were popular on stoner wall posters in the late '90s.

"What picture do you see here?" she asked.

"Circle," Marie replied.

"What about here?"

There was a pause. "Horse," she said uncertainly.

"And this one?"

No response.

"Marie, can you see a picture here?"

"Horse," she guessed again.

Dr. Smith passed the book and glasses to me. I put them on and could clearly see the progression of different pictures except for the last few in the series, which strained my eyes and kept trying to split into two separate rectangles of visual static.

"The eyes have to work together for depth perception," Dr. Smith explained, miming her hands like a gate opening and closing. "Each eye might be able to focus a sharp image on its own, so she technically has no prescription, but if the muscles can't coordinate their movements, their information won't match."

She placed a black plastic eye cover over Marie's right eye.

"Watch what happens to the covered eye." She used the penlight in her other hand to guide Marie's vision up, down, left, and right in the remaining eye, then suddenly flicked the cover away.

Marie's right eye had wandered far off to the side, completely asymmetrical to its partner. I watched it drunkenly wander back to center now that vision had been returned. It was eerie.

Dr. Smith performed the same demonstration with her other eye.

"The muscles on the left and right should be locked together in her brain so that they make the same movements even though only one eye can see. Instead the covered one doesn't know what to do, so it just relaxes. It's not the same as lazy eye, because with lazy eye the problem is that the muscle is not responding to the brain's signals. In her case the brain isn't sending the right signals."

In fact, Marie often looked at us with one eye closed. We called it her pirate face. I shared this with Dr. Smith, though I left out the part where we had accidentally taught her to say "Arr" whenever we caught her doing it.

"That's common with convergence issues," said Dr. Smith. "She is basically having double vision all the time, so she is deliberately cutting off the information from one eye. The danger is that over time, instead of strengthening her convergence, her brain will simply stop accepting signals from one eye even when it's open, and she could permanently lose depth perception."

She recommended that Marie begin receiving vision therapy once a week, which would use certain exercises to strengthen her eyes' responsiveness and train them to work in tandem. This proposition was more than a little inconvenient, as Dr. Smith's office was a half-hour's drive away. I had chosen her long ago, thinking we'd need to visit only once a year for an eye exam and glasses, not once a week indefinitely. But it would cost us several hundred dollars to do a complete reevaluation with someone closer, with no guarantee that they would be as thorough or skilled as Dr. Smith and her staff.

So every Thursday I picked Marie up early from PPCD and sped twenty-two miles south on the highway while she ate her lunch in the car. She spent an hour doing exercises with names like "Accommodative Rock" and "Randot Duction," sticking pegs in spinning boards and catching balls covered with tiny letters, sliding beads and colored lights and toy monsters in and out from her face, all with the constant reminder to "make it one." Over time I learned from the therapists how to tell when she was truly focused on an object by watching the angle of her irises and the dilation of her pupils. There were physical exercises for her body as well, designed to use alternating sides and strengthen the communication between the two halves of her brain. Then we would dash back out to the car and haul ourselves north to Building BLOCS, just in time to start her three hours of daily therapy there.

I deducted a lot of medical miles on our taxes that year.

After nine months Marie could pass all the eye-convergence tests with better scores than I could. At her final checkup she again looked through the book of gray stereogram images and was able to name every single picture hidden within. During this time she also became a fluent reader, though it's hard to say how much was due to the therapy and how much was just her own hyperlexia. Paul, too, had learned to read at this age, after all. What was more interesting, though, was the effect vision therapy had on her eye contact. Just as Marie had found it hard to look directly at the stick with the letter A on it when it was too close to her face, it turned out that her avoidance of faces was largely due to an inability to focus on them at the typical distances people placed themselves from her. By the time she was discharged she had no difficulty making eye contact with anyone.

As usual, whatever worked with one kid we tried on the other, and as usual, it was not relevant. Paul did need a weak glasses prescription, but it turned out his convergence and other visual skills were just fine. It was nice to know that we weren't dealing with the kind of clinic that automatically recommended services for everyone, but it was oddly disappointing to learn that his hand-eye coordination was normal and not in fact at the root of his daily tantrums over written work in his first grade classroom. At least then it would have been a problem we could have done something about.

His real problem was no mystery, of course, but the treatment was being withheld, albeit for very valid reasons. Steroids were off the table. It was like being told to push a row of nails in with your fingers while the hammer hangs beside you on the wall.

But what choice did we have? We tried to push in the nails and curb his stress and anxiety from whatever angles we could. Homework became typed instead of handwritten; he was allowed to leave class to meditate in the hallway whenever he wanted. And every single day and night we worked on emotional regulation strategies and exercises.

We talked about feeling like a 1 or a 2 instead of a 4 or a 5. We talked about taking the bomb outside the classroom so that it wouldn't hurt his friends if it exploded. We read him books that described worries as a weed that must not be watered with attention, as a little monster on his shoulder that must be physically brushed off, or as a beloved item that could nonetheless be closed inside a treasure chest for safekeeping and brought out only when appropriate.

I created a notebook full of pages that read, "Today I _____. I was this good at it, but not perfect." Each line was followed by a box ranking for him to fill in, and we had him score all sorts of mundane activities each night to drive home the idea that none of us are perfect at anything. He could run, but only at a 5, because Daddy could run faster, couldn't he? He could eat, but only at a 7, because he had stains on his shirt just like all boys his age, didn't he? He could see, but only at a 9, because he needed glasses, right? He could take a math test, but only at a—nope, time to freak out.

And so it went.

Around this time I learned about a charter school in the area called Meridian, which used the International Baccalaureate curriculum of inquiry-based learning. It was the kind of place that encouraged open-ended projects following the students' interests and didn't give out grades on report cards. The school ran from kindergarten through twelfth grade all in one building, and a core list of social profiles such as independence, tolerance, and creativity was tied in to every lesson at every grade level. If you were learning about George Washington, for example, you might also be asked to write down your thoughts on why crossing the Delaware showed these core traits, or not. Critical thinking skills were taught; test-taking was not.

In short, it seemed like the perfect place for Paul.

During the information session I attended, the principal of Meridian stressed again and again that this school was not for everyone and that it would save a lot of time if parents really understood what Meridian was about before deciding whether to fill out an application.

"By law we do have to administer the state standardized tests," she said. "But unlike district schools, we do not spend weeks or months preparing the children for these tests. They are just a thing we do one day; then we go back to our regular curriculum. Because of this, yes, if you compare our lower elementary test scores with other schools in the area, you will sometimes find that we rank lower. You will also find, however, that by high school our students are performing far above their peers because the only thing some of their peers ever learned was how to take a test."

Some parents were nodding while others were raising a skeptical eyebrow. *Good*, I thought. *Go away. More room for us.*

"We don't do math drills, and we don't do weekly spelling lists," the principal continued. "Please, please don't come in expecting that we are like some other charter schools in town, who pride themselves on giving hours of homework each night, because you will be disappointed. That's not what we're about. Most homework, in fact, is optional here at Meridian. And what we do assign is very open to choice. The teacher may give a list of ten things and ask for the students to pick five that interest them. Or the parents may talk to the teacher and agree that a different arrangement is appropriate for a particular student, maybe focusing it all on one skill that they are really struggling with and setting the rest aside to be addressed only in class. The only hard rule is that we want parents to be engaged in their child's work and really understand where they are and where they're going."

"How long is the wait list?" someone asked.

The principal tilted her head apologetically. "Long," she admitted.

The only requirement for admission was to live within the county, and practically no other information was even requested on the application form. Unlike private schools, there were no transcripts or interviews and, more importantly, no tuition. Meridian was publicly funded, just like any other school in the district, and as such it was not allowed to select students by any method except random lottery. The only exception, as written into the school's charter and approved by the state before it could open, was that siblings of existing students were given priority so that families could have all their children at one school.

The principal went on, "I think we had, what was it, about 550 applicants for kindergarten last year? And this year it's already surpassed that, with several weeks left before the application deadline."

"For how many actual spots?"

"We bring in 110 new kindergarten students each year, but I expect that at least a third of those will be filled by incoming siblings of students who are already here at Meridian. So call it roughly sixty to seventy open seats."

Faces dropped as parents did the math.

"But we call students up from the waiting list all year long," she added quickly. "You know, life happens. People move, or are asked to leave for disciplinary issues, or even pull their kids out after the first week, when they discover all the things they missed by not coming to one of these information sessions and realize that Meridian is not for them. We call kids off the wait list right up until the last day of school, and once you're in, you're in. You know, I had a parent last year who got called in May, and she said to me, 'Oh, it's just the last two weeks; I don't think it's worth it to transfer now.' But folks, you take those last two weeks, and then you're in for next year! Otherwise you go back in the drawing, and who knows where you'll come out?"

"So the lottery starts over every year?" asked another parent.

"Every year." The principal nodded. "Maybe you're number 247 this year, no chance of getting to the top, but then we draw again next year, and now you're number 5. Heck, we usually have that many turn down their spots over the summer just because plans change; you never know. I always tell parents, the first ten to twenty spots on the kindergarten wait list are almost guaranteed to get in before the end of the school year."

"What about other grades?"

"I'll be honest; it's a lot harder to get into the older grades, because of course all the slots are already filled by the last year's class aging up. One or two kids from each grade will usually leave over the summer, or sometimes we add a whole new teacher like we did with fourth grade this year, so that's twenty-five brand new seats. But in general the lottery for older grades is just to find out who is first on the wait list. Kindergarten is always going to be your best shot of getting in."

Another parent raised her hand. "So let's say I have a kindergartener and a second grader. And the kindergartener gets drawn. . . . "

"Then that kindergartener is now considered a Meridian student," the principal finished, "and your second grader would instantly get moved to the top of their wait list, since siblings get priority. Well, I should say to the top section of the wait list, behind any other students who are also siblings who got there first."

So far all of this information could have been found in one place or another on the school website, which I had been obsessively poring over ever since I'd heard about it. I had only one question to ask.

"In the handbook it says that there is a 'no birthday party' policy," I said. "How strict is that?"

The principal's face hardened. "Oh, we're very serious about that," she said, perhaps assuming incorrectly which side of the debate I was on. "Allergies are a big issue, not just as far as safety is concerned but with regard to students feeling included. But frankly, the bottom line is that cupcakes simply have no place in a learning environment. We encourage parents to have all the celebrations they want outside of school, and preserve this as a place of learning."

I wanted to press her further without seeming rude, and fortunately another mother said the exact thing I was thinking.

"At our current school they have a policy like that," she said, "but the reality is that parents just show up, and the teacher doesn't feel like she can turn them away when the kids have already seen the cupcakes."

The principal smiled contentedly. "Doesn't happen here. Another issue we take very seriously is security, being close to the highway as we are. All doors coming off the lobby are electronically locked at all times, and visitors must be buzzed in by a staff member at the front desk before they can get anywhere near a classroom. Those cupcakes will turn right around and go back to the car, and the kids will never even know they were here."

"And Valentine's?" I asked, already smiling.

When Paul's first grade class had had their party, Ms. Pallick had sent home a list of all the children in the class and helpfully noted on it that Paul's valentines should not contain any candy for dietary reasons. Most parents complied, but there were a handful who paid no attention. As I traded each red lollipop for an SCD-legal honey candy after school that day, Paul had looked up and asked in a quavering voice, "But why would they do that to me?"

It wasn't the loss of the candy he was upset about; this trading ritual took place any time a piece of candy crossed our path and by the fistful on Halloween. It was the fact that these friends had known he couldn't have candy but had chosen to give it to him anyway. I tried explaining that their parents probably attached the candy after the kids wrote the names, but he wasn't convinced. In his mind the kids should have overruled their parents, if not in the home then on the way to his desk, and the fact that they hadn't meant they either didn't care if he got sick or didn't care if he felt left out. I had thought he was quite used to this sort of thing by now and was surprised to see how hurt he had been by their small indifference.

After hearing the Meridian principal's firmness on the subject of birthday parties, I realistically knew the answer to my question already. But I wanted everyone else in the room to hear it in case there were some candy lovers present who might decide not to attend over the issue. *Go away. More room for us.*

The principal nodded at me. "The same goes for Valentine's Day. We encourage pencils, stickers, small toys, but no candy is allowed on the valentines exchanged at school."

I wanted to be in this school so badly. I yearned for it as much as I yearned for recovery, perhaps because I knew one could help lead to the other. This was the place for Paul, as surely as if it had been designed with no one but him in mind. The odds were stacked against us, but they always were. I remained optimistic. Marie was going to be drawn for kindergarten, I decided; then Paul would get in as a sibling. I decided it just like I'd decided on recovery, and I thought about it every single day leading up to the lottery. I told myself it would happen because we needed it to happen.

And it did.

The day they posted the lottery results on the school windows, I forced myself to arrive fifteen minutes past the deadline because I didn't want to have to watch it go up page by page if they were running late. In the end there had been almost 1,500 applicants across the whole school, and a list that long takes up a lot of paper. The parking lot was busy, with a dozen parents already peering up at the tinted glass, running fingers down lists and whispering quietly to each other. No one wanted to show too much excitement or disappointment in front of their competitors. Many seemed to be parents of existing students who were only checking to see if friends or anyone else they knew had gotten in. Everyone was pulling out a cell phone as soon as they turned away from the wall.

I slowly scanned the section of pages taped under a giant letter K and let out an involuntary gasp as I saw my daughter's name in slot number 60 out of 110. She wasn't just high on the waiting list; she was *in*. Then I looked back. Number 52 was a boy we knew, the youngest in the family that had originally told us about the school. He was an existing sibling.

I didn't know the names in between, but even if this friend's child had been the very last sibling on the list before they had begun the real lottery, that meant that Marie had been no more than the eighth name drawn, out of six or seven hundred. And whether first or eighth or somewhere in between, she had been the first one drawn with a sibling going into second grade, because Paul was in the very first spot on his wait list.

Two months later we received notice that someone would be withdrawing over the summer, and Paul took their place in time for the first day of school.

Chapter 28

State of the Industry

In March of 2013, just a couple of weeks after winning the literal lottery, a mild stomach virus made its way around our house, infecting all of us in turn. Paul was one of the last and most strongly affected, but just when we thought it was finally clearing up, he took a sudden turn for the worse.

"I think . . . maybe my stomach hurts," he told me one evening.

"Does it?" I asked with wary surprise. Speech fluency notwithstanding, Paul was still generally unable or unwilling to express abdominal pain, even when he was obviously suffering from it. He was still pretty stoic about all forms of pain, and I couldn't remember any time when he had ever told me that his stomach hurt, even in the throes of his trimonthly vomiting.

"Maybe," he said again.

"Let's see if we can find it," I said. I carefully prodded his midsection, but he made no reaction. When I moved over to his right side, however, he immediately leaped off the couch and walked away from me.

"Paul, did that hurt?"

"No," he said firmly, even as he refused to let me come near him and touch it again.

"Listen, it's okay, it's okay," I said. "I want you to think very carefully about your body, okay?" I touched his leg. "Does this hurt?"

"No."

I moved to his shoulder. "Does this hurt?"

"No."

I touched his elbow, his head, his nose, and all were an easy no.

I gently placed my palm on the right side of his stomach, without pressure. "Does this hurt?" I asked.

"Maybe," he said. "I think . . . maybe it hurts just a little."

"Hmm. Do you want some juice?"

He thought for a moment. "I think I don't."

That was certainly a red flag. "Well, maybe if we go start your shower, you'll feel better."

"I think maybe I just want to lay down on the couch for a little while," he said.

I went downstairs to talk to Andrew.

"Part of me wants to take him to the ER," I said. "I swear, I think he might have appendicitis."

Andrew was doubtful, but he had to admit that Paul discussing any level of pain, not to mention turning down juice and lying on the couch, was extremely unusual.

"But why appendicitis?" he asked. "Why isn't this just more of the stomach virus?"

"I don't know," I said. "I feel like this is different. It's on the right side, like appendicitis is supposed to be. And really it's just a bacterial infection that happens to get into the appendix, so with all his gut problems I have to assume he's at a higher risk for it than most people. Plus, it happened to my friend Laura—you know, biomedical Laura? Her son Colton was acting a little sick like this over Christmas a couple of years ago, and she took him in and it turned out he had major appendicitis and they had to operate immediately. It's the kind of thing that can kill you out of nowhere."

We poked our heads upstairs and saw that Paul was still flopped listlessly on the couch. "This is just so out of character for him," I said, "it makes me really nervous."

"Okay." Andrew shrugged, realizing that even if the facts didn't convince him, he wasn't going to be able to talk me out of it. "You guys go ahead and go; I'll put Marie to bed."

The ER is a truly terrifying place for me, so the fact that I was willing to go proved just how serious I thought the situation was. It may be hard to understand for someone who has never had anything but kindness from doctors, but I knew that scorn and dismissal of my concerns weren't nearly the worst things that could happen to us there.

Both biomedical and general autism message boards were full of the horror stories. It is all too easy to get yourself accused of Munchausen by proxy when you insist that your child is hurt, yet the child does not express pain verbally. Dr. Shikari had merely thought it to himself and shooed me away, but in hospitals there are social workers and psychiatrists right there on site who can be called in at a moment's notice by any well-meaning but ignorant staff member. One mother I knew online had brought her son in for a broken arm, and while the X-rays hadn't disagreed, the nurse on duty had been suspicious of the child's special diet and many supplements listed in his medical report and called Child Protective Services. This woman's autistic child was actually taken away and put in foster care for three days—a standard holding period, she was told, while they investigate any accusation—simply because some triage nurse thought he took too many vitamins.

I had actual nightmares about this sort of thing happening to us. The general recommendation on all the message boards was to keep it simple. Do thorough research about potential drug interactions yourself, and don't tell them about any supplements that won't matter one way or the other. Do all the talking, so they may assume the child is more nonverbal than he really is and won't try to ask him about his pain level. Don't demand X-rays or lab tests; rather, mention your good insurance coverage at every opportunity and act like you don't mind ruling everything out because hey, it's paid for.

Above all, don't look desperate, even if your day-to-day life is one long stream of desperation.

The ER was slow that evening, and we were moved into an exam room immediately. The doctor who came in was very friendly, and he even commented, "Well, we do get a lot of autistic patients with GI problems, so I understand your concern."

The times, they are a-changing, I thought.

He took our information, including a history of GI problems and several food allergies, but I made no mention of a special diet or any medications beyond what was prescribed by Dr. Krigsman.

"Stand up for me, buddy," he said to Paul. "I want you to jump up and down for me once, like this."

Paul hopped a couple of inches and winced.

"Can you do it one more time?"

He did, then was allowed to lie back down on the bed. By now he had finally started holding his arms over his stomach and readily agreeing that it hurt, but the doctor told me he still wasn't sure the pain level was enough to indicate appendicitis.

"I mean, normally, if a kid's in that much pain, you tell them to jump again and they won't do it, you know?"

"Oh, but he's had a ton of behavioral therapy," I said. Everyone knew that good autism moms put their kids in intensive therapy, so this lie would bolster my credibility. "He'll do absolutely anything an authority figure tells him to do."

Because approval is like a drug to him, I didn't say.

"Ah, I see. Well, to me, the physical exam doesn't show anything major, but what I hear you telling me is that the outward symptoms aren't going to be reliable."

"They really aren't." I sighed. "It's so hard to know what's going on inside his world."

That would win me points, too, though it pained me so much to utter the sappy words. Everyone loves the "in their own world" metaphor for autism. I wanted to be the perfect image of a mom doing everything right, not one hair out of the mainstream.

"Unfortunately, if that's the case," he said, "the only way to definitively rule anything out would be to order a CT scan."

I pretended to consider it for a moment. "I'd be okay with that," I said. "Just to be sure."

Paul got an IV, which he only barely whined about, and held perfectly still as they passed him through the noisy ring of the CT scanner. Thirty minutes later the doctor was back with the results.

"Well, the good news is, it isn't appendicitis," he told us. "However, the radiologist did locate a short intussusception in his small intestine, which is probably what's causing his pain."

I had never even heard the term, which was surprising given how much I knew about GI disorders. The doctor circled one hand in front of the other, forming a tube.

"Imagine a pirate's scope. It can extend outward, right? Or it can contract down, with the smaller piece of the tube sliding inside the larger section." He pulled one fist back, wrapping the fingers of his other hand around it. "That's what an intussusception is like. A portion of the intestine contracts inward and gets stuck inside itself."

"So what causes it to happen? Is it just a freak-accident kind of thing?"

"It's mostly a spontaneous occurrence, but inflammation can make it a little more likely, so I'd say it's probably a secondary effect of the virus he had. It's much more common for part of the small intestine to slide into the large intestine, with the obvious size difference," he said, "but sometimes they happen up high in the small intestine, too."

He made a dubious face. "The thing is, they often resolve themselves, just pop right back out. But they can also be very dangerous. If the outer part of the intestine starts squeezing on the inner part—and that's the one thing intestines do best, is squeeze—then it could put pressure on the blood vessels and cut off blood flow to the inner part. That leads to cell death pretty quickly, and if a portion of the intestines dies, it's a very big deal. It can be fatal."

Not my favorite word in the English language, *fatal*.

"On the other hand," he continued, "the only way to fix it is surgery, which is obviously a major decision. So it's kind of a game of chicken, giving it a chance to hopefully resolve itself but staying under close supervision in case surgery becomes immediately necessary."

For the next several hours we experienced the kind of high-stakes boredom the doctor had described. We had to travel by ambulance to Dell Children's Hospital for overnight observation, but it drove at normal speeds without the siren and lights. Once we arrived, doctors from several different specialties checked in with us, and each made sure to explain the grave seriousness of the situation, but one by one they left us again to continue doing nothing.

I called Dr. Krigsman's emergency pager, and even though his office was closed for the Jewish holiday of Pesach, he called back immediately. He told me that it seemed to be bad luck for the most part, as he'd never known intussusceptions to be more common in autistic kids than in anyone else. It was indeed as serious as we were being told, he said, and he urged us to follow the hospital's recommendations if they thought surgery was necessary.

I promised to have the radiologist send him a copy of the CT results and to call him again if anything changed.

As the night dragged on Paul became steadily more agitated and eventually started to display real levels of pain like a normal child, which I had to assume meant that he was in complete agony. By midnight he was crying and writhing on the bed, and if my heart wasn't broken for him before, it certainly was after he whimpered, "I don't think I can do this anymore."

Of course the secret only I knew was that he had almost certainly picked up that phrase from somewhere on TV. His echolalia choices these days were professional grade. That didn't diminish the sincerity of it; he truly felt the despair behind the words. He had just used a shortcut to express it.

The next doctor who came to check on us agreed to give him something for the pain. He noted that it would also be useful as an anti-inflammatory, since any reduction in swelling might help the intussusception pop out on its own.

Paul finally fell asleep, but I had no such luck. Aside from the fear of surgery, my horrible fold-down vinyl couch was no better than the offerings at hospitals geared for adults. Around 2:30 in the morning I dozed off, but at 4:00 a new doctor came on shift, to once again ask me for Paul's entire medical history and a detailed breakdown of the events so far.

"All right, well, I can tell you right now," she whispered in the semidarkness, so as not to wake Paul, "we are most likely looking at surgery in the morning. If he wakes up still in pain, that will be our answer."

And with those words she guaranteed that I was not going to be able to go back to sleep. I lay flat on my back, alternating between tense rumination and trying to distract myself with my phone for the rest of the night.

Around dawn Paul woke up. He peered at me curiously, then said in a chipper voice, "Mommy, I'm hungry. When can we go home?"

As abruptly as it had started, the terrifying adventure was over. The morning doctor agreed that surgery was now off the table, and they didn't even bother to do a repeat CT scan. Paul had woken up without the slightest pain; therefore the medicine must have worked and the intussusception had resolved itself. Just to be sure, they made us stay under observation for the rest of the day while Andrew brought us some food and they confirmed that Paul was successfully eating and pooping without any return of the pain.

Dr. Krigsman called to check in and was thrilled to hear the news.

"So let me ask you this," he said. "How have they been treating you there? I mean, you've got an autistic kid and you're talking about GI disease; what kind of reception has that gotten? I like to keep tabs on kind of the state of the industry, as it were."

"It's been surprisingly good," I admitted. "Most of them have just accepted it, either as coincidence or as an actual correlation. The first doctor even said, 'We get a lot of autistic patients with GI problems.'"

"Wonderful!" he declared.

"There was one nurse here at Dell Children's who wasn't on board, but she didn't argue about the GI stuff; she just kept implying that he didn't really have autism. She asked me what his diagnosis was, and I said autism, and she was like 'But what was the actual diagnosis? Asperger's? Or PDD? . . .' And I had to tell her no, he was diagnosed with high-functioning autism at the age of two and a half. And you could tell she wasn't buying it because he wasn't bashing himself in the head or whatever. But definitely no one has tried to tell us he doesn't really have GI disease. It's been nice. I assume you heard about the thing from the AAP a couple months ago?"

In November 2012 the American Academy of Pediatrics had suddenly pulled a complete about-face and released a two-hundred-page special supplement on the medical treatment of autism in that month's issue of the esteemed journal *Pediatrics*. In the opening summary the authors had stated the gastrointestinal connection in no uncertain terms:

> Despite the magnitude of these issues, potential GI problems are not routinely considered in ASD evaluations. This likely reflects several factors, including variability in reported rates of GI disorders, controversies regarding the relationship between GI symptoms and the putative causes of autism, the limited verbal capacity of many ASD patients, and the lack of recognition by clinicians that certain behavioral manifestations in children with ASDs are indicators of GI problems (e.g., pain, discomfort, or nausea).

The following pages contained even more potent statements.

> Increasingly, evidence supports a combination of changes in gut microflora, intestinal permeability, inappropriate immune response, activation of specific metabolic pathways, and behavioral changes.

> Autoantibodies could indicate the presence of inflammatory processes and/or an autoimmune component that could . . . contribute to decreased mucosal barrier integrity.

> Nutritional status and nutrient intake are inextricably related in children with autism.

> Autoimmune responses in children with ASDs and a familial history of autoimmunity have been reported.

Endoscopic analyses of children with ASD and GI symptoms have revealed the presence of a subtle, diffuse inflammation of the intestinal tract.

There was even a table labeled "Biomarkers as potential outcome measures," which included lab test recommendations, including calprotectin for intestinal inflammation, blood tests to assess gluten sensitivity, food allergy panels, intestinal permeability tests to assess leaky gut, organic acid testing for B12 or folate deficiency, and analysis of gut microbiota.

Perhaps most shocking of all was the use of the phrase "leaky gut," the informal term used to describe how undigested gluten and casein molecules could escape a damaged intestinal tract and ultimately make their way into the brain. Until now the only way the AAP would have ever printed the phrase "leaky gut" would have been alongside the word "charlatan," despite literally hundreds of medical studies from the past three decades demonstrating a variety of biomarkers for autism, including the presence of intestinal permeability.

Better late than never, but it only highlighted the fact that for fourteen years, they had actively ignored the science of treatment solely because they didn't like what Wakefield had said about causes back in 1998. In doing so they had allowed hundreds of thousands of children to suffer permanent brain damage. It was enough to make one just a little bitter.

"Yes, I saw the report," Dr. Krigsman said. In fact, it turned out he had been one of the consulting physicians on the paper, but they had included only his data and not his name in the final publication, in order to avoid controversy. "I'm glad to hear that other doctors are apparently reading it as well! Listen, if anyone does give you any crap, we've just gotten some new studies published about the enterocolitis specifically. You can give them the link or just open it up right there on your phone if you have to."

He gave me instructions on how to find the medical journal online. "Don't let anyone push you around. I know you won't." He chuckled.

It amused me that Dr. Krigsman always gave me more credit than I was due. History had shown that I most certainly would let people push me around, at least before I went stealthily behind their back to get what I wanted anyway. Maybe he had all autism moms on a pedestal, or maybe he really did understand how beleaguered we all were, and his regular pep talks were meant to bolster our courage.

It always worked.

Chapter 29

Autism Awareness

THE SUMMER AFTER the intussusception, two years after beginning treatment with Dr. Krigsman, both children had follow-up colonoscopies. Marie's was vastly improved, almost in complete remission,
and at the same time it was clear that her kindergarten teacher was
very skeptical of the IEP accompanying this otherwise typical-looking
child into her classroom. Paul's scope, on the other hand, showed only
slight improvement, if any. Some parts that had been inflamed were
healed, but new inflammation had appeared in areas that had previously been healthy.

"I'm telling you, if we had scoped him a year ago, when he was
just coming off the steroids, he would have looked like Marie," I told
Dr. Krigsman. "Entocort is his magic medicine."

Having taken a year off, Paul was allowed to do another round of
Entocort, just in time for the start of second grade. As predicted, he
did wonderfully from the very first pill. At his first ARD at Meridian, the staff were baffled to read the behavioral assessments that had
transferred with us from his old school.

"I wasn't even sure we had the right paperwork at first," his teacher
admitted. "We're not seeing anything like this, just nothing at all."

Of course I gave a certain amount of credit to the alternative teaching style and environment of the school. As just one example, Paul still

286

refused to accept that reading at his desk could be done silently. Rather than admonish him or redirect him to a quieter task, his teacher gave him a small piece of curved plastic piping that he could hold like a telephone handset, which allowed him to hear his own voice loudly in his ear while still keeping quiet enough not to disturb his classmates. This solution, aside from being clever, was something she already had in her cabinet, ready to go. They were used to dealing with problems differently here.

I warned everyone, however, that at least part of his good behavior was due to medication that the doctor would almost certainly make him stop taking again in a few months.

"We always cross our fingers that maybe this will be the time he's able to taper off the meds without flaring up again," I said. "But it hasn't happened yet."

It wasn't full remission this time, either. The meltdowns had stopped the day he started back on the steroids, but the odd speech mannerisms, the generalized anxiety, the awkward body movements, and the obsessions with certain topics remained. He was not the stark outcast he had been in first grade, but neither was he just one of the gang, as he had been in kindergarten.

His best friend, in fact, was a boy he hadn't shared a classroom with since he was three. Timothy was a year older than Paul and had been in Mrs. Allison's PPCD class for a mild speech delay and some obsessive behaviors. His was the kind of borderline case that likely never would have been evaluated were it not for the fact that Timothy's older brother, Aidan, was significantly autistic, so his mother had picked up on the much more subtle symptoms Timothy showed.

Lola and I had hit it off very well, and we continued to get the boys and ourselves together even through several school changes and house moves. Aidan required constant supervision outside his tailored home environment, so Lola relied on friends who could come to her. Our arrangement generally involved me bringing her wine and her cooking me fantastic meals.

One day while driving home from a late-afternoon play date, Paul asked, "Why does Aidan do that?"

"Do what, honey?" I asked.

"Like, go all crazy sometimes."

"Well, Aidan has something called autism. It makes it hard for him to talk and hard to stay calm sometimes."

"But when I was in the hospital, you told the doctor that I had autism."

Oh, crap.

Suddenly I was in very deep. Parents often discussed online whether, when, and how to tell their children they had autism, but like the birds and the bees, it always seemed to come up when you were least prepared for it. Not that I'd ever intended to keep it secret from him, like my friend had with her daughter, Lilah, but I admit that I had hoped the conversation could be put off until it was about something he used to have.

"Well," I stammered, "you're right, I did. I didn't know you were listening. But your autism is not like Aidan's autism."

"Why not?"

"Well, there are a lot of different kinds of autism. Kind of like wearing glasses: some people don't need glasses at all, some people need them just a little, like you, and some people need them a whole lot, like me."

"What does it do?"

"Well, you know how sometimes you have a hard time thinking of the words you want?"

"Yeah, it's like I just, I just, can't think of, like, what I mean!"

"Right." I chuckled. "So, that's because of the autism. It kind of gets in your brain and makes the words hard to find. And it's the reason you sometimes have worries about things that are no big deal, and the reason it's hard to stay focused on other people when you're talking."

"Okay . . . " Paul pondered. "So I just have a *leeeetle* bit of autism, and Aidan has a whole lot of autism."

"Right. But I'll tell you what, when you were little, like two and three years old, you actually had a lot more of it. You were pretty crazy, too."

"I was?"

"Yeah, you used to shout a lot, and run away all the time, and you couldn't answer any questions or tell us about your favorite things."

"Oh, yeah, like in those videos!"

Another thing I hadn't realized he remembered. The last time he'd seen them on my computer was when I'd made the final recording, after his first day of kindergarten. That had been a little over two years ago.

"Do you remember what it felt like back then?" I asked.

"Kind of. I really liked my toy cars."

"Yes, you did."

"Can we watch those videos when we get home?"

"Okay," I said.

He watched all of them in order, excitedly pointing out his own behaviors and noting that he didn't do this anymore and didn't do that anymore. When the last video ended, he turned to me.

"I want to make another video to let everyone know that I'm all better now. Well, *mostly* better," he said, holding up his finger and thumb very close together. "I need to tell everyone about how my poop isn't cloudy anymore."

"Well, maybe people don't want to know about that."

"Why not?"

"Some people might think it was kind of gross. That's one of those things we don't talk about unless people ask first. But you can tell them about your diet if you want to."

"Yeah! My SCD diet! I can tell people about being healthy and eating lots of healthy foods, and, and . . . "

He started to leap off the chair, and I gently took his shoulders. "Hang on. How about you write down whatever you want to say, get all your thoughts in order first. And then when you're ready, I'll film it."

"Okay!" He nodded a little too frantically.

He got distracted, though, and I didn't bring it up again. There was a difference between filming his uninhibited actions and having him consciously practice and deliver a message. The latter smelled too much of exploitation to me. At some point this all becomes his story to tell, and if he chooses to, it won't be because I pushed him into it.

Not long after that the steroids ran out, and the roller coaster went down again. As his behavior plummeted and his self-awareness dulled, he stopped talking about his own autism entirely. Apparently he could only know he had it when he barely had it.

The environment at Meridian was less stressful, and his maturity was always inching upwards in the background, so the meltdowns were not quite as bad as they had been in first grade. Nonetheless, they continued to worsen through the winter. We apologized to his teacher, we kept working on coping techniques, we switched immune suppressors, all to no avail. Before long the standard question when I picked the kids up from school became "Any tears today?"

The answer was yes most days.

While recounting one particularly rough day to me, Paul once again managed to rattle me with a comment lobbed casually from the backseat. He was staggering incomprehensibly among the details of at least three different incidents, not quite able to separate them from one another, let alone identify causes. He was already in tears just trying to recount them all when he muttered, "But I only punched him a little."

"Wait, what?" I cut in. "Go back. You punched someone?"

"Only a little!" he cried defensively.

I spent the next twenty minutes delicately prying the relevant details from the emotional cauldron he was swirling in, asking and reasking questions from different angles until I was sure of two things.

One, Paul had definitely punched another student in his class that day.

Two, he had been upset about mostly unrelated events, and that particular child had done nothing at all to provoke him.

Granted, the attack had been weak enough that the other boy hadn't even reported it to the teacher; otherwise I certainly would have heard from her. But this was a very dangerous first step. Many of my friends had high-functioning boys who would lash out physically when overwhelmed, and it was a bigger concern for them than all their children's other difficulties combined. It's one thing to scream and disrupt the class but quite another to potentially hurt another child. Violence, even nonmalevolent violence resulting strictly from sensory or anxiety overload, was a sure ticket to a self-contained classroom.

Or, in the case of Meridian, a ticket out the door and back to your district school. A public school had to deal with you on one level or another, but charter schools had a lot more leeway when it came to ejecting students in favor of those who wouldn't break the rules. I absolutely could not let him get kicked out of this school, could not even let him get pointed in that general direction.

With an aching heart, I made an appointment with a child psychiatrist.

It was a disaster. Within the first two minutes Dr. Rodney told me that Paul "clearly" had ADHD and wanted to put him on a combination of three medications. When I refused, saying that at most we would be trying one medication at a time so we could determine what was helping and what might be causing side effects, he calmly informed me that Paul's teacher would be the best one to determine whether his symptoms had improved or not.

"We're not here because his teacher complained," I said pointedly. "And I assure you, I know my son's symptoms better than anyone."

"Of course, of course. Well, if you want to slow the process down, that's fine."

He gave us a prescription for Prozac but again reiterated that he would be adding a diagnosis of ADHD to Paul's chart.

"Whatever," I said. "Labels don't bug me."

Four weeks later we were back. "His anxiety didn't improve at all," I told him. "It just made him hyperactive."

"So are you ready to add the Focalin, as we discussed last time?"

"No," I said. "I thought we were going to try a different anti-anxiety medication."

"But you said his problem is hyperactivity," he said, sighing.

"Only as a side effect of the Prozac. Which we're going to stop, because it didn't help."

"Listen," he said, "it will probably take several months to start helping. You have to layer these medications; each one covers one piece of the puzzle."

I shook my head. "I mean, if it had helped a little, and you were saying the effects would grow over time, maybe. But we saw zero improvement over the whole month. There are dozens of anxiety medications out there. I guarantee you one of them is going to work better than not working at all and also making him worse."

"Prozac, Focalin, and risperidone are the only drugs that are FDA-approved in this situation," he said.

I made a face. "I know literally hundreds of autistic children on other prescribed meds. Lexapro, Concerta, Clonidine, Xanax, Abilify . . ."

He shook his head. "They are being used off-label if that's the case. Paul is a classic picture of ADHD with maybe a little autism in the background, and I promise you, the Focalin will help. You can ask his teacher."

This was what I got for using a doctor without a wait list. Of course we had sought out all the recommended doctors first, but they all had waiting lists, and I had foolishly thought we might get somewhere with an average doctor while we waited for our eventual appointment with the WIGWAK doctor. Stupid.

I did try the Focalin without the Prozac for three days, just because I hate leaving any stone unturned, but it made him worse as well. We canceled our follow-up with Dr. Rodney and hunkered down to finish waiting for our first choice.

Dr. Ada, in contrast, was fantastic. Or at least her nurse practitioner was; we were never actually escalated to the doctor herself. The nurse practitioner spent more time talking to Paul than she did to me and administered several standardized tests during the hour we were in her office. These included an ADHD test, which ruled that he very conclusively did not have it.

She recommended we start with risperidone, which I was instinctively against. Not just because it had been one of Dr. Rodney's choices but because I was very uncomfortable with the potential risks and side effects. I had done my research, and risperidone was a drug I had crossed off in my mind even before we had our first appointment. But she spent a long time convincing me it was worth a shot and promised that if we didn't see improvement from it within one week, we would take him off and investigate other avenues.

"I do not believe in adding one medicine on top of the other," she said. "Different medications to treat different symptoms, yes. But not pills to treat the side effects of other pills."

She had earned my trust, so we reluctantly put Paul on the lowest possible dose of risperidone. Sure enough, it helped. Not perfect, but better.

When Dr. Krigsman heard about our foray into psychiatric meds, however, he balked.

"You should have told me that. You could have come back for that, if it was that bad. We would make room for an early appointment!"

I shrugged. "The only thing that helps him is steroids, and you said he couldn't have them."

"Look, there are side effects from the steroids, yes. But there are side effects from the other meds, too, and we don't even know what they all are yet. If it has to be one or the other, my recommendation would be the steroids, absolutely. Maybe we can taper and get him down to just half a pill and let him stay on that long-term."

He leaned forward, pleading. "Being a doctor, I have lots of doctor friends, you know. And some of them are child psychiatrists, and what they tell me about those meds is . . . well, they would never in a million years give them to their own kids, no matter how bad it was. They'll prescribe them for other kids if the parents want, but never their own. That's not my opinion; that's what they tell me. It's really not a good situation."

"Look, we'd love to stop taking them," I said, "*if* you're telling me he can go back on Entocort. The psych meds don't work nearly as well as the Entocort anyway. But something has to keep him from lashing out physically at other kids."

"That's what we'll do, then," said Dr. Krigsman.

I still have the bottle of risperidone in the medicine cabinet, though, in case we need it in the future. Because I freely admit that I don't have all the answers, and the questions almost never get easier.

Chapter 30

No Such Thing

RECOVERY IS A tough concept to pin down. Autism is not just a spectrum within the artificial boundaries of the diagnosis; the hallmark symptoms continue to trail off into nothingness even on the other side of the clinical line. If you've ever quoted a line from a movie to make your friends laugh, you've engaged in echolalia. If you've ever straightened a crooked picture on the wall, you've edged a sliver closer to the realm of the obsessive-compulsive. On the other hand, if you live in chaos and never correct, clean, or straighten anything, you probably qualify as pathological in the opposite direction. Mental and behavioral health doesn't start at zero and count upwards; rather, we huddle together in the middle and point at others in the distance in all directions. There's really no such thing as symptom-free, only a measure of how your symptoms compare to the average of everyone else's symptoms.

What's more, it is a moving target. We can't agree on what is strictly normal from one generation to the next, let alone among the huge diversity of cultures that have ever existed. And even as we try to stake down the place where most of us clump together and define it as normal, American society today encourages us to inch outward, to be "true to ourselves" and celebrate the diversity among us. This is ultimately self-serving, of course, since most of us would prefer to welcome diversity in others rather than step boldly into an environment where we are the minority and hope for the best. The few who declare themselves proud deviants give the rest of us permission to engage in our small deviations.

It is a pattern as old as civilization. A minority group, be it rooted in religion, race, sexuality, disability, or any defining characteristic, begins as a rejected "other," mistrusted and abused by the clump in the middle. Martyrs emerge, fighting for empathy and awareness of their plight, educating the majority by exposing common ground and revealing their inherent humanity. Finally, a tipping point is reached, and the clump relaxes a little, accepting its outer members and, if not moving the line of normalcy, at least being willing to acknowledge the minority as a part of the larger whole. Every group throughout history has had to go through these phases of rejection, education, and acceptance, often more than once as societies break down and are replaced, and sometimes even with minority and majority in reversed roles.

Today, in this country, we are in the midst of an acceptance tipping point for mental illness. The cultural rhetoric no longer voices a need to protect ourselves from these individuals. First the call was loud and angry, resulting in the mass institutionalization and abuses seen in previous generations. Then it quieted to social rejection, more subtle but no less menacing. Now, finally, the most common rallying cry is to help those who suffer from mental illness, to provide them with the tools and love they need to overcome their demons. To a large degree this has been facilitated by improved medical treatment, but more important is the elimination of blame, the understanding that these are true diseases and not choices or personality flaws.

In some ways autism is a part of this movement, but in many others it stands obdurately apart. Certainly the awareness of and empathy for those with autism reached its tipping point years ago, if only by sheer numbers, but there is an urge among many to classify autism as a permanent otherhood, like race, rather than a group that deserves help to achieve normalcy, like schizophrenia. There are no touching documentaries highlighting the beautiful gift of schizophrenia, nor are there television dramas implying that schizophrenic children are privy to an enlightened or even spiritual realm, as there are so many with autism.

Ari Ne'eman, cofounder of the Autistic Self-Advocacy Network and the first autistic appointee to the White House's National Council on Disability, believes that recovery is not only impossible but unethical. His group largely popularized the neurodiversity movement, or the belief that autism is never something to be cured, only to be embraced and celebrated.

"Not too long ago," he wrote in 2011, "a colleague commented that I should be proud for being so nearly 'indistinguishable from my peers.' Only in the autism community would anyone consider that a compliment. . . . Those kinds of statements define our worth as human beings by how well we do looking like people whom we're not. No one should have to spend their life hiding who they are."

Certainly I can agree with this sentiment and acknowledge the banality of being truly indistinguishable. But to assume the most literal definition of the word here is disingenuous. Yes, perhaps better phrasing could be used in the autism community at large: "deficit-free," for example, or "unencumbered." But the spirit of the word, as it is used today in my considerable experience, is never to eradicate a child's personality, only to reveal it—to be indistinguishable in the sense that one is *as fully* connected and engaged with the world as one's peers, rather than connected in exactly the same way. Andrew and I never would have considered wrapping up sports equipment for the boy who wanted anatomy posters for Christmas. Our accomplishment was that he was able to ask for them at all, indistinguishable from his peers who could ask for the things they wanted.

There is a difference between personality and neurological symptoms, despite Ne'eman's attempts to fuse them. As a personal example, I find most people to be emotionally irrational to the point of foolishness, and, like all humans with a fully developed ego, I would never want to normalize my judgment on this matter because I believe with all my heart that I am *right*. I may be on the far-flung edges of the clump in this regard, but I've genuinely considered the opposing side and still see no benefit in budging. Logic is better than emotion, period.

On the other hand—or perhaps the other side of the same hand—I am not good when put on the spot with unexpected information. I need time to process, to react appropriately, to form the words I need to say in the way I want to say them. Catch me off guard with news of a personal tragedy, and rather than tear up or offer a hug, I will most likely just stare blankly at you. I have often thought that it would be terrible to have the police inform me of my husband's tragic murder, aside from the obvious reasons, because my lack of reaction would surely be interpreted as guilt.

Everyone has skills that are harder for them to master than others, and this is one of mine. It is a question of what we want to do, versus what we are capable of. My ability and preference for thinking logically are strengths, and a part of my personality. I do know how to think emotionally and can predict the emotional reactions others will have, yet still I choose logic as superior in most cases. My inability to perform a particular social skill when it is called for, however, is clearly a weakness. Perhaps if I did master the skill, then chose to hurt others anyway by not employing it, you could say it was a reasoned preference and thus part of my personality after all, but in that case I would also probably qualify as sociopathic.

There are some in the neurodiversity camp who would say my goal is reprehensible; that by trying to improve my social skills, I am not only sewing my own sheep suit but insulting those who apparently revel in their own inabilities. Yet I think it does a great disservice to us all when, in the name of acceptance, we declare weaknesses to be inherent.

My parents put me in my first pair of glasses when I was three years old. Does this mean they didn't accept me for who I was, a person of limited sight? That their love was reserved only for a perfect child who could see? On the contrary, it is precisely because they loved me that they did not equate my deficits with my fundamental sense of self, nor did they search for some higher insight hidden within my "different way of seeing the world." They recognized that this myopia was neither a character flaw nor a spiritual perspective on life, but simply a bodily weakness that could be—ought to be—overcome with the right investment of time and resources. In the same way, I understand that my children are not being obstinate or belligerent when they are overwhelmed by certain emotional or sensory situations, but I also insist that we work together to overcome these problems, no matter how long it takes.

We must not choose to self-identify with traits in order to mask their distastefulness. We must not be the emperor declaring that our new clothes are, in fact, just what we ordered. I can strive to be socially better without losing myself, just as I can learn calculus and still be the same person who opened the textbook to chapter one.

So if recovery is not merely a loss of "context and community," as Ne'eman says, what then is it? Most would agree that recovery from the clinical deficits of autism must include at least three major factors:

First, the ability to live independently, providing for one's own leisure as well as daily responsibilities.

Second, the ability to work at a job with a reasonable career trajectory, not makework set aside for the less capable in society.

And finally, the ability to maintain a healthy set of close relationships, including long-term loving commitments. Children are not a requirement, but the decision not to have children needs to be a conscious one, not an avoidance out of fear or an inability to find a willing partner.

Beyond these basic requirements, however, my personal definition of recovery would best be summed up as "the kind of person for whom no one makes excuses."

Of all the message boards and groups I have been a part of, the most frustrating and depressing were those that specified themselves as being for Asperger's syndrome rather than autism in general. These were often collecting grounds for the parents who had convinced themselves, or been convinced by others, that their children were miniature Einsteins. Splinter skills, such as early reading or prodigious math calculations, were held aloft as evidence that their children couldn't be disabled and that they were to be judged on an entirely different metric. More distressingly, it was a foregone conclusion among this type of parent that the Asperger's had inherently *caused* these talents, and that without it their children would lose whatever made them impressive and sink into obscurity. They rebranded their children's social problems as not just excusable but necessary.

"Yes, my son threw his french fries at you. But you know what? He's a genius, so you can damn well just get over it."

This is an actual quote from a mother of a child with Asperger's, writing about an incident her son had caused at a fast-food restaurant. You dared not call it autism in front of this woman, even though Asperger's was already defined as part of the autism spectrum in the DSM-IV, and as of 2013 it has been completely eliminated from the DSM-V, along with the disorder formerly known as PDD-NOS. They are no longer valid diagnoses that can be given in this country. It is all one long spectrum, and if you had Asperger's, by medical definition you now just have autism spectrum disorder.

Which ought to be fine, if these parents were celebrating their children's uniqueness as they claimed. Either your child is truly special, in which case all labels are irrelevant except his name, or your child was special only because he belonged to a small yet uniformly understood and elevated group. It was the exclusivity they sought, the accolades for having a prodigy, and they used it as an excuse to be lazy parents.

While many autism parents rejected medical evaluation and intervention because they were afraid of the work involved, the parents on these Asperger's boards were far more likely to cite a fear that their child would change, no different than the fears parents have of psychiatric medications. A child on a special diet, a child who didn't have diarrhea or injure herself, would somehow be as foreign and unappealing to them as a child spaced out on high doses of risperidone.

What if Einstein had never been pushed to talk? There are some who refute the posthumous assumption that he was on the autism spectrum at all, pointing out that he was not a delayed talker, merely a reluctant one. His immediate relatives recalled that at the age of two and a half, Einstein asked, "But where are its wheels?" in reference to his new baby sister, whom he thought was supposed to be a toy. Assume, however, that Einstein was autistic to some degree. What we do know for a fact is that his parents put him in a rigorous German school at the age of six, and that he received poor to moderate grades at first but was excelling by the end of the first year. He rose to meet the demands of his environment.

What if the next Einstein is indeed alive today, but he will never manage to restrain himself in school long enough to learn, or stay employed at his first inspiring job that drives him into new fields, because his parents believe that his genius is inseparable from his tantrums, or that eliminating his health problems will make the numbers fly out of his head? What if the next Einstein's parents demand accommodations and acceptance rather than finding ways to overcome his struggles in order to enhance his talents?

There is nothing to be done about parents who refuse to curtail even obviously negative symptoms, but with those for whom terminology is the most divisive issue, perhaps a middle ground can still be reached. I would be willing to give up the word "recovery" entirely in favor of "remission." We could stick with 299.01, autistic disorder residual or inactive state.

Are my children in remission, then? Some months yes, some months no.

Just as the target moves with the shifts of society, so, too, is it moving with advancing age. We may reach a certain plateau that once seemed impossible, but if we stop climbing, we will soon fall behind once again. Or we may even be ahead for a time, but one common infection can cause a regression that takes us back to the bottom of the hill.

Each of my children was in remission—quirky but unencumbered—at the start of their kindergarten years, but each was regressing again by the second half of that time frame. Marie's teacher noted the difference when she came back in January, but we ascribed most of her regression to a severe illness over the winter break, and it wasn't until the end of the school year that we realized her visual strength had weakened again as well. It would seem that just as Paul's condition needed to be maintained with steady medication, Marie couldn't do a round of therapy and walk away permanently fixed, either.

So we began doing the eye exercises at home again, and her eye contact has been slowly coming back. She sometimes speaks as if she learned English as a foreign language, putting adjectives out of order or conjugating verbs incorrectly, but some of her classmates do this as well, and she's catching up. Meanwhile her ability to learn an actual foreign language, Spanish, has proven shockingly advanced. The more we work on her English, the more the Spanish seems to logically follow suit in her brain. Correcting her deficit has enhanced her talent, not diminished it.

Her digestion did eventually dance two steps forward after the one step back of that winter, but I don't need a popular fantasy series to tell me that another winter is always coming. She is still on a low maintenance dose of GI medication, but we successfully weaned off the oxytocin years ago. She has many friends at school and is above average academically. For now, at this exact moment, my daughter can claim my definition of the word "remission."

Paul is not so lucky. His digestive disease barely manages one step forward, one step back. Recently I connected several of his seemingly unrelated symptoms—including a severe intolerance to bananas, poor reaction to fat-digesting enzymes, and a historically very positive response to the supplement Quercetin—to some emerging studies on histamine intolerance and mast-cell cytosis, and together with Dr. Krigsman we are exploring this potential new avenue for him. His initial reaction to the treatment has been encouraging, but we don't know yet if it will grow into something more and allow him to get off the steroids and immune suppressors for good.

What I do know is that closure is mostly a fiction. Memoirs are supposed to tie themselves up neatly with a defining moment of satisfaction, as if the made-for-TV movie script were already in the works. But life is rarely like that.

Back in October of 2010, *Scientific American* published an article with the charming title "Desperation Drives Parents to Dubious Autism Treatments." The content was as one would expect, condescendingly dismissing all manner of dietary, probiotic, anti-inflammatory, and gastrointestinal treatments for autism as not just scientifically unsound but somehow dangerous. Yet less than four years later, in September 2014, that same venerated magazine published another article called "Gut Bacteria May Play a Role in Autism."

A flip-flop worth celebrating, no doubt. But by the third sentence of this new article I had a bitter, if not unfamiliar, taste in my mouth.

"Scientists have *long wondered* whether the composition of bacteria in the intestines, known as the gut microbiome, might be abnormal in people with autism and drive some of these symptoms."

Emphasis mine. Either the editorial staff at *Scientific American* take a very liberal definition of the word "long," or they are resting safe in the knowledge that almost no one pays the fee to read their archives in depth.

So it has been with a dozen other publications. Attitudes change, the bad data gets weeded out, and science advances: these are all wonderful things. But there are never any blockbuster "We Were Wrong!" headlines, and there are certainly never any apologies. In the real world martyrs do not get vindication; they just get absorbed. When it becomes clear that the tides are shifting, most will quietly switch sides in the darkness of night and act as if they have been correct all along. The core strength of the scientific process is the ability to admit when the evidence proves us wrong, yet the core weakness of the very humans performing that science is the need to save face. Humility is too quickly wrapped with the gilded ribbon of trustworthiness. You can wait a lifetime for a single admission of past foolishness, let alone culpability, and all you will ever hear is "Ah, *now* we are right." We are never to acknowledge that yesterday's idiots who thought bees couldn't fly and today's geniuses who figured out the secret are in fact inhabiting the same bodies.

The good news is that science can be done by anyone, if done properly. Trust firsthand evidence over theory. Figure out a way to test what you think is true until you can get repeatable results. Those results may apply to no one's case but your own, but unless you're looking to publish, your case is all that should matter to you. Be rigorous in your observations, objective in your interpretation, and open to being wrong. Half of the things I discovered about my children's health came about only after I first noticed what wasn't working and questioned why.

Someone will always try to tell you that Italy is in the other direction, or doesn't exist at all, but you must avoid the impulse to turn back and argue that you can hear Pavarotti in the distance. Even those who can hear it may call it a hallucination, may insist that the honey can't be real even with the *struffoli* still sticky on their lips. Words may motivate the angry mob, but they don't affect the complacent masses, and the best leaders are often silent. Simply decide where you're going to go, and move a little towards it every day, even if it's just three steps before you have to put everything down again to rest. Soon you may look back and see that everyone else is following you after all. And if the only vindication you ever get is to hear the naysayers cheer that they had your back all along, well, it doesn't matter anyway. At least you aren't where you started.

Epilogue

THE ALARM GOES off at 5:45, and I ought to get up and take a shower. Instead I snooze for another twenty minutes, like most days, before awkwardly jabbing my limbs into some workout clothes and tying my hair back in the pitch blackness. I'm not going to work out, but it helps legitimize my disheveled look. Weave a bunch of Lycra into what are effectively pajamas to begin with, and all of a sudden I look like I've got standards.

The lights go on in stages. First is just the laundry room, spilling a tiny ray of dull orange light across the kitchen floor as I begin to assemble breakfast plates. Paul's eyes are even more sensitive than mine in the morning, and he uses a special "sunrise lamp" alarm clock to slowly brighten the room over the course of thirty minutes before waking. It was expensive, but better than listening to him moan every morning while he tried to eat breakfast with one arm pressed over his eyes.

Marie jaunts down the stairs, wide awake and already dressed, and tucks into her apple slices eagerly.

"Oh, what a pretty dress you chose," I tell her with a big smile. "But you know what? I think you forgot something, silly!" This goofy, gosh-darn attitude is not at all my preference this early in the morning,

305

but it's necessary for what I'm about to say next. "Today is Monday, and we go back to school! Do you want to go change into Meridian clothes, then eat, or eat first and then go change?"

It's not the drudgery of school uniforms that has the potential to set Marie off but the implication that she has made a mistake. She's a perfectionist and does not like to have her errors pointed out. She eyes my plastered-on grin with wariness for a moment, too smart by a mile for the false choice I've presented to her, but apparently decides to buy my "I bet you did this on purpose just to make me laugh" act.

"Eat first, then change into Meridian clothes," she says primly.

I dump the morning's pills into two cups, with Marie taking about one-third as many as Paul does. Just last week we were able to wean her off another one with no return in digestive symptoms, and I am trying not to let myself split into two mothers again, this time with Marie's mother the champion and Paul's the impotent wretch. We are trying some med changes for him yet again, but at this point change itself is not enough to offer me hope. The next couple of days should reveal whether we've found another piece to his puzzle or merely ruled out another item that doesn't belong.

Marie is halfway through her breakfast by the time Paul finally shoves his weighted blanket off and staggers blearily into the kitchen, but he will still finish before she does. He eats methodically and with purpose, ready to chug his probiotic-infused smoothie the moment I have it prepared.

He wears a white polo shirt, as he always does on Mondays. To those who notice his pattern, he is quick to point out that it is actually two weeks long, because although Monday through Thursday are always the same progression, he has two different school T-shirts that he alternates each Friday. In the past he's been willing to break the pattern if there were no clean shirts of the appropriate color, but recently he's been digging in harder.

"I just need the right color shirt to help me feel organized," he insists these days, a hint of the old panic in his throat. I know how to pick my battles, and this is one that I win by default when he is on the upswing, so there is no point in training it out of him. For now I just make sure not to fall behind on his laundry.

Some medications are topical creams instead of pills, and the kids rub these into their chests as I double-check backpacks and homework folders. Normally they enjoy doing a few left-brain-right-brain exercises before we leave the house, but I skip them today because the wind has picked up outside and I know it's going to start raining any minute.

Sure enough, a few droplets have begun falling by the time we have shoes and socks on, and Paul cries out in shock and anger as he runs to the car and flings the door open. I pull some napkins from my large stash in the glove compartment, and he carefully dabs them over his entire body, including the tops and bottoms of his shoes.

"Can we listen-en-en, ah . . . listen to Weird Al?" he asks, handing the slightly damp napkins back to me as if they were infected with plague.

"No, thank you," says Marie. "How about Pharrell Williams?"

"No, thank you," says Paul. This is one of their most well-established routines, thanks to their incredibly eclectic tastes in music and my refusal to play referee. They will agree on something, or we will listen to nothing. "How about JPP?" he continues.

"Okay," Marie says, and I comply. I'll put up with anything as long as the two of them aren't fighting about it, but I'm pleased with this choice. JPP is a string quartet from Finland, and the mellow classical folk tunes are a nice fit for the weather and my sleepiness. Paul likes it because the harmonies and rhythms are surprisingly complex, and Marie enjoys anything involving her instrument of choice, the violin. She began demanding to play the violin a little over a year ago until finally I rented one for her on a monthly basis, figuring surely the obsession would peter out soon. Instead she begged to know when she would meet her violin teacher.

"How do you even know that there is such a thing as a violin teacher?" I had whined, but I dutifully signed her up for lessons nonetheless. The people at the music school were reluctant to take on a five-year-old, but I assured them that I was not some demanding stage mom, and we were going to be doing it only as long as it made her happy. So far it still makes her very happy.

The roads are almost empty because it's Columbus Day and the neighborhood elementary school is closed. Meridian just got finished with a weeklong fall break, so we were not given the extra day. No one has ever mentioned it, but I suspect there also might be some deliberate anti-imperialist overtones to their downplaying of Columbus.

Fifteen minutes later, in front of the school, a line of volunteers helps kids get out of their cars six at a time. We are lucky to pull up in front of a friend of mine who has a special needs child herself. Paul doesn't want to get out, but she offers to walk him in under her umbrella, and he relaxes. I shoot her a grateful look.

He has to lean to one side to counterbalance his heavy lunch box. Banging against his legs are chicken pancakes with honey, cucumbers with homemade "ranch" dip, blueberries, almond crackers, pistachios, homemade gummy bears, and three vegetable smoothies. When I pick him up this afternoon, it will be empty and he will be starving.

As soon as I've merged back into traffic, I eject the JPP disc and put in one containing profoundly offensive musical comedy. This is what Mommy listens to when the kids are not in the car. There was a time when I couldn't tolerate anything but comedy in my life, because this camel's back was already broken without the added weight of television dramas or mournful music. Nowadays there's an even mix, but still, my trip home from school in the morning is always something fast and upbeat. I have to get myself energized for the work awaiting me.

Unlike my farm-matron ancestor, I can at least put my laptop on the kitchen counter and stream my favorite shows during the endless hours of cooking. Recently I've been catching up on *Supernatural*, but Netflix suggests a new stand-up special, and this morning I agree. I am tense over whether Paul's first day back will go better or worse than normal with his recent medication changes. (And if worse, will it truly be due to the meds or only because of the rain? That will take a few more days to tease apart.) If he does have a bad day, he won't be allowed to have any screen time when he gets home, a consequence that he makes at least as hard on me as it is on him.

Yes, it needs to be comedy this morning.

I fill a pot to the brim with smoothie vegetables and put it in the lower oven to roast for an hour while I bake a batch of coconut-flour muffins in the top oven. I pluck and wash a couple of pounds of grapes, wash and cut three pints of strawberries, and chop up one whole pineapple. Then I dump a cup of homemade marinade, the second half of a batch I boiled down a few days ago, into a ziplock bag with some short ribs for tonight's dinner.

Pausing for breakfast, I pop out my Invisalign mouth guard. I have finally stopped grinding my teeth at night again, so hopefully this yearlong treatment for my intense jaw pain won't need to be repeated once my molars are back where they belong.

I pour the last of the cashew granola into my bowl, mentally adding it to my to-do list of foods. I've been eating on the Specific Carbohydrate Diet along with my kids for a little over a year now. The decision came about partly because my digestion had never been the same after I had to take a round of hospital-grade antibiotics and partly because Paul asked me outright if I would be his special diet buddy.

How could I say no?

The change was nothing short of revolutionary for me, and though I have cheated a few times when the kids aren't around, I have always regretted it afterwards. I don't just walk the walk for solidarity's sake; I do it because I can feel the difference. Andrew is on the same path, if a few steps behind. He went fully gluten-free in solidarity with the kids several years ago, and the improvements in his health were enough to convince him to stick with it. Now instead of GFCF with the family and whatever he wants while he's at work, he eats SCD with the family and gluten-free at work. I don't expect he'll ever go fully SCD, but crazier things have happened.

After a quick shower I cue up another comedy series and set up shop at the kitchen table. Paul's Sulfasalazine dose is three-quarters of a tablet, three times a day, and I long ago figured out that it is easier to prep the doses beforehand in empty gelatin capsules rather than keep a pill cutter in my pocket at all times. I spend an hour cutting every tablet in half, cutting a third of those in half again, then cramming a half-tablet plus a quarter-tablet into each capsule in the specialized tray. The tablets are artificially colored, and my fingertips will be stained yellow for the rest of the day. I long to get him off this med, but frankly, I'd be happy if he could just grow enough to increase his dose to one full tablet.

A little freelance audio work and one batch of gummies and crackers later, and it's almost time to pick the kids up from school. I've forgotten to eat lunch again.

I snack quickly on an apple with some cashew butter, but I'm no good at doing just one thing at a time anymore, so I instinctively decide to pay some bills online while I chew.

There is a deposit into our bank account from Google, of all places, for just over $100. This makes no sense. My website gets a few dollars a month in advertising from Amazon, but I don't run Google ads. I log in, dig around, and eventually figure out that this is ad revenue from my YouTube videos. They've been sitting in the background adding up pennies at a time all these years, and apparently I finally crossed the minimum threshold for a payout.

Turns out my channel has over seventy-four thousand views now. I had no idea.

The weather has cleared into an absolutely stunning fall day, and I have to decide between driving with the windows down or continuing to listen to my profanely funny music. I choose the music. The afternoon pickup line is long and slow, and I get almost to the end of the disc, ejecting it at the last possible second just as the volunteer is grabbing my door handle.

The kids climb into the car, Marie already chattering about the exciting details of her day. Finally, she takes a breath, and I cut in.

"And how about you, Paul? How was your day?"

"Great!" he says, as if just realizing it himself. "I got my signature, and I had no tears at all."

I can't help but notice that he says this with almost no stuttering.

"That's great news! And what special did you go to?"

"Spanish," he groans. He finds learning a foreign language to be a particularly egregious waste of time.

"And how was it?" I ask cautiously, afraid of the answer.

"Um . . . it was okay, actually. Kind of fun. Hey, Marie, do you want to listen to some music now?"

And just like that, the roller coaster is up again. I can see for miles.

Acknowledgments

First and foremost, to my children, whose hard work and suffering have overshadowed mine by an order of magnitude, yet still they smile. You are the strongest kids I know, and "proud" is too small a word.

To my husband and family, whose unwavering love and support have manufactured courage out of thin air more times than I can count. Loaves and fishes have nothing on you.

To Dr. Arthur Krigsman, who takes the hard road and stands up for what is right, every day. You are a mensch.

To Brandy Windham, Christie Layton, and the many talented therapists at Building BLOCS. Your generosity helped my daughter to speak, yet leaves me speechless.

To Lucas Ramirez, Kirsten Bell, and everyone past and present at the Johnson Center. I am living proof that you are the change you wanted to see in the world.

To Melanie Bergeron. Thanks for wrestling with this little boy.

To the teachers: Ms. Allison, Ms. Debbie, Ms. Anita, Ms. Jill, Ms. Laurie, Ms. Michelle, Ms. Katelyn, Ms. Miller, Ms. Pallick, Ms. Bryan, and the entire staff at Meridian School. No matter how much patience we asked for, you always came up with more.

To Dr. Melba Lewis, who has the heart of Orpheus and the feet of Hermes.

To our vision therapists, London and Maggie. We made it one.

To Jim Helm and Nikki Day, who never met but would like each other. You both kicked me in the pants when no one else would, and I am grateful.

To all the moms on all the message boards. Thank God for the Internet.

And finally, to the pioneers: Elaine Gottschall, Dr. Sidney Haas, Dr. Sidney Baker, Dr. Bernard Rimland, and all the doctors who fight for us. It is worth it, and we are winning.

Bibliography

The two-hundred-page autism treatment supplement from the American Academy of Pediatrics, referenced in chapter 28, can be found online in its entirety here: http://pediatrics.aappublications.org/content/130/Supplement_2/S160.full

Atladóttir, H. O., M. G. Pedersen, P. Thorsen, P. B. Mortensen, B. Deleuran, W. W. Eaton, and E. T. Parner. "Association of Family History of Autoimmune Diseases and Autism Spectrum Disorders." *Pediatrics* 124, no. 2 (August 2009): 687–694. Epub July 5, 2009.

Brimberg, L. A., Sadiq, P. K. Gregersen, and B. Diamond. "Brain-Reactive IgG Correlates with Autoimmunity in Mothers of a Child with an Autism Spectrum Disorder." *Molecular Psychiatry* 18, no. 11 (November 2013): 1171–1177. Epub August 20, 2013.

Coury, D. L., P. Ashwood, A. Fasano, G. Fuchs, M. Geraghty, A. Kaul, G. Mawe, P. Patterson, and N. Jones. "Gastrointestinal Conditions in Children with Autism Spectrum Disorder: Developing a Research Agenda." *Pediatrics* 130, supplement no. 2 (November 1, 2012).

Gesundheit, B., J. P. Rosenzweig, D. Naor, B. Lerer, D. A. Zachor, V. Procházka, M. Melamed, D. A. Kristt, A. Steinberg, C. Shulman, P. Hwang, G. Koren, A. Walfisch, J. R. Passweg, J. A. Snowden, R. Tamouza, M. Leboyer, D. Farge-Bancel, and P. Ashwood. "Immunological and Autoimmune Considerations of Autism Spectrum Disorders." *Journal of Autoimmunity* 44 (August 2013): 1–7. Epub July 15, 2013.

Gottschall, Elaine. *Breaking the Vicious Cycle: Intestinal Health Through Diet.* Baltimore, MD: Kirkton Press, 2007.

Guastella, A. J., and I. B. Hickie. "Oxytocin Treatment, Circuitry and Autism: A Critical Review of the Literature Placing Oxytocin into the Autism Context." *Biological Psychiatry* (July 2, 2015), pii: S0006-3223(15)00543-0.

In the United States Court of Federal Claims Office of Special Masters: Child, a Minor, by Her Parents and Natural Guardians, Mom & Dad, Petitioners, V. Secretary of Health and Human Services, Respondent. 2007. Print. "In sum, DVIC has concluded . . . the vaccinations CHILD received on July 19, 2000, significantly aggravated an underlying mitochondrial disorder . . . and manifested as a regressive encephalopathy with features of autism spectrum disorder."

Jepson, Bryan, and Jane Johnson. *Changing the Course of Autism: A Scientific Approach for Parents and Physicians.* Boulder, CO: First Sentient Publications, 2007.

Müller, N., B. Kroll, M. J. Schwarz, M. Riedel, A. Straube, R. Lütticken, R. R. Reinert, T. Reineke, and O. Kühnemund. "Increased Titers of Antibodies Against Streptococcal M12 and M19 Proteins in Patients with Tourette's Syndrome." *Psychiatry Research* 101, no. 2 (March 25, 2001): 187–193.

Ozonoff, S., G. S. Young, A. Carter, D. Messinger, N. Yirmiya, L. Zwaigenbaum, S. Bryson, L. J. Carver, J. N. Constantino, K. Dobkins, T. Hutman, J. M. Iverson, R. Landa, S. J. Rogers, M. Sigman, and W. L. Stone. "Recurrence Risk for Autism Spectrum Disorders: A Baby Siblings Research Consortium Study." *Pediatrics* 130, no. 3 (September 2011): 488–495.

Scheele, D., N. Striepens, O. Güntürkün, S. Deutschländer, W. Maier, K. M. Kendrick, and R. Hurlemann. "Oxytocin Modulates Social Distance Between Males and Females." *Journal of Neuroscience* 32, no. 46 (November 14, 2012): 16074–16079.

Singh, V. K., and R. L. Jensen. "Elevated Levels of Measles Antibodies in Children with Autism." *Pediatric Neurology* 28, no. 4 (April 2003): 292–294.

Singh, V. K., S. X. Lin, E. Newell, and C. Nelson. "Abnormal Measles-Mumps-Rubella Antibodies and CNS Autoimmunity in Children with Autism." *Journal of Biomedical Science* 9, no. 4 (July–August 2002): 359–364.

Trifiletti, R. R., and A. M. Packard. "Immune Mechanisms in Pediatric Neuropsychiatric Disorders: Tourette's Syndrome, OCD, and PANDAS." *Child and Adolescent Psychiatric Clinics of North America* 8, no. 4 (October 1999): 767–775.

Walker, S. J., J. Fortunato, L. G. Gonzalez, and A. Krigsman. "Identification of Unique Gene Expression Profile in Children with Regressive Autism Spectrum Disorder (ASD) and Ileocolitis." *PLoS One* 8, no. 3 (2013): e58058. Epub March 8, 2013.